Praise

*The Ultimate Guide to Creating Your Soul-Aligned Business:*
*25 Practical Strategies from the Experts...*

"Camille, an extraordinary mentor and soul-aligned leader, has compiled an anthology of some of the most brilliant minds. Instead of reading a ten-step method, you can now learn from the personal experiences of these conscious creators of life. You will also be learning how Camille got the inspiration to create her unique business. Go dive in now!"
~Solera Cheng, Executive Coach & Spiritual Channel, SoleraCheng.com

"As a lifelong learner, I have a B.S in Computer Science. My M.B.A degree hangs proudly on my wall. I have more letters and designations than most people. And with all this education, The Ultimate Guide to Creating Your Soul-Aligned Business: 25 Practical Strategies from the Experts, provides more real-life information to help someone build their own business, on their own terms, and thrive doing so. This is not a book to be read and put on a shelf. Each author provides practical ideas and exercises that every business owner should complete. Not only will you learn more about running a business, but you will also discover more about yourself, what holds you back, and just as importantly, how to catapult yourself to the next level."
~Paul B. Taubman, II, Chief Online Strategist, DigitalMaestro.com

"[This book] represents hope and health for the future of "work." The stories within invite us to dismantle our society's imbalanced relationships with overdoing, striving, and conforming. Each chapter shares practical and actionable steps for individuals and businesses to realign their relationship with money from a soul-driven place."
~Safrianna Lughna, LCPC, MS, Living LUNA, LivingLunas.com

"This is a book of wisdom. A book that will be passed down to each eager entrepreneur who wants to experience more joy, purpose, and profit, and understand the truth of leveraging their mindset, heartset and soulset to succeed. It is a book full of magnificent insights about the power of possibility and prosperity and how to be centrally soul aligned in our business and life. I loved this book, and I am so grateful that these courageous business leaders chose to share their brilliance to restore the Soul in business at its highest form."
~Carolyn Cooper-McOuatt, Inspired Business Development & Co-founder of the Grand Connection, grandconnection.ca

"If you are looking to build a soul-aligned business, you must work on your inner relationship to business and money! Implementing the strategies in this book will serve you for a lifetime and result in a bigger impact. If you are being called to master these skills, grab the book and see what magic it can bring you"
~Tyson Sharpe, Spiritual Business Coach & Founder of the Serving Circle

"This compilation of soulful writers OVER-deliver, and inspired me to search into the depths of my soul and come out more alive personally and professionally!"
~Dr. Lance Knaub, Author of *The 4% Break-Thru,* Founder Denali Consulting and Breakthru Physical Therapy + Fitness

"This is a wonderfully inspiring book and perfect if you need to give yourself permission, encouragement, and/or pathways to create the life and business your heart desires! It is time to go for it and do it in your unique way, so allow this brilliant book collaboration of wisdom teachers to support you moving forward now!"
~Deb King, Cofounder of The Wisdom Playground

"*The Ultimate Guide to Creating Your Soul-Aligned Business* is a practical guide that supports the entrepreneur as a whole person. Our businesses are an extension of our desire to express and support others in the world. This book is filled with real life women who are walking their talk as they navigate the wild world of entrepreneurship. As the world changes so does our requirements to show up in a "Soul-Aligned Business" and offer our clients, communities, and ourselves the gift of what that looks and feels like. The authors shared the brilliance of the human spirit as seen through the expression of their businesses."
~Danielle Marggraf, Somatic Business Coach and Wealth Activator

"Get ready to create real transformation in your business when you buy this book. With 25 strategies to choose from you will definitely find new ways to make money AND ensure that you are running your business in alignment with your higher self in a more profound and deeper way. Go big or go home as they say!"
~Jen Coken, Comedian/Coach/Speaker/Author, Jencoken.com

"I've been in business for ten years now, and I can honestly say that this book is a great collection of real stories, real successes, and real insight. This is a perfect read for business owners who want to infuse more SOUL into their businesses—and lead from a place of love, service, and abundance."
~M. Shannon Hernandez, Founder of Joyful Business Revolution

"I met myself in these pages. As each chapter in this anthology of soul stories unfolded, I read the reflections of my struggles to hold onto my soul truth throughout my own journey - as a woman, a business owner, a leader, a wife and mother, and as a soul traveler trying to navigate through the ever present financial rat race, with its constant pressures and stresses to always be multi-tasking at genius levels of performance. Thank you to the many encouraging, beautiful stories of hope, for giving us this sacred time to meet ourselves and to explore the power and possibilities of our own inner power."
~Susan Schöning, CEO, Coach Automator

"I absolutely love the personal story journeys ALL the writers share and then their breakdowns of strategies to help YOU implement from their life experiences. Very inspiring and knowledgeable and DEFINITELY recommend (Shout out to Jackie Roby, Chapter 18) She is amazing if you don't know her!"
~Jackie Zuckerman Delorey, Founder of NEXTonSCENE Media

"In this highly personal and very engaging work, Lily Gibarac (Chapter 23), provides a clear roadmap on how to step into your power and transcend the core wounds that hold you back from your full potential. She shares personal stories that powerfully debunk the myth of the superwoman that so many consider "success" - one that looks happy and successful on the outside but is plagued with negative and harmful traits like people-pleasing and the need to over-achieve. By revealing what's really going on behind the mask, Lily shows how you, too, can change and move forward with confidence and impact."
~Alex Raymond, CEO of Kapta and host of The Conscious Entrepreneur Summit

The Ultimate Guide to Creating Your Soul-Aligned Business

25 Practical Strategies from the Experts

Camille L. Miller

Published by Brave Healer Productions

All photos of Camille Miller courtesy of Andrea Phox.

Paperback ISBN: 978-1-954047-61-7

eBook ISBN: 978-1-954047-60-0

# ULTIMATE GUIDE TO CREATING A
# SOUL-ALIGNED BUSINESS

## 25 PRACTICAL STRATEGIES FROM THE EXPERTS

## CAMILLE L. MILLER

FEATURING: LINDA BERGER, COCO ALEXANDRA CHAN, HALA DAGHER CHIBANI,
MICHELLE CLIFTON, SARA FINS, AMY FLORES-YOUNG, LILY GIBARAC,
LISA E. GIBBS, GAYLE GUNN, CLAUDIA HALLER, DESIRAE M. HALUK, MERYL HAYTON,
DR. SONIA LUCKEY, KIKI MAGNUSON, ROBIN MOONEY, NICOLE PARKER,
SUSAN PRESCOTT, BARB PRITCHARD, JACKIE ROBY, MEGAN SMILEY,
KRISTI H. SULLIVAN, SYDNEY TYLER THOMAS, LARA WALDMAN, ERICA ZYGELMAN

# DISCLAIMER

This book offers words of wisdom with regards to physical, mental, emotional and spiritual wellbeing and is designed for educational purposes only. You should not rely on this information as a substitute for, nor does it replace professional medical or business advice, diagnosis or treatment. If you have concerns or questions about your health, business or mental wellbeing, you should always consult with a physician, other healthcare professional or business professional. Do not disregard, avoid or delay obtaining medical or business related advice from your healthcare or business professional because of something you may have read here. The use of any information provided in this book is solely at your own risk.

Developments in research may impact the health, business, and life advice that appears here. No assurances can be given that the information contained in this book will always include the most relevant findings or developments with respect to the particular material.

Having said all that, know that the authors here have shared their tools, practices, and knowledge with you with a sincere and generous intent to assist you on your journey to being unstoppable in business and life. Please contact them with any questions you may have about the techniques or information they have provided. They will be happy to assist you further!

# DEDICATION

I dedicate this book to my three greatest achievements.

**Casey, Julia, and Victory**

You're the greatest gift I have ever received. You allow me to see
the world from a different angle, and with loving eyes, you always
see the greatness in me, even when I don't see it in myself.

I am so proud of everything you do, the creative souls you are,
and that I get to be your plus one when you hit that red carpet!
You truly make the world a better place, and I'm so very proud of
each one of you and the fine adult you have each become.

# TABLE OF CONTENTS

# ACKNOWLEDGEMENTS

None of my accomplishments would have been possible without the journey I took to get here and the many people I met along the way. I strongly believe everyone has crossed my path for a reason. So, I sincerely acknowledge every single person who has touched my life, even in the smallest way.

I'm forever grateful to all our NLBP members. Especially those who joined in the early years and who saw my vision and helped spread the word. We have become the business incubator I saw in my head back in 2015 but going global was a bonus I never planned for, although I'm immensely grateful. I sincerely thank you for believing in my vision and for continuously showing up and sharing the community with others.

To my closest friends, especially Mike, Nicole, and my Rochelles, who stood beside me in my darkest hours and continued to believe I was meant for bigger things even when I couldn't get my sh*t together, you gave me hope and encouraging words to help me see my potential. You gave me the needed spark to ignite my own torch so I could cast light upon the path for others. I stand today as a beacon of light for others and the pioneer of the Soul Professional Movement because you loved me.

To my sister Tracy, and parents, Bob and Phyllis, who backed loans and lines of credit against their own homes for my survival and to build this global enterprise.

To the 24 other authors of this book who took the chance to collaborate with me on this vision project, I'm grateful for your trust and the incredible words of wisdom you've shared so others may see their potential.

To Laura Di Franco and the amazing staff at Brave Healer Productions, I could not have pulled this together without your incredible organization and the sheer confidence you gave me from day one.

To those who said I couldn't do it, I thank you too. You gave me a reason to prove myself.

# A LETTER TO OUR READERS

Dear Reader,

I want you to know you can do this! Yes, you. It's your birthright to create a life and business you love from the moment you wake up to the moment you fall asleep and every moment in between.

Your job should not make you feel stressed and overwhelmed or not in alignment with your purpose and core values. I'm here to tell you when you believe you can create your dream business, you will, but the change must happen in *you* first.

I can hear my dad telling me at a very young age, "Make sure you love what you do so much that you would do it for free if you could." It took me a while to find my lane of joy, but when I did, there was no stopping me and no better feeling of fulfillment than when I am in flow. That feeling of sheer happiness and joy that comes from helping others and paying my bills is like nothing else I can describe.

I always loved building businesses but never liked running businesses, so I created a job that allows me to do just that. I get to teach people how to create their dream lifestyle business *and* make money doing it every day through the Natural Life Business Partnership (more on that to come) and in my private work as an Alternative Business Engineer. You can do it too.

If you're reading this book, it's likely because the title resonated with you, and you are searching for a change, a better way, or the answer to: What is my purpose? This book will help you create, design, and strategize your business, so it's aligned with your soul and how you want to work. You don't need to follow what others are doing; you just need to believe you can have it all. Find your *purpose beyond profit*.

This book was created to remind you that you are worth it. You are deserving. You are worthy. You *can* and *will* make the money you need once you create the life and business you love.

Thank you so much for picking up this book. I wish you all the success you can dream up.

With much love and gratitude,

Camille

# INTRODUCTION

Throughout my 55 years of being on this Earth, I have held many jobs, from a short-order cook at age 13 (yes, they allowed that in 1980) to CEO of a non-profit at age 44. In between, I was a cashier, server, mental health counselor, fundraiser, sold real estate, became a business consultant, opened a few companies of my own, then went back to non-profit work. I always loved what I did. I used to move around a lot and job jump because I got bored very easily once I mastered something (this is a trait I now see in a lot of soul-aligned entrepreneurs). I used to say, "Every two years, I move up or I move out," which meant if I'd been with a company for two years, I better be promoted to a different job with a higher salary, or I'd go find it elsewhere. For me, it was a great strategy. I loved learning new things and conquering the next challenge.

My greatest work (other than my three kids) began in late 2015 when I founded the Natural Life Business Partnership (NLBP), a global professional organization and business incubator for the soul-aligned entrepreneur, business owner, and conscious leader. I had a deep knowing of what the world would need, and in 2020 it all came true.

## THE SOUL PROFESSIONAL MOVEMENT

We've been taught that being professional is a certain way of life: What you wear, how you present yourself, whom you know. Some of that is true, I pride myself on being professional, but I also embrace my spirit. I speak from my heart. I do things differently. I believe in the Law of Attraction. I use alternative medicine. I talk about abundance and allowing. I'm not into the transactional side of a relationship but more of who a person is on the inside. It takes courage to align yourself with others that think differently, and it takes confidence to shift to this new way of doing business. All of this led me to create NLBP.

As a long-time not-for-profit executive, my heart was always driven to help others. In my last role before creating NLBP, I was a natural health and organic food advocate working extensively in raising awareness around food and farming issues at the local, state, and national levels. In that role, I witnessed many people in all different professions living a holistic lifestyle but not embracing those same values in their everyday work. It was like they felt less than a professional if they embraced both science and soul. However, for the first time in my life, I felt I could be authentic both personally and professionally because I was in a role that allowed me to be me.

Unfortunately, that job was defunded in late 2015, and I found myself searching for my next position. I was a bit lost after experiencing my dream job, a place where I felt aligned each day and knew I was making a difference. I was searching for my soul tribe, both personally and professionally. I didn't find the same level of professionalism in holistic business organizations (a bit too woo-woo for me), so I started asking people where soul-aligned professionals met, and I always got the same answer, "We don't." That was early December 2015 when I felt a strong calling to make a change. I wrote my business plan that night and three months later trademarked and launched what is today the Natural Life Business Partnership (NLBP).

My mission was always to create an incredibly unique professional organization, with the hopes of someday aligning NLBP with the likes of the American Medical Association, the Bar Association, or any other trade association where like-minded professionals hold themselves to a higher standard. I wanted all soul-aligned entrepreneurs to be recognized and respected in the professional world. It was about who you are, not what you do. I wanted to give credence to those who embraced both their logical and soulful sides and provide tools and a safe space to develop their business authentically so the world could benefit. I did not know what was going to happen next, but I felt a clear calling to create a community like I had never felt before. *This is what I am supposed to do.*

We started as a local coffee club but quickly spread throughout the Northeast with morning, afternoon, and nightly meetings. I was on the move. As a single, full-time mom of three teens, I knew this was not sustainable. By the end of 2017, I received a phone call from someone in California who said, "I can't wait for you to get out here," and I knew at that moment I had to make a change.

By January 2018, we launched online via Zoom and began the first no-chapter all-inclusive organization we are today. And yes, that woman in California joined, so we became bi-coastal overnight!

Over the next few years, we grew solely by word of mouth. It was a slow crawl. In February of 2020, I declared we would target the high-achieving soul-aligned entrepreneur and tripled our prices. The idea was to stay small and to work as a tight boutique community. 30 days later, we were in a global pandemic.

Just a few weeks into the pandemic, we started attracting those who had been watching us over the years, who wanted a safe place to talk about their fears, desires, and business and get the skills and confidence to shift what they were doing to a virtual model—something we had been teaching since 2018. We were already an established online global organization, so we did not need to pivot to be something else. We grew rapidly.

Fast forward to July 2021, a brand strategist approached me and said, "I love what you're doing; however, your website doesn't reflect the size and potential of your organization. You need to rebrand and go big." It took me until September to embrace this idea, but I hired her. After months of challenging work refining our vision, purpose, and manifesto, it all dovetailed when we claimed and trademarked *Soul Professional*™ as the title for our membership and launched the new website and branding. This time we added levels to our membership so we could help more budding entrepreneurs as well as our Six-Figure Souls® with mentorship and resources at every stage of their business. To date, we have created a magnificent business incubator in which any Soul Professional, regardless of their field, can thrive.

This year, 2022, we added micro-communities to deepen the member experience and allow our higher-tier members to serve as mentors and community leaders within NLBP. We also launched our Six-Figure Soul Inner Circle for those that have crushed that six-figure ceiling, are scaling their operations, and remain soulfully aligned in their leadership. I am filled with joy that we now have members surpassing the $1M mark.

As Barbara Marx Hubbard stated in her book *The Conscious Revolution,* "Real power to change happens when we connect what is working and empower one another to be the change we all want to see in the world."

# SOUL PROFESSIONALS

### MANIFESTO

---

## SOUL PROFESSIONALS

SOUL PROFESSIONALS are a Global Model of Evolved and Authentic Business Owners, Entrepreneurs, and Conscious Leaders.

## LIVE IN A HIGHER VIBRATION

Soul Professionals are Fully Aligned, Eternally Grateful, and Abundantly Generous.

## HAVE AN ALTERNATIVE APPROACH TO BUSINESS

Soul Professionals lead with their heart, are non-conforming, and purpose-driven.

## ARE HERE TO REPAIR THE WORLD

Soul Professionals Serve Others, Live in Abundance, and Inspire Humanity.

---

# WHY THIS BOOK NOW

I've been teaching business for many years now. I even got a local county college to allow me to teach a course once a semester called Creating Your Holistic Business. Now, post-pandemic, I hear one-in-four Americans are not going back to their corporate jobs. They have seen that working from home allowed closer relationships with their family and the things that were important to resurface. There was a paradigm shift happening before the shutdown; however, since 2020, the business world has shifted to a global marketplace. People are comfortable with video, and more people want to feel connected to their work. It's become a more heart-centered world where purpose beyond profit feels right.

I hope this book makes you feel inspired to create your ultimate dream job. Each one of these authors was chosen with you in mind. Each author has a specific talent, knowing, or story to share to make it easier for you to take that leap to create your soul-aligned business. If you are already on your way to six-figures, use this book as a resource and handy guide to grow and scale.

Remember, you are loved, supported, understood, valued, respected, accepted, and gifted. The world needs you. My mission in leading this book project is to help you align your soul with your work to achieve your *purpose beyond profit*.

# CHAPTER 1

# STAYING IN YOUR LANE OF JOY

## CREATING YOUR ULTIMATE DREAM JOB

Camille L. Miller, MBA, Ph.D. ABD

## MY STORY

When I found myself out of work in 2015 due to the USDA defunding of the program I was leading, I had to make some hard decisions in my life. I saw it coming but didn't entirely embrace that it was actually going to happen. I *loved* this job, the people, and what it stood for. I loved the changes I was making and I loved my staff.

I wasn't ready to go back to a corporate position where my two worlds, spiritual and professional, would once again be torn apart so I could make money. I wasn't quite finished with my doctorate classes either, so I needed to have time to continue my education. I had some nice offers to lead fundraising efforts from two major hospitals and an institute for higher learning. And even though the money was excellent, and I'd have the benefits I needed for my family, there was something inside of me that just didn't want to go back to that lifestyle.

I was turning 48, and it was abundantly clear that organizations can hire cheaper leaders, and I'd be aging out of the non-profit executive world in the next few years. An increased number of non-profits were merging, and there was an abundance of qualified leaders available. On top of that, after being in my dream job for so long, I couldn't grasp the idea of a commute again and long hours away from my three kids. Worse yet, *what if I spent the next few years overworking myself, missing my kid's teen years, and then was defunded again and lost my job? What would I have gained?* It seemed money was no longer my driving force. I wanted something more in my life. I dug deep and felt creating my own position was the best hedge against any risk.

Although I knew I wanted to work for myself, I didn't exactly know what was next. I talked to a lot of people, went on many interviews, even went house shopping, and considered a major move. None of it felt quite right. Then one day in early December 2015, about six weeks into my unemployment, I saw an ad for a meet and greet at an integrative pharmacy about an hour from my home. I thought it would be a good place to search for a clue. *What would be next for me?*

Walking in, I immediately noticed a room filled with holistically-minded professionals. However, they all seemed a bit lost and not interacting. They were all quite quiet and noticeably uncomfortable. I'm an introvert too, so it was painful. I wanted to find my clue, so I started a few small conversations to learn what others were doing and where they came from. I loved hearing these people's stories and could feel their passion for their work, but I couldn't help noticing how unsure they were about themselves when speaking to me. So, I asked, "Do you have other meetings like this?" The answers were all very similar "No, this is the first time."

Everyone seemed disconnected other than advertising in the same natural health magazine, but I knew they likely had a shared client base. An integrated doctor should know an organic farmer. A massage therapist should know a homeopath. A health coach should know a chef. They should all know the social media professional specializing in natural health or the holistic attorney doing contract law. So why didn't they know each other?

Leaving that night, I *knew* I had the power to help. I was gifted at creating communities and building unique business structures. Helping this group was clearly a need in the market, plus it was a group of professionals I understood both scientifically and spiritually. I felt deeply connected to their work and a calling to help bring their gifts to the world that needed them. *Was this my clue?*

The idea became clearer the next day, and then I received a download—that's the best way to describe it. It was a knowing like I had never felt before. *I should create a membership organization, a safe space, for people like me, who walk two paths in life and want to dovetail their holistic lifestyle with their professional life—those who embrace both science and soul.* I certainly knew how to build and design unique businesses from my own experience, plus I had in-depth knowledge of running large organizations from my non-profit experience. My rare job journey and nonlinear degrees uniquely qualified me to create this unconventional professional organization. *That could not have been a mistake!*

For the next two days, I wrote out my business vision without thinking anything was impossible—the entire long-term dream of what this organization would look like. How would we launch? What programs would we need? What was the financial forecast? How would it look in two years, five years, and ten years? Then I called a few close contacts from my previous position and shared my vision to see if it resonated. They all loved it!

I launched three months later in April 2016. I built a drag and drop website, created brochures, bought trademarks, and hit the road to talk about my vision to anyone who'd listen. It was exhilarating and exhausting, but slowly I found people who saw my vision and helped me grow. Within the first year, I secured enough members to pay the bills but not myself. That would continue for the next three years.

My decision to not work a traditional job and build a business around my dream life came with much criticism from my then-husband. *Note: friends and family are not always the best supportive partners when they see you growing!*

Starting my own business made him uneasy, to say the least. His deep-rooted love for money, coupled with his fear of never having enough played hard on both of us, but I was determined to build this community. He had just come into a multi-million-dollar inheritance, so money wasn't the issue, at least I thought. So, I asked that he support me in my entrepreneurial endeavors. His response was, "It's *my* money, not *our* money. You still need to support us."

A year later, I filed for divorce. We were married for over 21 years. He was the love of my life, my best friend, and I thought my soulmate for all of time. In the proceeding 20 years, we never raised our voices at each other and never woke up angry or held a grudge, but something definitely snapped in the end. I think it was his own self-worth story, but I'll leave that for the experts.

Sometimes I look back and wonder how the hell I survived. My divorce was vicious. He became a narcissist who did everything in his power to stop my success. I was thinking "conscious uncoupling" while he cleared out bank accounts, took car keys so I couldn't leave the house, tried to make me sell the company and my trademarks in the divorce settlement, ran up credit card debt, siphoned money off our stock accounts, came after me for alimony, and then refused to pay child support. He was manipulative and calculating. When the court ordered him to help with the bills, he intentionally paid late to destroy my credit—*everything* was in my name since I was making the money. I was taught a man would save me, so I continued to allow this to happen without fighting back until my friend Mike said, "You know, he's not going to stop." Somehow in my brain, I thought he would snap out of it and do what was right because he loved me.

To top it off, I hired my own abusive attorney, who mercilessly fought for power against his backbiting attorney, but not always in my best interest. *Talk about the law of attraction!* I paid six times what he did in legal fees to get less than half of the assets I owned just a year before while he retained the inheritance. I learned a lot about myself in that mess, the most important lesson being, I create my own reality, and I alone have the power to change my situation by how I allow it to affect me. That's when things started to change.

I was in counseling for over a year, raising three children full-time with little financial support, finishing my doctorate classes at night, all while trying to run a start-up company on what was left of my savings from the sale of my house. I'm *very* thankful for the friends and family that had my back, who held me up day after day, and allowed me to see the light at the end of the tunnel when I did not have the strength to hold the candle. I self-funded this crazy venture because I believed in it. At times, I received food stamps and public assistance to help feed and clothe my kids. I remember my child counseling me one day as we searched for food, "Don't be embarrassed Mom, the food bank is here to help." It was all worth it too.

This isn't a rags-to-riches story. I never told my story or shared what I was going through or how bad it actually got with anyone. I didn't want to live from a place of anger or as a victim. I wanted to stay above it all for myself and my kids. It's merely a story of determination and to let you know you can do anything if you have the mindset to keep moving toward the light. Release your story of why you can't do it. I'm not saying it's easy. I'm saying it's the only way to move forward.

I have fully released any anger around my divorce and my ex-husband. I have also released any debt I once felt owed because of this situation. I truly only wish him the best, and in our limited contact, I can still see the good I always saw in him and still have a flicker of light from a distant love. I know his issues are because of his story. I attracted him because of mine.

So what story are you telling yourself that you can let go of right now? Do you have an idea for a business or a passion you want to do every day of your life from your home on the Riviera? Has a business idea been placed in your head, and then that small voice inside you said it was crazy? Yup, that's how this started for me too. But knowing it would work out and that I'd be successful kept me moving toward my goal even in the face of all that debt. That doesn't mean I didn't have huge doubts and scary moments wondering if I could pay the bills! I had lots of them. I still do. As you and your company grow, the same problems arise, just bigger, but I'm saving that story for the next book!

I used an envisioning strategy to create my ultimate dream job, and I challenge you to do the same. I carefully laid out the steps below to help you find your passion. Your everyday work should be dovetailed with who you are and what you believe, and then, you need to find a community that supports and encourages you to follow it.

I can't wait to hear your stories!

# THE STRATEGY

When I set out to create NLBP, I wanted to create a job I'd love as well as one that would support my kids and me for many years. As I said earlier, I was a job jumper. I loved building companies but hated running them. Still do. So, I sat with a piece of paper and wrote down my ultimate dream job. I didn't second guess or tell myself no for any reason. I just wrote it all out. These are some of the things I knew I knew about myself:

- I knew a lot about building companies.
- I knew I did not want to report to a board that could make decisions to override me.
- I knew I definitely needed the wisdom of an Advisory Board.
- I knew I worked great in a team environment.
- I knew I needed time with my kids and lots of flexibility for their teen activities now that I was a one-woman show.
- I knew I loved working in a group atmosphere.
- I knew I needed recurring income so I could travel.
- I knew I needed a business that could move around the world because I want to live in Italy for three months each year.
- I knew my business must reflect my true inner self and come from a place of purpose.

These are all things that were important to me. What's important to you? Do the tasks below to start to develop your ultimate dream job. Take as much time as you need to start to discover what you like and don't like.

I recommend getting a new notebook so you have a record of all your thoughts. I still have my original notebook. It has all my thoughts, names I thought of using for the business, URLs I thought to purchase, words I'd use, and people I'd contact. Get yourself a big notebook and write with an ink pen, not on a computer. You think differently when writing longhand—a little trick I learned from my dissertation chair.

## STEP 1:

On a fresh sheet of paper in your new notebook, draw a line down the middle of the page to make two columns. On one side, write what you absolutely want in your dream job, and on the other side, write what you don't want. Be very clear and precise. If you don't want to work five days a week, nights, weekends, or nine-to-five, write it down. Know what that dream job is and what it's not. Don't be afraid to write things that are non-traditional, like, "I only want to work two days a week from 6 a.m. to 6 p.m. and make $100,000." I literally helped someone design a business like this.

Come back to this list over and over and adjust whenever you like. You will find things change over time too. It took me a long time to adjust to taking off weekends, and now I take half days on Friday and don't even open my computer on Sundays.

Fully complete this step before moving on to step two.

## STEP 2:

When designing your ultimate dream job, you need to think beyond what you think is possible. Think long-term like recurring income and the ability to move anywhere in the world. If money didn't matter, what would you do all day? Who would you help? Where would you live?

Next, write out the answer to the above questions and others that come to you in longhand. Yes, with a pen and piece of paper.

As you write each line, feel it. If you're writing, "I want to spend my summers on the beach," feel what that feels like to be on the beach. Smell the saltwater. Hear the waves and the seagulls. If you're writing, "I don't want to post on social media," feel the shift in your energy when you don't want to do something. You are *releasing* the burden of whatever you thought you needed to do to be successful.

After you write it out, review it for a few days and add and delete whatever you want. Refine it. Think of every little thing that matters and plan for the long term so, in a few years, you have recurring income or can spend a week with the grandkids at Disney without worry. For me, it's having income to pay medical bills in my very old age, so I'm not a burden to my children and family. I also want to live in Italy for three months every year and be able to send plane tickets to my kids so we can still have family time.

Here are some questions to get you started:

If money didn't matter, what would you do all day?

Who do you help?

Where do you live? Where are you working?

Who do you surround yourself with?

Who works for you to make your life easy?

What structure is your business? Virtual, in-person, group, 1:1?

What new opportunity do you create?

Why do people seek you out?

How do people see you?

How do you feel working in this dream job?

What do you hear people saying about you?

What do you say to yourself?

If you could paint a picture of what it would look like when you reach this goal, what would it be? Be very descriptive.

Add your own thoughts and questions.

## STEP 3:

Once you have that all together, the next part is to align yourself with others who have the same dreams and desires you do that can help you grow personally and professionally. Share your vision with those that want to support and encourage you on this new path.

I invite you to join the NLBP Global Collaborative on Facebook and share your vision with me and others using the hashtag #MyUltimateDreamJob. It's a great place to connect with other soul-aligned individuals and the other amazing authors in this book. Go to www.facebook.com/groups/nlbpglobalcollabortive/

## STEP 4:

Join me at a meet and greet to see if you're a good fit for membership at NLBP. Our free bi-monthly meet and greets are open to those exploring membership. This is a small roundtable-style event to meet me, Camille Miller, and to introduce yourself to other members who have aligned who they are with what they do. It's the first step to seeing if you're a good fit for NLBP. Go here to find the next meet and greet: www.SoulProfessional.com

**Camille L. Miller,** MBA, Ph.D. ABD, is the Founder and Chief Visionary of the Natural Life Business Partnership and pioneer of the Soul Professional Movement. Her professional experience includes over 30 years in senior-level leadership with extensive experience in operations, sales, marketing, and brand management efforts in both for-profit and non-profit organizations. In creating NLBP, she has dovetailed her strength in business with her passion for living a natural lifestyle.

As an Alternative Business Engineer, Camille helps you shift from business owner to entrepreneur as well as find the courage to align your business with your values through her Six-Figure Soul® Strategy Sessions. Camille is also an intuitive, PSYCH-K facilitator, and host of the Six-Figure Souls Podcast: Doing Good and Making Money®, which highlights entrepreneurs who crushed the six-figure ceiling while remaining in alignment with the Universe and their purpose.

Her mission is to help you align your soul with your work to achieve purpose beyond profit. Camille believes there is no great secret to creating a massively profitable business that aligns with your soul's purpose. There is, however, a need to shift your mindset to get there.

Connect with Camille:

Become a Soul Professional: https://SoulProfessional.com
Book a Private Session: https://CamilleLMiller.com
Follow Me on TikTok: https://www.tiktok.com/@camille.l.miller
Subscribe to our YouTube Channel: https://NLBP.tv
Subscribe to my Podcast: https://anchor.fm/nlbp-tv
Find Author Interviews: https://sixfiguresouls.com/
Connect with me on LinkedIn:
https://www.linkedin.com/in/camillelmiller/
Read my Blog: https://www.soulprofessional.com/blog
Connect with us on Insta: https://www.instagram.com/naturallifebp/
Connect with me on Facebook:
https://www.facebook.com/camille.miller.756/
NLBP Facebook Business Page:
https://www.facebook.com/thenaturallifeorganization
Join Our Global Collaborative on Facebook:
www.facebook.com/groups/nlbpglobalcollabortive/

# CHAPTER 2

# STOP OVERWORKING AND START OVERFLOWING

## HOW TO BUILD YOUR SOUL-ALIGNED BUSINESS USING HUMAN DESIGN

Kristi H. Sullivan, Human Design Expert, Author, Speaker

# MY STORY

### EXPERIMENTING WITH MY HUMAN DESIGN

I carefully walked into the office, worried I might be interrupting a conversation. I was invited to close the door and sit down at the small conference table. My intuition immediately kicked in and told me, *Breathe.* I noticed the breath in my body and tried to take some slow, deep inhales and exhales like I'd practiced and taught in so many yoga classes over the last 20 years. But I still felt uncomfortable and soon realized that my annual performance review was not about to happen.

My blood drained, my hands got cold, and I began to feel my head sort of separate from my body as if I was in a dream. Like the feeling you have when your head gets heavy and seems caught in a thickening fog, eventually floating away and disconnected from your neck and shoulders.

I tried listening to the words spoken, using all my effort to follow what was said while painfully and somewhat reluctantly storing it into my memory. Especially since I know my open head center doesn't always remember things easily. Then, anxiety and panic in my emotional center started to increase along with my heartbeat as I received the news of my job elimination.

*How can I be feeling disappointment, anger, and rejection while also experiencing excitement and freedom?*

A few days later, my friend Robin and I were sitting at a corner booth table, having lunch at our local Indian restaurant. I was sipping a warm cup of chai, enjoying the combination of sweet and spice. *Yum, my favorite!* We were catching up on things, and I explained my recent unexpected turn of events.

While I often welcome change, I felt tired and overwhelmed after having just experienced the latest of threes crises in a little over two years. To be honest, I'd been working hard to keep things together, especially at keeping myself together. But frankly, I was burned out, and sitting with Robin provided me with some of the much-needed spiritual counseling she usually offered.

"My guides are telling me to gift you a spot in my writing program that starts next week," she said. Up until then, I hadn't thought about writing a book. In the 20-plus-year marketing career that I was leaving, I much preferred editing over writing, and journaling was not my favorite pastime.

Ironically, two years later, I found a bio that I'd previously created for the future, pre-noting that I'd written several books; so perhaps this was predestined?

Despite my mind chatter, something inside me lit up at the idea of responding "yes" to her offer. Without thought or explanation I felt the immediate, solid gut response coming from deep inside my lower belly. My sacral was communicating, *uh-huh.* I envisioned an image of being a member of Robin's writing group over the next six weeks and receiving guidance and inspiration, hopefully, to lead me towards my next step, which was unknown at that moment. So, I said, "Yes."

Then, ideas started swirling in my head to figure out what might evolve as the result of my acceptance. Like most of us do out of habit, it was easy for me to start thinking about the possibilities and try to figure out what I wanted and what my next steps would be. It was so ingrained in me to use my head to analyze, plan, and strategize the direction I should take, where I should focus my efforts, and what my future career would look like.

It wasn't until six months later that I fortuitously learned about an opportunity to write a chapter in a collaborative book (my first of three that year), and 12 months later, I started coaching with a book publisher to expand my new business endeavors further. Then, 18 months later, I eventually produced my own anthology with 25 other authors whom I enlisted.

I didn't create a vision of my new career path in that transformative year. I didn't set goals of what I wanted to achieve or expectations of what needed to happen. I didn't even dream of the opportunities that would be presented and what I'd say "yes" to. It was a life-changing year, and instead of panicking about the unknown, I stepped into uncertainty and leaned into a tool that I'd learned five years prior. It is called Human Design and helps me navigate my life's direction.

Human Design is like astrology on steroids. Your design is based on your birthdate and explains your unique energetic blueprint or operating system. It's who you are at the core—your true, authentic nature that lies beneath the layers of your personality influenced by upbringing, conditioning, trauma, and programming.

Learning about my design taught me that I was a Generator whose energy was meant to respond. This was very different from the work hard, just-do-it mentality that I was taught, and many of us learn in this day and age. Before discovering Human Design, I wasn't consciously honoring my unique ability to attract the right opportunities, to do the right kind of work, and vice versa. Nor was I aware that doing the right kind of work also attracts more opportunities for me to respond to.

The more I align to my unique Generator energy, the more I allow, trust, and receive. Opportunities easily and effortlessly come to me. Part of my journey to create more ease and flow is in the inner work I am doing. I become aware of conditioning that is not in alignment with my design or my true nature and work to shift and clear the self-limiting beliefs, past wounds, and old, outdated programming.

Based on my own experience, I believe that personal growth and self-care are key ingredients to a successful business and life in general. They are as important, if not more, than your business plan, financial goals, or marketing strategy. Inner work and personal development *must* be part of your business if you want to create the best version of it and of *you*. These go hand-in-hand.

Now, as I mentioned, I have 20-plus-years of experience in marketing and communications, which means I learned the formulas that supposedly must or need to be followed to create business success and what should happen to achieve goals and metrics. I was taught that strategy is the recipe for success, and measurement validates the effort. I used to manage projects and provide consultation to clients on these formulas and how to fit them into these frameworks.

But if we're each uniquely designed, specifically encoded to be different than others, then why follow the same formula? Yes, we can adhere to some general guidelines and use data to inform, but there's a magical, mystical ingredient that is the key to merging our life purpose and path to the reality that we create. It's our unique design, and understanding yours provides the secret recipe to your specific success with ease and flow, according to your true nature!

In the same year of my career transition, which coincidentally happened during the pandemic, I was invited to be part of two virtual masterminds, and I started attending many networking meetings remotely. I quickly began expanding my network, a natural expression of the Opportunist profile in my design. I started connecting with several online communities, which include women entrepreneurs who are on a path of personal development. Many are also focused on spiritual growth, like me.

I enjoyed my new routine, despite the unexpected global shutdown that coincided with the shift in my career. This new identity of mine was naturally unfamiliar and took some time to get used to. I utilized my knowledge of Human Design to help me learn self-acceptance and to explore my deeper self.

While sometimes I worried about past experiences or the future, most days, I was in utter surprise and gratitude at how my life was unfolding. My days filled me with deeper connections to my divine spirit while I was surrounded by like-minded women on similar journeys.

As I began following my design more purposefully, I learned about a program to coach women to become better speakers. I was interested and decided to say yes to the opportunity. During the program, I developed several speeches about Human Design and self-care, tools that I was using on a daily basis to cultivate self-love and honor my authentic self.

One day that year, I was suddenly asked by a friend to speak about Human Design to her networking group. I spoke my mind instantly, saying, "But isn't that something you know about more that you should present on?" And she replied, "No, my dear, you're supposed to speak." Perhaps she was getting a message from her inner guides as well.

The book opportunities and the invitation to speak, which also aligned with the open throat center in my design, became the foundation of my new soul-centered business once I followed the stepping stones that appeared. I embraced the idea that I didn't need to follow a formula to make things happen but instead wait to respond to the right opportunities that light me up, an important strategy for Generator types.

As of this writing, two years into my solopreneur business, I am so fortunate and grateful that I am experiencing amazing success. I have five books under my belt once this one publishes, plus a sixth in the works. I also have done more than a hundred podcast interviews, numerous speaking opportunities, and many workshops to teach others and share my expertise. I am experiencing more abundance and satisfaction than I could have imagined when sitting at that conference table at my former job.

I continue to use my Human Design to guide my success in alignment with my uniqueness and hope to inspire you to make similar shifts in your business or career path. I'm now on a mission to help you stop overworking and start overflowing!

# THE STRATEGY

## EXPERIMENTING WITH YOUR HUMAN DESIGN

Human Design is called a rabbit hole for a good reason. It's complex and can take years to study. Mastering your design is an ongoing process. I recommend peeling back each layer carefully, and my mentors suggest experimenting with the information to allow time to integrate and embody the unique aspects of your true nature.

I often get asked, "Where do I start?"

I have identified five initial steps to help you navigate the rabbit hole with ease and flow:

1. Explore Your Design (Type, Strategy and Authority)

   First, I recommend going to MyBodyGraph.com or Google, a similar website to, look up your Human Design. In your chart, take note of your energy type (Manifestor, Projector, Generator/Manifesting Generator, or Reflector) and your specific strategy and authority. These are perhaps the most important, life-changing aspects of your unique blueprint, which, when followed correctly, can have transformative effects.

   There are many valuable resources online to help explain the numerous elements of your design and provide a lot of information for self-study. I also suggest engaging with a Human Design practitioner who has studied the system and can provide you with guidance and interpret your chart.

2. Evaluate Your Conditioning (and Decondition)

   Your true nature is how you were encoded at birth, but there are layers from life experiences and generational/cultural programming that affect the expression of our Human Design. We want to understand these layers, particularly those that may have an adverse effect, and identify the shifts that can help us become more authentically ourselves.

   This process is very important to help your true nature to be expressed. Do your inner work to decondition any not-self programming, including self-limiting beliefs, negative effects from past traumas, and ancestral and cultural blocks. The more you can heal, shift and release, the more your design will naturally align and bring you energetic ease and flow.

3. Expand Your Self-Care (and Inner Work)

In addition to making it a priority to follow your Human Design strategy, authority, and understanding your conditioning, it's also equally important to prioritize your self-care. I believe self-care also has to be unique to you, based on your needs and what feels nurturing.

In some of my other books, I describe self-care in three categories: Occasional (temporary, time-bound, or sporadic actions), Daily (everyday practices with commitment), and Spiritual (deeper activities to evolve and heal, including inner work, mind-body-spirit practices, and self-love). Follow these tips as you expand your self-care:

- Make It a Priority - put yourself (care) first, create a schedule and block times, take frequent breaks, say no, and set boundaries when needed.

- Keep It Simple - don't make self-care overwhelming, time-consuming, or expensive, do it in small increments, maybe several times daily, or bookend your day with a few minutes.

- Make It Essential - don't treat self-care as a luxury or reward, not even a task. It's a necessity, like the oxygen mask.

  (Receive my free PDF to create your customized self-care plan on my website: www.KristiHSullivan.com.)

4. Experiment with Your Design

Understanding the elements of your chart is just the first step. The next is living your Human Design. Bring awareness to how you're living in alignment, or not, with your energy type, strategy, and authority.

Let's look more closely at the Generators, for example. About 70 percent of the population are Generators (including a subset called Manifesting Generators). While the majority of people are of this type, the general advice here can also apply to other types.

Generators have consistent life-force/workforce energy because we have a defined Sacral center (whereas other types are non-sacral beings). This makes Generators ideal for being the busy worker bee. We are designed to get things done and feel satisfied when we do the right kind of work that lights us up. When we are not doing the right work, we usually feel frustrated or burned out and are out of alignment with our design

Be aware of functional burnout. This may look like overworking or overdoing, being too busy getting things done, or feeling chronically overwhelmed—but continuing to function daily. This misalignment can lead to frustration, potential health issues, and even doing work that does not align with your life purpose and path.

In alignment, Generators feel healthy, sleep well, are rested and energized, and thus, are a magnet for opportunities and have clarity and wisdom to decide about responding to those opportunities that feel right—and saying no to those that don't.

5. Experience Consistent FLOW

   Use the first letters of FLOW to remember these steps as you continue on your Human Design Journey!

   - **F**ollow Your Strategy and Authority

   - **L**ove Your Self (Care)

   - **O**vercome Conditioning

   - **W**ork In Your Design

For more information about Human Design, I invite you to take my self-guided, 60-minute mini-course, which introduces the energy types and strategies. The course also includes an interactive exercise to help you develop your personalized self-care plan, tips, and handouts for creating daily rituals. The course is available at KristiHSullivan.thinkific.com.

I also offer monthly introduction to Human Design webinars and workshops, which you can learn about in my Facebook group: Kristi's Human Design and Self Care Community, or by joining my email updates at www.KristiHSullivan.com.

Please reach out and connect, and may you find the FLOW in life!

XO

**Kristi H. Sullivan** is a Human Design and Self Care expert, author, and speaker on a mission to help busy women stop overworking and start overflowing! She hosts a virtual community for female personal development junkies (like herself) to create better wellness, improve relationships, shift mindsets, and manifest more success, wealth, and freedom—to live their best life by design.

Kristi is the lead author of a best-selling Amazon book called *Stop Overworking and Start Overflowing: 25 Ways to Transform Your Life Using Human Design,* published in October 2021 with Brave Healer Productions, in collaboration with 25 other Human Design practitioners.

She teaches workshops internationally, both in person and virtually, and is co-author of three best-selling collaborative books produced during the 2020 pandemic; *The Ultimate Guide to Self-Healing, Vol. 2, The Great Pause: Blessings and Wisdom from COVID-19,* and *Transformation 2020.*

Kristi has been featured on dozens of podcasts, workshops, and conferences, including the Women in Business Summit, Women Future Conference, Wealthy Healer Conference, Coping with Trauma Summit, Forgiveness Summit, Awakening to a New World Summit, and EmpowerConn.

Her journey for mind, body and spiritual development began nearly two decades ago as a yoga teacher (RYT200). During the pandemic, she retired from a marketing communications career, and became a full-time solopreneur, developing her business online, where she connects her community to resources and support for transformation. She encourages her clients and students to be inspired and empowered, to authentically align with their true selves, to manifest abundance, and live their best life.

Kristi is a 4/6 Generator with a passion for connecting with like-minded, inspiring souls and sharing her experiences and lessons as a role model to other life-long students.

To connect with Kristi, visit KristiHSullivan.com, join Facebook.com/groups/KristiHSullivan or follow @KristiHSullivan.

# CHAPTER 3

# MONEY ON PURPOSE

## CREATE A SOULFUL, SUSTAINABLE, AND SUCCESSFUL 6+ FIGURE BUSINESS

Lara Waldman

# MY STORY

### PAIN TO PROSPERITY

On March 21, 2020, the lockdown began here in the United Kingdom, and I started experiencing a lot of anxiety around the uncertainty of what the pandemic would bring.

I was running The Living Abundance Mastermind, my 12-month program, and was stretched in my leadership. *How do I support women with financial success during these unprecedented times? How can we talk about making money and thriving in business when this could be the end of the world as we know it?*

I went back to my practice, my money manifestation mastery strategy, and the steps that have always supported me through change and uncertain times. I sat with this fear, held the uncertainty, and tuned into my inner guidance.

After the fear calmed down, waves of calming energy came rushing through me. I felt this beautiful light and saw doors opening in my mind's eye. *Lara, you will have your most successful year in business if you follow this flow. You are here to guide others to stay on purpose and succeed during these turbulent times of change. Stay focused.*

I know this inner voice well. I've been creating my business from this space for many years, and it's always led me to beautiful and unexpected experiences. But this time, with the world falling apart, I wasn't so sure.

I felt guilt and shame around what I was being shown. I questioned this guidance. *Why should I thrive when so many are experiencing such devastation: loss of work, lifestyles, and loved ones?*

The answer came through clearly. *Lara, we need you to thrive. We need guiding lights through these times of change. Walk through the doors and show others how to do the same.*

I was at a choice point; go down in flames of fear or step through the doors of possibility and lead courageously from this place.

Then on July 1, 2020, I was doing my morning meditation when one of my best friends appeared in my mind's eye. *Lara, I have died,* she said to me. I was very confused by this message and visitation from Kim. I thought she must be going through an inner death of sorts, as she had been visibly stressed and struggling with her masters, working, and homeschooling her three young girls.

I finished my meditation and went on with my day, not thinking much of it.

Two hours later, I got a text from Kim's husband informing me that Kim had died. Kim had an undiagnosed brain tumor and died suddenly overnight. There was no warning or preparation for her death.

Over the next month, Kim came to me every day with instructions on how I was to support her three young girls and husband. She told me she was here to help me with my work and explained how her purpose would continue beyond her physical life.

Kim's messages to me were peaceful and positive, but I felt angry toward her. *What does all of this mean if you're not here?* I argued with her. *It's good that you're at peace, but what about us left behind, especially your three daughters?*

I could not sense the value of this spiritual information in the midst of such a traumatic loss. For the first time in my life, I questioned the spiritual world and my connection to it. What does it all mean?

Deep down, I knew Kim was right, that there was a new level of my purpose opening up through this immense pain. But initially, I was in too much shock, grief, and anger to process the information when it came through.

In time, it became clear that Kim's sudden death was not just a tragedy in its own right. It also brought up trauma from my childhood. When I was 12 years old, my godmother committed suicide, leaving behind her three young children. My mum sunk into a deep depression after losing her best friend. Then when I was 14 years old, I came home one day to find out that my mum left, with no warning.

Here I was, almost 30 years later, grieving my dear friend, who left us suddenly, without warning. This experience was strangely familiar. I had a sense that this was my opportunity to heal the past, but I had no idea where this awareness would carry me.

For the next five months, I was on autopilot. I was drinking every night, waking in the middle of the night with terrible anxiety, crying every morning, struggling to get going, and dragging myself through the day. I supported Kim's children where I could while trying to run a business and remain present for my family.

Then on November 10, 2020, COVID-19 came to visit our house. My husband, two teenage daughters, and I were all hit with the virus.

I felt like I was on fire as COVID made its way through my brain and body. I experienced a dark night of the soul with this virus. I felt the old burning away, intense sensations both physically and emotionally. I surrendered and let it take me.

We did not fully recover after making it through what we believed would be the worst part of COVID-19.

January 1, 2021, I developed vertigo. I lay sobbing in my bed, my head in a huge amount of pain, unable to move from the dizziness. I was scared. *Did I have an undiagnosed brain tumor? Was I going to die?*

I was due to run a big online event, The WEALTH Retreat, in ten days. I had 250 people signed up, but I had no idea how I would deliver.

I sat with these fears and eventually calmed down enough to receive a clear message. *Go on an anti-inflammatory diet. Show up for your event. You will be okay.*

My family started an anti-inflammatory diet, and after four days of detoxing, all of the brain pain symptoms and vertigo stopped. I still felt wiped out, but there were signs of improvement.

I didn't know how I was going to run my event, but my inner guidance was clear that I should go ahead, so I did. I hired extra support, and I did the bare minimum I needed to get by. There were many things I felt I should do, but I had to focus my limited energy on the most important tasks. I let go of anything that wasn't essential.

I managed to show up live and deliver the retreat. It felt like a miracle. By the end of the event, I had the best sales of any launch I'd run before.

I was so overwhelmed by the success of this launch that I spun out in anxiety. How has this happened? *How did I have my best sales ever while in such a mess?*

On reflection, I can see that being floored by grief and the long-term effects of COVID-19 forced me to slow down. I couldn't continue as before. The only thing I could do was surrender.

My inner guidance told me to continue showing up to my business and showed me how I could sustainably do this. This meant getting more support than I ever allowed myself to receive before. I hired another assistant, outsourcing everything that drained my energy and let go of things that weren't working.

I had no choice but to rest, surrender, and let go.

In this forced slowing-down process, I felt the grief of losing Kim and the old trauma that came along with it. I refer to this as a death process. This death process felt like the end of the world where I was in deep questioning of so many things. But the one thing I knew I had to do was go with it and let it take me. Besides, I didn't have enough energy to fight.

In this letting go, I had no idea what would remain. I was moving through the pain of old trauma, and the death of old ways of being in my business and in life. In grieving Kim, I was processing old trauma patterns that no longer served me.

I received all the support I could get to keep going. I looked after my physical, mental, and emotional health. I kept leaning in and letting go.

I listened to what I needed to do in my business and what I needed to let go of. It wasn't about whether or not I felt like it, but whether or not I was guided. I stayed committed to following my inner guidance. It was the one thing I knew I could rely on.

In 2021 I experienced one of the hardest years of my life, but I also had my most successful year in business. I hit my first six-figure year, and my business grew to a whole new level.

How did this happen?

From where I sit now, I can see that these results happened by letting go and surrendering to success. To birth in the new, you need to be willing to let go of the old wounded trauma patterns that unconsciously block success in your finances, business, and life.

During this time, I connected to a new level of vulnerability, finally surrendering to the fact that I couldn't do it all and hold it all alone. I opened up to help, support, love, and connection in every area of my life, including my business.

Kim was right, and she helped me step into the next level of my purpose and power by staying present with the pain of grief. Because I am inspired by how she lived her life and the tragedy of her early death, I am now braver, I love harder, and make the most out of the precious time we have on this Earth.

Pain can be a portal to prosperity if you're willing to work with it mindfully, consciously, and with the right support. Through grief, there is growth if you let it move through you.

In life, there is death. In love, there is loss. After winter, there is spring, there is pain and pleasure, joy and sadness. We live in a world of light and darkness. If we can embrace it all, learn how to hold it all, we can be freer to live and love wholeheartedly.

I want to share with you the steps that I used during this hard time, my Money Manifestation Mastery strategy, to help prosper on purpose, activating the next level of your power and prosperity through whatever life may bring.

# THE STRATEGY

## LARA'S MONEY MANIFESTATION MASTERY STRATEGY

1. Commit

Carve out time and space for this Money Manifestation Mastery process.

This is a daily practice.

If a daily money manifestation practice is not possible or realistic, then I recommend a minimum of four times per week to experience results over time.

Consistency is key.

What can you commit to on a regular basis?

5, 10, 15, or 20 minutes each day?

Decide on how much time you can commit to on a regular basis.

What is the best time of day that you can commit to this practice?

Put this time in your diary.

2. Create Sacred Space

Your fortune is in your focus.

Find a comfortable place where you won't be interrupted.

Switch off all distractions before you begin.

Sit up somewhere comfortable.

Now it's time to consciously enter this prosperity portal.

3. Relax

This next step is designed to calm and balance your nervous system, mind, and emotions. Being relaxed allows you to become receptive to this process.

Start by closing your eyes and taking slow deep inhalations and exhalations.

Inhale on the count of four and exhale on the count of four.

Do this for one minute or as long as you need to relax and slow down.

4. Call in the Soul of your business

Take a moment to acknowledge the consciousness of your business.

Declare: *I welcome the soul of my business here now.*

Welcome the intelligence of your business into this Money Manifestation Mastery session.

Take slow deep inhalations and exhalations with your business's energy for one minute.

Be present with what you feel.

5. Welcome in the Wealth Frequency of Your Business

How much money are you and your business calling in for the next year?

i.e., consistent $10k per month or $100K per year.

Write this amount of money down on a piece of paper in front of you.

6. Connect to this Amount of Money

Acknowledge this amount of money and welcome it to this session.

Declare: *I welcome* (amount of money) *into this session now.*

Breathe with this amount of money for one minute.

Be present with what you feel.

7. Identify Your Money Blocks

Meditate or journal on this question:

What is stopping you or blocking you from welcoming in this money now?

Identify your unconscious money blocks and belief systems.

Money blocks can hold trauma patterns.

Be kind, gentle, and patient with yourself through this step.

8. Release Your Money Blocks

Decide and declare that you're releasing these money blocks now.

"Anything and everything stopping me or blocking me from receiving this money, I release and let it go now, through all time and space, with ease."

Breathe with this step as the releasing process happens.

Allow at least one minute for releasing but take as much time as you need.

Stay present with whatever comes up for you.

9. Embody Your Wealth

You are growing into a new level of empowerment and leadership with the amount of money you are calling in. An inner transformation is required to prepare you for this new level of money in your business and life.

Journal or meditate on this question:

Who do I need to become to receive this money?

10. Rewire to Receive

The next step is to prepare your nervous system, body, mind, and emotions to feel safe and ready to receive this amount of money. It's now time to welcome this money into your body, business, and bank account.

Imagine breathing this amount of money into your body.

Declare: *I am ready to receive $_____ into my life now.*

Open up to receive.

Breathe this money into your body.

Do this for at least one minute.

Your money blocks may come up with this process. Keep releasing and opening to receive.

Stay present with whatever comes up for you.

11. Meet Your Needs

The part of you that experiences lack, scarcity, and not enough is where your unmet needs are. Learning how to meet your needs is an important key in receiving this amount of money.

Meditate or journal on this question:

What do I need to feel safe to receive?

Write down what comes through your inner guidance and commit to meeting that need.

12. Become Money

Welcome the energy of this money into every cell of your body.

Become this amount of money now.

Become the vibrational frequency of this amount of money and welcome it into every cell in your body.

You're now becoming this amount of money.

Feel this through your body.

How does it feel?

Connect to the version of yourself you need to become to receive this money.

Be this now.

Become this version of yourself now.

Do this for at least one minute while inhaling and exhaling on the count of four.

13. Aligned Action

Now it's time to connect to the practical action steps that you need to take to welcome this money into your life. Aligned action is the action guided by your wealth consciousness and the soul of your business rather than action inspired by fear, lack, and scarcity.

From this new alignment with your wealth consciousness, meditate or journal on these questions:

What action do I need to take to welcome this amount of money?

What is the next best step that I need to take now?

This step is helping you get clear on the practical action or strategy required to grow this heart, soul, and body-aligned wealth.

14. Repeat

Repeat these steps every day.

A minimum of four times a week is required to experience consistent results.

The most important thing is consistency.

Commit to 5, 10, 15, or 20 minutes a day for this practice. It's not about how long you put aside; it's about how consistently you do the practice.

To receive my free Money Manifestation Mastery guided meditation, visit this link:

www.subscribepage.com/moneyonpurpose.

I hope you have enjoyed this process. I would love to hear how you get on with this practice. Feel free to reach out and connect to me on any of my social media platforms or send me an email. I would be more than happy to hear from you.

**Lara Waldman,** a.k.a The Abundance Activator, is a conscious wealth expert and coach, abundant business mentor, and author of Money Manifestation Mastery.

She draws on two decades of experience as a healer to help business owners achieve financial success guided by the soul of their business and their wealthy inner wisdom.

Lara's passion is helping the world's leaders create authentic success and the impact they are born to make. She'll teach you the mindset, practices, and strategy you need to build the wealth and freedom you desire without the grind.

Originally from Vancouver, Canada, Lara lives in London, England, with her husband and two teenage daughters.

Contact Links:

https://larawaldman.com
https://www.instagram.com/larawaldmanofficial
https://www.youtube.com/channel/UCxYz6GHZ2rFrhthpCXmBHU
https://www.linkedin.com/in/larawaldman
https://www.facebook.com/abundanceactivator
mail@larawaldman.com

# CHAPTER 4

# DAYDREAMS TO DESIGNS

## YOUR STRATEGIC BRIDGE FROM EMPLOYEE TO ENTREPRENEUR

Megan Smiley, Esq.

# MY STORY

"I've never recommended this before, but for some reason, I want to tell you to do ayahuasca," said my career coach.

*Are you serious? How uniquely fucked up am I that this is the advice I'm getting. Not "fix your resume" or "broaden your search," but "crack your soul open with a mind-altering substance."*

The truth is, I think I intuitively knew what I needed was more on the *crack your soul open* side of the spectrum than on the *tinkering with job applications* side. It's why I picked this particular holistic career coach in the first place.

When I had that call, I happened to be visiting my best friend, Sarah. I was sitting on a bean bag chair in her daughter's room among a community of stuffed animals, all of us enveloped in a world of pinks and purples. It was the same room that'd been Sarah's growing up. It was a place I spent much of my childhood before I became a responsible adult and took the stable albeit unimaginative road to law school. A lifetime of possibilities was still ahead.

But then, I was almost 40 and feeling as rudderless as ever.

*Is it too late to start over?*

*I don't even know how to think outside the box.*

*What will people think if I abandon my law degree?*

Quiet tears started down my cheek, which I quickly wiped away.

*You're supposed to be okay.*

*You've always been the strong one, the one no one had to worry about.*

Minutes later, I was downstairs googling Peruvian ayahuasca trips.

Although somewhat confused at this being the outcome of a career coaching call, Sarah was supportive:

"Megan, you've always been brave and created your own path. I have no doubt you'll do it again."

It's funny how the people who care about you most see you in the best light, even when you struggle to see yourself that way.

And I was struggling.

I'd left my corporate law position years earlier; an existential crisis of its own. But then I happily landed what was then my dream job in international programs at a law school. It was a sensible post-legal career. It aligned with my interest in all things international. I thought I'd figured it all out and was set for life.

Four or five years in, however, the shine started to wear off. Although I still loved interacting with all of my foreign colleagues, the truth was I mostly sent perfunctory emails from my windowless office. All of the programs we ran recycled each year, making them increasingly rote. I looked at my boss's job and realized I didn't want it. And that was the only place to go from my position.

Years without change, growth, or any sense of profound impact took their toll. Walking to work in the mornings, I used to bask in birds singing and sun twinkling on the leaves, thinking how lucky I was. Truly, I was like an annoyingly happy Disney character. But then, everything turned muffled and gray. The New York City skyline view from the B-line train running over the Manhattan Bridge used to inspire awe. Then, it was just the unremarkable background of my commute.

It was like in *National Lampoon's European Vacation* when they couldn't get out of the traffic circle, and Chevy Chase kept saying with each rotation, "Look kids: Big Ben. Parliament." A few rotations in, the excitement dwindles precipitously.

Optimism and a sense of possibility had always come easily to me. This dulled version of life felt so alien. Even when I was miserable as a corporate lawyer, I intuitively knew I had another act coming. I never lacked hope that my future would be better, even when the present was awful.

But I couldn't see beyond the fog that time.

I came home after work and sunk into the couch to watch reality tv. My husband asked from the other room,

"Are you okay?"

"Yeah, why?"

"You're sighing very loudly."

"Am I?"

But as he mentioned it, I noticed that my chest constricted. I couldn't get enough oxygen without taking a deep sigh. The heart palpitations got stronger as the evening went on. It's difficult to fall asleep when your heart is beating out of your chest and you're gasping for air.

My body was in revolt. It was trying to send me a message. It took me a while to decipher, but I eventually did.

*This can't be all there is to work and life.*

*The clock is ticking, and you're wasting time.*

*Did losing mom at 11 teach you nothing? You're supposed to live life to the fullest. And this sure as shit isn't it.*

I tried looking for other jobs, but every description I read triggered the tightness in my chest. The truth was that my position at the law school was better in many respects than any other job I came across. That sounds like it should be a plus, but it felt like a painful dead-end given how unfulfilled I was.

From that space, I had the call with the career coach. I desperately wanted someone to give me the answers. But, following the rules, and considering only standard career options is what got me into this mess in the first place.

So, after that session with the career coach, I took her advice. I didn't go to Peru or do ayahuasca, but I did throw out my job search and start from ground zero.

I allowed myself to burn down all of my assumptions around what I thought I wanted or was realistic.

This is very hard for a lawyer. We're trained to see all of the possible problems. We want to mitigate risk. We solve problems from a left-brained, analytical perspective. I wasn't sure how else to go about solving a problem.

But, to start, instead of asking myself *what job would be a natural extension of what I've been doing?* I asked *what I would do even if no one paid me? What feels easy?*

To my logical brain, these questions felt indulgent and unproductive. But I had no better plan, so I went with it. I then asked myself *if anything were possible and, despite being almost 40, if I were to start over at square one, what would I want my work and life to look like?*

Answering that question was not straightforward. It put me on a path of deep reflection and personal growth.

Every day I meditated, journaled, and read personal development books—all-new practices for me at the time.

I took classes in things that interested me, even if they didn't seem career-related. I took a photography class, a graphic design class, and a voice-over class. I dove into renovating our apartment. I started a podcast, and I created a travel blog.

I took all of the eye-opening personality assessments. They gave me interesting new perspectives on how I function best and my natural strengths beyond the skills I'd acquired from my jobs.

Through this process, I was able to identify a few core themes and values I knew would be important pillars of a fulfilling life and career.

Freedom. The first thing that came through clearly was that I wanted freedom. As I've come to realize, freedom is my top personal value.

I wanted control over my daily schedule. This business of having to arrive at 9:00 a.m. on the dot and sit in an office for eight hours felt arbitrary and stifling. I wanted to have a leisurely morning, drinking my coffee in the sun, and enjoying my morning routine. I wanted to exercise in the middle of the day when I found it easiest. I wanted to be efficient with my work and then do something else.

I wanted the freedom to do my work from anywhere, and ideally in a room flooded with sunlight.

I wanted the freedom to live wherever I wanted at any given time and the freedom to change my mind and move. Set up camp in Montana or Mexico for a month? Yes, please!

I wanted to travel the world and visit family and friends without constant worry around limited vacation days.

Creativity. I had the sense that I wanted to create something. I wasn't sure what. But I knew I wanted to build something and put it into the world. I could feel my right brain calling out to be included. It was a part of me I'd undervalued and abandoned for so long.

Autonomy. I never thought of myself as a rebel. But I realized that my preferred modus operandi wasn't consistent with working for anyone else, at least not in the traditional professional world. I knew I was done being a worker bee for other peoples' priorities, which I found boring at best, and highly problematic at worst.

Purpose and Connection. I wanted my work to have purpose and a meaningful impact. It wasn't that I needed to save the whole world. But, in my small corner of the universe, I wanted to feel connected to people and for my work to genuinely make a difference.

This vision did not amount to a specific plan. It wasn't a computer program that spits out my perfect career. But I had started to create space to connect the dots.

I was patient. Somehow, I developed faith that as I did this internal work and exploration, clarity on the what and how of my next step would come.

And it did. When it did, I knew it was the right next step because it all lined up with that vision I'd laid out.

I now spend my days running my own business and coaching people with big dreams and high standards for living by design, not by default. I help budding entrepreneurs design heart-centered businesses that allow them to show up as their best selves, live their best lives, and ditch their nine-to-fives. I even launched a private podcast called Daydreams to Designs that shows people how to make the jump from employee to entrepreneur.

Although a few years ago, I wouldn't have even known this was a career track, I've never been more proud of any work that I've done. Plus, I get to wake up without an alarm every morning. I have my coffee and meditate in the sun. It's almost always sunny in San Diego, where I live now. I work from the light-filled office that I've wallpapered with a monkey garden design, which brings me daily joy.

# THE STRATEGY

## CLARIFY YOUR NORTH STAR VISION

When you're preparing to make a big leap from employee to entrepreneur, the first step is clarifying your goals and defining your success. What is your ideal destination? It's like setting the GPS in your car. It helps keep you on track and make all of the correct turns. It also helps ground you into why this journey is important to you and what the payoff will be. That vision will help pull you forward on your journey.

The way I like to do this is to write out a vision statement. It's a one-to-two-page written exercise, envisioning your life in three-to-five years.

## GETTING SET UP

Give yourself at least 45 minutes for this exercise. It's not something to rush through. Grab your drink of choice, put on some calming music, take some deep breaths, and feel present. You can hand-write the vision statement or use the computer.

## BEING IN THE RIGHT MINDSET

It's important to come at this exercise with an open mind. Don't censor yourself with thoughts like "I shouldn't want that," "that's not realistic," or "I can't imagine how that would happen."

The goal is to uncover what you want if you strip away all you've been programmed to believe is possible. Please remember that you're allowed to want what you want.

## WRITING YOUR VISION

Now it's time to write. Imagine it's three to five years in the future. Daydream about what your life looks like. Remember to incorporate both work and life elements. It's okay if you're not exactly clear on your ideal work. You can describe aspects of work that you know are important to you. Write it as a journal entry in the present tense. It must be in the present tense, and include both external and internal experiences. All of this will make it as rich and tangible as possible.

Inspiration Questions:

- Where are you living?
- Who are you with?
- How do you feel?
- What do you see, taste, smell, hear?
- What does your daily routine look like?
- What are your favorite aspects of the work you do?
- What does your workspace look like?
- What is the impact you're having on clients?
- What motivates you in the work you do?
- What does success look like?
- What are your relationships with clients, family, and friends?
- How are your core values being embodied in your life?

## REVISITING YOUR VISION

You don't want to write this vision and never look at it again. The experience of consistently revisiting it is important. It serves as a litmus test for your decisions moving forward. Does that job, move, or experience take you closer or farther from this vision?

Some options for keeping your vision top of mind are:

- Framing your vision on the wall
- Laminating your vision and hanging it in the shower
- Setting a weekly reminder to read your vision
- Voice recording your vision and listening to it weekly

Revisiting your vision is also important because if you continue telling yourself this story as if it's the truth, your brain will start to believe it. It will build a new neural pathway, and when it does, your brain subconsciously goes to work to make that truth a reality. It sees opportunities you might have otherwise missed. It sees how seemingly unrelated puzzle pieces go together, and your reality will move closer and closer to your vision.

If you'd like to learn more about my framework for designing your heart-centered business, you can access my Daydreams to Designs private podcast and other resources at www.megansmiley.com/resources.

**Megan Smiley,** Esq. is the founder of Megan Smiley Coaching and the host of The Lawyer's Escape Pod. She is herself an escaped lawyer, having practiced corporate transactional law. Before taking the big leap into entrepreneurship, she took a baby step away from practice by working for a law school, where she was the Director of International Programs. She first launched an interior design business and then pivoted into coaching. She now primarily helps people design their own creative or coaching businesses through her one-on-one coaching.

Her mission is to help people who feel stuck in unfulfilling professions launch businesses that align with their life vision, natural talents, and values. It can be hard when your identity and sense of success are tightly bound to a profession. But Megan wants to help open your eyes to the world of possibilities and help you create a life and career by design rather than by default.

In her free time, you'll find Megan traveling the world. She's been to 58 countries and counting. She also loves hiking, sailing, and drinking ice-cold beer with friends. All things she can do year-round in her new home of San Diego. After deprogramming from the legal world, she's fiercely committed to creating space for fun and joy in her life, not just work.

Connect with Megan:

On her website: https://www.megansmiley.com
On her private podcast, Daydreams to Designs:
https://www.bit.ly/daydreamstodesigns
On her podcast, The Lawyer's Escape Pod:
https://thelawyersescapepod.podbean.com/
On LinkedIn: https://www.linkedin.com/in/megansmileyesq/
On Instagram: https://www.instagram.com/megansmileyesq/

# CHAPTER 5

# OWN YOUR MAGIC

## BECOME MAGNETIC WITH A SOUL-ALIGNED BRAND

Barb Pritchard

## MY STORY

"You're going to have to conform, Little Girl." I heard this so frequently in my late teens and early twenties, that after all these years, my mom's heart-felt wisdom still rings in my ears. She truly meant well. My mom had the perspective of a woman working in the corporate world, but I knew very early on that wasn't my destiny.

Looking back, I see how conflicted and confused this left me. My loving, strong, and protective mom was also the same woman who created a safe space for me, she empowered and encouraged me to explore my individuality, creativity, and self-expression. She was doggedly determined to have her girls form their own opinions and feel safe expressing those thoughts in respectful ways because she wasn't allowed to when she was growing up. "My girls will be both seen and heard." But her original advice to conform left me floundering. I was like a proverbial square peg, forcing my way into a round hole to be accepted and offered a corporate position.

As the years passed, I found success in the corporate world. I figured out how to play the game and climb the ladder. I learned the strategies, secrets, and tools that set businesses up for success and visibility.

But feeling unsatisfied and stifled, I longed to blaze a trail of my own. Many times, I tried to spread my wings and become my own boss. And many times, I failed. Though I always picked myself back up and tried again. I learned lessons and eventually discovered that, ultimately, one thing held me back.

Conformity.

It's the same culprit that holds many heart-centered entrepreneurs back from finding their success. It manifests itself as fear, doubt, second-guessing, and paralysis. It resembles throwing spaghetti at the walls, desperately hoping something will stick. It results in showing up as watered down, muted versions of ourselves, generalized expression, and speaking to everyone but attracting no one.

I get it. I experienced this myself with each failed attempt at a successful business. In a society where conformity is considered polite and, well, right, busting that mold and owning what makes you unique, your magic, as I call it, takes genuine bravery and courage, and it's scary as hell! What I found to be true is that owning your magic is an absolute necessity for success in today's crowded marketplace.

Standing out from the sea of sameness has never been more important for soul-aligned businesses. According to the US Census Bureau, in 2020, 4.4 million new businesses were started, only to be surpassed by a massive 5.4 million in 2021. These numbers provide ample opportunity for us all! There are a lot of businesses that need us and need to receive our message—but it's mission-critical to be visible. After all, you can't get noticed if you don't stand out.

How do we distinguish ourselves from the sea of sameness? Your magic, and how it manifests within, is the special sauce that no one can replicate. It magnetically attracts, initiates engagement, builds genuine connections, and creates superfans. Your magic is the connection that makes you memorable amongst the mundane.

But how do we know what our magic is, and how does it relate to our star clients? You will find your magic in those defining moments in life where your strength, purpose, and values are forged in fire. It contains emotion and is infused with passion. It's a turning point in your life that defines the "why" behind what you do and who you help. Its focus is on your star client, not you, your accomplishments, or your expertise. Your magic truly makes you unforgettable and is the reason your star client chooses to work with you.

The key is to surface your magic story and infuse that magic into your business by sprinkling it into everything; your branding and all it touches, every client interaction, and the many ways you show up in the marketplace.

The beautiful thing about your magic story is it's unique to you. The lessons you learned, the growth you experienced ground you in your magic. Your magic is the beacon of light you tap into to guide you through any storms or challenges you or your business may face. Your magic story is emotional, personal and paints a picture of the journey your star clients can relate to, establishing the authenticity and credibility they connect to. Stories are sticky. When shared from the heart, it's where your unique vantage point lives.

As an example, I'll share my magic story with you. When I finally quit conforming just to be accepted and please others, and when I discovered my magic and stood strong in it, I had a significant growth experience. I adopted the man who'd raised me since I was two and was no longer desperately seeking approval from my biological father.

To give a little context, my parents divorced when I was two. From as far back as I can remember, I tried my damnedest to earn the attention and affection of my biological father. He was inconsistent in my life, at best.

At the time of this magic story, I was 19 years old and a recent college graduate with my web design degree. I sent my father an invitation to my graduation, and he was a no-show. But I love the ways Spirit shows up and shows out. In that invitation, I felt compelled to include a little something extra. I enclosed a letter that shared aspirations and goals that I purposefully hadn't shared with anyone else. I also enclosed my first business card with my very own website and email address for my brand-new freelance web design business.

A few short weeks after my graduation, Father's Day rolled around and my sister, ever the dutiful daughter, dragged me out of town to visit him.

Throughout the entire visit, my father and stepmother brought up things I'd mentioned in the letter I'd included with my invitation. For example, we were on the way to grab lunch together, and my father pointed out a brand new, teal green Mercury Cougar as we passed a dealership and asked, "Is that the car you've got your eye on?" Indeed, it was. It was the same car in the exact color I'd described in my letter. I can still see the side-eye my sister gave me many times throughout the visit, wondering what the hell they were talking about. I also noticed my business card sitting on the mantle. It was hard to miss. My face was on it, and my hair was just as bright red back then as it is now. I knew early on he received my graduation invitation but didn't bother to show up or acknowledge it. By the grace of Spirit, I somehow managed to keep my cool.

At the end of the visit, as the sun was setting on a hot summer day, I had a rare, brief moment alone with my father. It turned out to be the last. It was as if time stood still. My father faced away from me, marveling and commenting on the magnificent sky's vivid oranges, pinks, and purples. He had his hands resting on the railing and his shoulders bunched up to his ears as he leaned over to take in as much of the scene as possible. As if compelled by Spirit, and before I could stop myself, I asked my father if he had received my invitation.

Instantly, his shoulders sank, and his grip on the railing tightened. The tension in the air was suddenly thick and palpable. Without ever looking at me, my father paused for what seemed like a million lifetimes and whispered, "no."

Something in me shifted at that moment. I finally saw what kind of man he was, especially his lack of integrity. I didn't feel wounded; instead, I was emboldened. I stood up straighter, raised my chin high, and replied with a simple, "Okay."

I was done.

A flurry of painful memories rushed through my mind as I watched him struggle with the awkwardness of the situation. Time seemingly slowed further as the hot summer breeze stung my cheeks. It was as if to keep me present and not focus on all the times he forgot me, my birthday, my dance recitals, and graduations. Instead, I felt relief and sensed that it was as much closure as I was ever going to get from him. I didn't argue or point out his blatant lie. It finally dawned on me that he wasn't worth my energy, time, or tears.

Not long after this revelation, I began the process of changing my last name to that of my dad, the man who loved me as his own, unconditionally, from the age of two. It was one of the greatest gifts I'd ever give myself and this wonderful human that I began to call Dad from that day forward.

## SURFACE YOUR MAGIC STORY

To surface your magic story and uncover the magic you hold within, I invite you to create a quiet space to reflect, get grounded, invite Spirit in to guide you, and let your intuition take the lead. Focus on a defining moment in your life where your strength was forged in fire. Chances are, when you've found it—you'll feel it. It's likely to be emotionally charged and passion-filled, resulting in a lesson learned, healing, clarity, and drawing a line in the sand to take a stand.

There are four parts to this magic story moment:

1. Struggle
2. Turning Point
3. Realization
4. Connection

## PART 1: STRUGGLE

The struggle provides context and backstory about what was happening and what wasn't working, leading to the turning point.

My example:

The inconsistent relationship with my biological father plagued me with doubts and insecurities throughout my life. I would bend over backward to be who I thought he wanted me to be just to win his love.

## PART 2: TURNING POINT

The turning point is the crossroad where a decision was made, and a significant change is about to take place.

My example:

After years of my father floating in and out of my life on his whim, I had a feeling he wouldn't bother to acknowledge my college graduation. I felt called to test his integrity, a quality that I require for those in my inner circle. When the opportunity presented itself to confront him with his most recent no-show, what I suspected was true, and I was finally able to see his true colors.

## PART 3: REALIZATION

This is your A-ha moment! The clarity, healing, or lesson learned as a result of the turning point. At the heart of this realization is your magic.

My example:

Over the years, I did my damnedest to conform to an ideal that I thought would win my father's affection. This defining moment showed me that I wasted a lot of time, tears, and energy over the years on a person who didn't value me. But that wasn't my fault. My big a-ha moment was realizing that I am enough, exactly as I am. I can be all of me and still be loved and appreciated. I don't have to water myself down or round out my edges just to fit into a mold that wasn't meant for me in the first place. I noticed that Spirit showed up and showed out by inspiring me to take action and truly open my eyes to love me for who I truly am and to own that magic I have within. As time passed, there would be more opportunities to truly step into my magic and develop more self-love. But the lesson remained the same: I am enough. I am magical. I am loved exactly as I am. And I don't have to be a muted version of myself to please anyone.

## PART 4: CONNECTION

The connection bridges the gap between your story and your star client. It creates that connection between them and how your magic relates to them.

My example:

It can be a huge leap of faith to go all in and own your magic. As spiritual entrepreneurs, we have likely seen or experienced firsthand the alienation that comes with our woo-woo walk. And as such, many of us water that down out of fear of rejection.

In my work with heart-centered businesses, I recognize a disconnect between my clients' passion, what lights them up, and how they show up in their business. Many hold parts of themselves back to play it safe, while others are more than ready to step into their magic but don't know how to surface it, let alone articulate it verbally or visually.

Spiritual entrepreneurs have the power to help others break out of their status quo and experience true, life-changing growth. My mission is to empower these beautiful souls to envision and embody their magic so they become magnetic to their star clients. It's my dream to perpetuate a world of do-gooders doing super goodness, paying that growth forward, and raising the collective vibration of the planet one person at a time.

# THE STRATEGY

## HOW TO INFUSE YOUR MAGIC INTO YOUR BRAND VISION TO STAND OUT

After you've unlocked your magic story, answer the questions below.

1. What is your magic story? I invite you to grab a journal or open up Word/Google Docs and let it flow out of you without editing.

2. Once you've finished letting your magic story pour out of you, identify the following:

   a. The struggle: the context and backstory about what was happening, what wasn't working, and what eventually led to the turning point.

   b. The turning point: the crossroad where a decision was made, and a significant change is about to take place.

   c. The realization: the A-ha moment! The clarity, healing, or lesson learned as a result of the turning point. At the heart of this realization is your magic.

    d. The connection: how your star client can identify with and relate to your story/magic and how it helps them experience transformation.

3. Focus on your A-ha moment! What was the realization, the clarity you gained, the lesson learned, and the healing you received from your magic story? This is your magic.

Once you've surfaced your magic, it's time to own it by infusing it into your brand and every client interaction. Below are a few ways you can utilize your magic, infuse it into your business, and share it with the world:

- Infuse your magic into your visual identity (Get the free workbook at the end of the chapter for how!)
- Add your magic story to your about page on your website.
- Write a blog post that describes your magic and how you discovered it.
- Share your magic story in a series of social media posts.
- Create a video explaining your magic and its relation to your star client.
- Create a podcast episode.
- Write about it in a book.

**Want to take your magic to the next level? Download the free Soul-Aligned Brand Vision Workbook.**

The free Soul-Aligned Brand Vision Workbook helps you put your magic into context by surfacing visuals that represent the essence of your magic. You can then utilize visuals similar to these and use them throughout your brand, website, social media, and launches. Think of this as a vision board for your business or next launch!

www.soul-alignedbrand.com

**Barb Pritchard** is a brand enchanter, website wizard, and book cover/launch magician for spiritual entrepreneurs. She helps soulful businesses look like the abundance they manifest, raise their vibe, and infuse their magic into their business through purposeful, empathy-focused design. Barb is a believer in the magic of marrying Spirit with strategy to create an impactful and remarkable business that attracts clients automagically.

With over 20 years of design experience with Fortune 100/500 clients and small businesses, Barb's passion is empowering heart-centered entrepreneurs to feel more fulfilled within their business and make a bigger impact by sharing their magic and infusing it into every client interaction in their business.

When she's not designing, Barb can be found snuggling with her mini-panthers, nerding out with her husband on video games or Dungeons and Dragons, or planning their next excursion to Europe to experience the culture, the food, and the history.

Connect with Barb:

Website: www.infinitybrand.design
Facebook: www.facebook.com/InfinityBrandDesign
Instagram: www.instagram.com/infinitybranddesign
LinkedIn: www.linkedin.com/in/barbpritchard
Free Soul-Aligned Brand Vision Workbook:
www.soul-alignedbrand.com

# CHAPTER 6

# BUSINESS ENERGETICS

## WHY DETOXING YOUR LIFE IS THE KEY TO YOUR BRAND'S SUCCESS

Coco Alexandra Chan, Co-Founder Voltage X,
Mystic Teacher, Soul Coach

# MY STORY

Being born fatherless and growing up with an absent mother created a huge hole of insecurity within me. It was a hole I would try to fill every day. I was scrummaging through external satiations in hopes of hitting that euphoric high you get when you're in love or feel loved.

I performed to receive praise.

I gave more in the hope of receiving more.

I said yes to people-pleasing so I would be liked.

And over time, I became a neurotic yes-woman.

I was available for everyone and anything except myself, and felt regularly tired, drained, grumpy, impatient, and annoyed. I was in meaningless and toxic relationships hoping that I would feel less alone. I drank into the wee hours to numb myself from feeling my soul-wrenching emotions of childhood abandonment. And I attended every glamorous city event in hopes of feeling included and seen.

That way of living eventually took a massive toll on me. One day at the office, as I was about to go out for a meeting, I collapsed. When I woke up, I found myself in a cold hospital bed. In what seemed like slow motion, a stern-faced doctor informed me, "You're being diagnosed with chronic anxiety, and I advise you to change your lifestyle habits. If you choose not to, the situation will only get worse, and your organs may begin to shut down one by one."

I was in my early 20s, and this shook me to the core like an earthquake internally erupting from within. Twenty-plus years of pain exploded into a tsunami of tears. That was my rude awakening—like a slap in the face from Spirit.

That moment changed my life forever.

I quit my job and began to search high and low for alternative healing methods that would free me of using lifelong prescription medication. After all, I wanted to revive the inner sparkle that I was confident would shine bright again. I didn't want to use medication as a crutch or to make myself feel numb. I'd already been numb for years. For long enough, I'd felt like a soulless bodysuit walking around aimlessly and without purpose. I wanted to feel the wide range of colorful emotions and experiences I once felt.

I spent months researching and traveling to the corners of the earth to meet with shamans and healers to find myself again. Then, I went through a soul-altering transformation. It wasn't an easy journey, as I witnessed my whole life crumbling. When I reached one of my lowest and darkest points, I experienced my loudest awakening.

I met a healer that cracked my heart open to see through the illusions and smokescreens that hazed my vision of life. She opened a doorway for me to see a way out of the darkness. It was then that I knew healing would be an instrumental part of my life.

As I sat in a room filled with crystal grids and thick sage smoke, the healer took me on a meditative journey through past lives that weaved into the present and catapulted me into future timelines. At that moment, a loving angelic voice spoke to me: *You have chosen to come into this life to experience trauma at a young age, for through these lessons, you will learn to forgive and love even more deeply. You shall embody these experiences and lead by example for many.*

That message vibrated throughout every fiber of my being. I knew I would dedicate my life to healing myself and supporting others on their personal growth journey.

The following years were filled with highs and lows. But with each wave, I learned to ride them with more ease and land more gracefully. I collected pearls of wisdom from teachers in the sacred arts of the Akashic Records, Holy Fire Karuna Reiki, shamanism, angel healing, channeling, quantum healing, light language and plant spirit medicine, divine masculine, and divine feminine teachings.

The woman I had become was hardly recognizable by those who knew me in the past. The once jaded black sheep became the high vibing cheerleader that everyone wanted in their corner. My energy rose and became infectious wherever I went. I became magnetic.

I learned how to weave together the energetics of the spiritual realm and embody it into physical form. After that my life fast-tracked. I founded one of Hong Kong's top PR and digital agencies in 2013 called, Voltage PR. Then I launched my coaching and healing business in 2017, got married to the love of my life in 2018, became a mother in 2019, and invested in my first home that same year. Voltage PR rebranded to Voltage X in 2022, and expanded its clientele globally.

This life I created was possible thanks to all the teachings of my mentors but, most importantly, energy mastery. Everything aligned when I learned how to shift energies and embody them to flow naturally into my personal and professional life.

Everyone's dream life is different, but each of you deserves to be living it! The first step towards this transformation is through energy management.

# THE STRATEGY

I have dedicated years to studying and embodying the arts of spirituality and energetics and their role in our lives. I realize that focusing on the mastery of balancing the divine feminine and divine masculine is how we, as *soulpreneurs,* healers, and coaches, co-create with the Universe to birth through our soul gifts/businesses and anchor it into reality.

The masculine is a part of life we are familiar with, the doing, the taking action, and getting results. But it's the divine feminine energies that bring balance and hold space for us to be able to create a strong foundation to build on, whether it's our personal life, relationships, emotions, or our soul business.

If we only know one mode, which is all push and go, then we are operating from a space of imbalance and quickly learn the lesson of burnout.

Our soul business is an extension of our energies. We must learn to balance the divine feminine and masculine to co-create a harmony within us that then overflows into our business. The universal law of polarity is always at play. So, I want to share the strategies and methods to weave together these two aspects of life so any *soulpreneur* can manifest their dreams into reality and create a thriving heart-aligned business that flourishes.

Practicing energy management will be a key element in creating a thriving business.

Before we dive into the step-by-step process, let's begin with what energy is and how it affects our overall vibes.

Everything is energy.

Quantum physicists have already proven that everything is matter. Everything is made of energy. We are energetic beings. At our cellular level, we are composed of atoms, and these molecules are constantly bouncing against each other, creating friction between them that creates a vibration. This vibration is our frequency. However, as humans, we have emotions, and therefore our vibration is continuously fluctuating. We have all had those moments when we enter a room of people, and there are certain people we gravitate towards and others we repel from, right? Cue all the vibes.

We have our good days and our off days, depending on how we feel. This is because our emotions interlink with our frequency—we emit that vibration, and others can feel it.

Again, we are energy, and everything we say, do, and create is also energy—which leads me to energy leaks!

Energy leaks are the byproduct of the lack of boundaries we have. When we do not have healthy boundaries, we create energy leaks. We leak energy everywhere. When we have energy leaks, we may feel tired, uninspired, unmotivated, impatient, annoyed, resentful, grumpy, drained, and the list goes on. So how can we shift these energy leaks, protect our vibes, and stay true to ourselves? The first step is to get radically honest with yourself and bring awareness to where your energy leaks are coming from.

Here is a list of examples:

- Over scheduling your calendar
- Constantly being plugged in
- Endlessly giving away your time
- Watching too much Netflix
- Addictions
- Working overtime—all the time
- Endless scrolling on social media
- Being with people who are negative and complain
- Not prioritizing yourself
- Poor diet
- Being in a toxic relationship
- Being in a toxic situation or environment
- Lack of sleep
- Lack of exercise
- Lack of connection

Do any of these sound familiar? Hey, I get it. That was me before. We live in a modern society where we are constantly conditioned to do more, crush those goals, and attain a certain level of status and success. We are regularly plugged in and always on the go. It's no surprise that we are experiencing the highest documented rates of burnout, anxiety, and mental wellbeing imbalances. This overloads our nervous system. Our never-ending to-do lists become our biggest enemies and energy drainers.

If you were drawn to this chapter, then your soul business is about to get an upgrade! As an energetic being, your soul business is an extension of your energy. So, let's dive in and take a closer look at your life and find those energy leaks to get you from an energetically depleted state and become a magnetic *soulpreneur* with the practice below.

## LOCATING YOUR ENERGY LEAKS

### What you'll need:

- Pen and paper
- An open mind
- Can-do attitude
- Resilience (lots of it)
- Consistency
- Radical honesty

Prepare a pen and paper to journal after this practice. Find a place free of distractions where you can be fully present and sit or lay down in a comfortable position.

Gently close your eyes, relax your body and connect to your breath. Begin inhaling deeply into your being, expanding the belly, exhaling, and sighing through the mouth. With each inhale, breathe in light and expansiveness, creating more space between every cell of your body. On each exhale, release any tension or heaviness held within all 12 parts of your being. Repeat this breathing cycle as many times as you need until you feel completely aligned in the present moment.

When you have arrived at your unique rhythmic flow through the breath, guide your breath down into your heart space and activate your sacred heart with three deep breaths. Your heart is a portal to your soul.

When you align with the energies of your heart, you see, sense, and feel with more clarity.

And now, with your mind's eye and the power of your intention, visualize what your aura looks like. What colors do you see, sense, or feel? Take a few moments to tune into it.

Now visualize your aura as threads of energies. Notice where your strands of energies have been left behind, whether in conversations, places, objects, habits, situations, experiences, or relationships.

Notice who pops into your mind, which experiences or interactions are present. Once you can see, sense, or feel where your energies have been left behind, use the power of your intention to release your energetic cords from these people, places, and situations—breath by breath and call back your energies strand by strand. Take as long as you need.

As your energies return to you, become aware of the increase of life force energy within you, aligning you back into a space of wholeness. When you feel calm, centered, and fully in your energies again, I invite you to graciously smile, place both hands over your heart, complete this practice in a state of gratitude, and then softly open your eyes.

Now take a few minutes to journal what came through for you.

Here is a few journal prompts to get you started. Feel free to add in your own.

- Where or who are your energy leaks coming from?
- Which energy leak felt the most draining?
- Are your energy leaks conscious or unconscious?
- What actionable steps can you take to eliminate these energy leaks?
- How can you integrate more energy-boosting activities or rituals into your life?
- What boundaries do you need to set in place to keep yourself in a positive, energetic space?
- What inspired action will you take after this practice?

This practice supports you in clearing out energy blockages and releasing energies that you may hold onto that are not yours. Those energies take up space—your space. When you clear them out, you create more space within yourself to do what you do best; create magic within your life and soul business to call in higher vibrational clients and opportunities. Yes, please!

You can come back to this practice time and time again. It's yours to add to your energetic support toolbox for life. I love it when clients add their own magic into the practices I share to make it their own. Perhaps you may feel called to evolve this practice over time, so it grows with you.

## SETTING HEALTHY BOUNDARIES

Boundaries are the essential building blocks of your energetic container for both your personal and professional life. This is where you get to practice authentic expression to communicate to yourself and others how you want to be treated, seen, heard, and loved. It shows others how you want to show up, where you choose to invest your time and energy, and, most importantly, how you value yourself.

Know that you're in the driver's seat when building and creating your life and soul business. You make the rules. Think of what your needs are. How can you respectfully communicate your expectations with others to create healthy and strong boundaries and operate at your best?

By doing this, you're creating an energetically high vibing life to live your best life and have time for all the things you love.

Remember, your energy is sacred. You get to decide who has access to you.

## ALIGNING YOUR ENERGIES TO YOUR SOUL BUSINESS

As you learn to master your energies, you create more space to build a grounded foundation to build your soul business. Your soul business is a part of you. If your energies are everywhere, they will reflect in your business. If you dedicate time and space to your energetic hygiene, stay grounded, set healthy and strong boundaries, and do the inner work, your business will benefit from it.

While you continue to work on yourself, your soul business will grow and expand with you.

There are no limits to what you create. The only limitation is your willingness to put in the work.

Lean into your gifts as a *soulpreneur,* master your energies, and it will align you to your authentic magnetism.

Your soul resonance emits a unique frequency when you're in alignment.

This is how you attract your soul-aligned clients, increase your opportunities, and elevate your soul and business expansion.

I want you to know that no matter what you've experienced in life, you got through it. You're here, and the future awaits you with open arms.

You have the magic inside you to create a life you have always envisioned.

Weave this practice into your professional and personal life to build your dreams and make them all become your reality! I'm rooting for you!

This is just the first step of many to integrate energetic mastery into your personal and professional life. It's deep and important work. It's stepping into bravery, facing your pain, and processing them in a healthy and safe container so you can embody your experiences and align with your dreams and thrive in life.

Clients I work with say that they value having an empowering cheerleader in their corner, and I love being there for them! But let's get real, intuitive healing and soul coaching support tap into realms of shadow work, and this is not always sunshine, rainbows, and daisies. But, if you choose to take that leap, the results are long-lasting, and it will change your life forever.

**Coco Alexandra Chan** is a Soul Coach, Mystic Teacher, and Speaker based in Hong Kong, serving clients globally. As the co-founder of Voltage X, one of Hong Kong's top PR and digital agencies, she bridges her 17 years of experience in the business world with the wisdom of spirituality to support clients through deep transformational healing and in creating soul-aligned businesses that thrive.

As a human design manifesting generator, she wears many hats in life and has the energy for it. She's a mom to a spiritually gifted child, a mentor to *soulpreneurs,* a public speaker, mental health advocate, and a conscious business investor.

She now spends her days coaching individuals/groups and advising brands to further expand their business, personal and spiritual growth through energetic management tools. Coco aspires to leave behind a legacy with her love of teaching and empowering others to live their best life.

Her work has been featured on Cosmopolitan, Marie Claire, Tatler, ESQUIRE, Sohohouse, SCMP, ELLE Singapore, TVB, Lifestyle Asia, Capital CEO, Hypebae, and more.

Connect with Coco:

https://cocoalexandra.com/
Instagram @iamcocoalexandra
https://www.linkedin.com/in/cocoalexandrachan/

# CHAPTER 7

# KNOW YOUR MONEY, GROW YOUR BUSINESS

## GET YOUR FINANCES IN ORDER AND TAKE YOUR BUSINESS TO THE NEXT LEVEL

Sara Fins, Accountant, Health Coach

## MY STORY

I sat at the big round table savoring my dessert and thinking about the delicious Shirley Temple I'd enjoyed earlier with my dinner. Then the waiter handed my father the bill, and as he looked at it, an expression of feigned shock and horror appeared on his face. I was eight years old, and we were out for a rare celebratory fancy dinner. My sister and I looked at each other and giggled at his silly behavior.

This reaction was not new. My father often made this joke when he was paying for something. Although it was meant to be funny, and we laughed every time, I often wondered why he acted so surprised.

*Didn't he know what the dinner would cost?*

To my young mind, the message seemed to be that money was not something you needed to pay attention to until you had to spend it, and when you did, you would hope that you had enough.

As you can probably guess by now, my family didn't talk much about money when I was growing up. My parents divorced when I was five, and my sister was three, and although we had what we needed, I always sensed an underlying tension around money. I felt it between my parents and in general in their homes. My response to that feeling was to never ask for money for something unless it was absolutely necessary. When I did ask one of my parents to buy me something, I always felt guilty about it, and it felt better to avoid doing it. Money was not something to embrace and appreciate, but something to be ignored and even feared.

I couldn't wait to earn my own money. So, as soon as I was old enough, I started babysitting. Feeling that crisp twenty-dollar bill in my hand from a night of watching my neighbor's kids felt like a relief. If I had money of my own, I wouldn't have to ask anyone else for it, and maybe I wouldn't have to stress over it or think about it at all.

As I got older, I went on to work in retail and as a lifeguard. The certainty of receiving an actual paycheck every few weeks felt liberating. I loved having my own money for personal expenses, like new clothing and gas for my car, and was so relieved not to have to ask my parents for it. I had a general sense about how much I had available to spend, but I didn't pay much attention to what I earned. I certainly never dreamed about buying anything beyond my basic needs and a few fun extras. In fact, I never even realized it was possible to think bigger. The money came in and went out, and that was that. I didn't need to think any more about it.

Although money management wasn't a regular topic of conversation as I was growing up, it was made very clear that getting a job that paid well was important. My mom always said, "It's your job to be a good student." I took that to heart and worked very hard in school, earning good grades and acceptance to a prestigious university. I was on my way to securing a job with a salary where I earned enough to cover my needs. That way, I could continue to avoid having to pay too much attention to my money and relieve the feeling of stress that always came with it.

I entered school as a general business major and quickly changed to accounting. I felt that pursuing a career in this field would get me to the goal of getting a good job after college. I wasn't wrong. I did well in my classes and earned myself an internship at a respected accounting firm for the summer before my senior year. After that internship ended, I was offered a job that would begin after graduation later that year. I accepted.

After graduating and starting my dream job, I also began living on my own and supporting myself fully for the first time. I could pay my rent, put food on the table, and go out with my friends, so I felt like I had my finances covered. Heck, I even set up automatic withdrawals from each paycheck to put part of my earnings into a retirement account, as the company advised.

I was doing all the right things, but something still didn't feel right. Why did I get so anxious when my friends would ask me to go on vacation, or when someone suggested going to a really nice and expensive restaurant, or a Broadway show? *Will I have enough money for that?*

Although it seemed at the time that I was checking all the boxes of smart finances, my actions didn't translate into true money management. Why? The awareness wasn't there. If only my present-day self could go back and speak to my twenty-five year-old self, she could have explained to her what was truly possible for her money and her dreams if only she were intentional about it. She could have told her: *If you pay attention to your money, you will be able to relieve the stress you are feeling while enjoying current experiences and also plan for even bigger things.*

After studying accounting for four years, earning my CPA license, and working at an accounting firm, I realize now that I still avoided *my* money.

While I knew everything about debits and credits and how to book a journal entry, I didn't have a clue about true money management. It's easy to feel like you have things under control when you have enough money to get by and pay your bills. But when you begin consciously and deliberately paying attention to and planning with your money, the world opens up for you.

When my boyfriend at the time (my now husband) and I began talking about marriage, I reluctantly came to the realization that I couldn't simply ignore money anymore. It was terrifying. The kinds of things we were talking about now like paying for a wedding, buying a house, and starting a family, simply couldn't be addressed with the money-in and money-out approach I'd been relying on for so long.

I spent the next year paying attention to my finances. Even though it didn't feel natural to me, I made a commitment. I looked at my income and where my money was going. Which expenses did I have that were non-negotiable and which did I have some discretion over? What would I need money for in the long run, and when would I need it? This wasn't an exercise in budgeting but rather an exercise in focus. Before I could start using tools like budgeting and investing, I had to create the right *mindset* when it came to my money.

Do you know the saying, "Where your attention goes, energy flows?" Putting that saying into practice changed *everything*.

My husband and I did not want to settle for a cost-conscious wedding, or live with the constant anxiety of coming up short when it came time to pay a bill. So, we patiently and purposely saved enough money to throw ourselves the wedding we'd dreamed of at a beautiful restaurant on the water. We also had money in the bank to put toward a down payment on a house when we were ready. The fear and anxiety that I'd unconsciously carried around about money for all these years were finally beginning to melt away.

Shortly afterward, we manifested an experience of living and working abroad. By applying that same mindset change, we were able to travel and experience life like we always wanted to. We enjoyed short weekend getaways, knowing what we could afford, and planned for longer and more exotic vacations to places that seemed out of reach to that financially fearful teenager of my youth.

When I became pregnant with my daughter, I decided that the time was right to take the next step in my life and leave the corporate world behind to follow my passion for health and wellness.

I went back to school to study nutrition, become a health coach, and opened my practice shortly after earning my certification. Since I was new to entrepreneurship, I had a lot to learn about running a business. However, the attention I'd been paying to my personal finances, coupled with my accounting knowledge, made the financial management of my business feel easy for me.

Over the years, I discovered that many of my fellow health coaches and others in the entrepreneurial space did not have this same ease around their financial management. It was something that they dreaded and often preferred not to think about, *just as I'd felt about money all those years ago.* While this mindset did not prevent them from helping their clients achieve amazing results, it kept their businesses stuck and prevented them from growing the way they wanted and deserved.

*You should teach this to people* was the thought that kept popping into my head over and over again. I ignored it. *I already have a business. I don't need a new one.* But, as I sat in the audience at a business conference watching a hugely successful business owner talk about how she used to feel so lost when it came to her business's finances, a light bulb went on. She explained, "Once I found someone to teach finances to me in a way I could understand, I gained the clarity I needed to grow my business exponentially." As I listened, I began thinking. *I know that I could help others feel this way about their money.* After all, I was already the go-to girl for friends who had small businesses and questions about organizing their finances.

After many months, I finally decided to listen to the message I had been getting from the universe. While waiting in the airport for my flight home from that conference, I wrote the plan for my new business and the outline for my new finance course. *Easy Business Bookkeeping* was born.

I've never felt so aligned with my business and purpose as I do now. I have moved on from health coaching and started focusing my time and energy on my passion. I am helping fellow solopreneurs learn to confidently manage their business finances so they can achieve their business goals. The key? Awareness coupled with simple, repeatable action.

In this next section, I will share with you five tips that you can get started with right away. I believe these strategies will have the most immediate impact on your business finances and allow your business to grow while you manage it with more ease and less stress.

# THE STRATEGY

Get Your Finances in Order and Take Your Business to the Next Level

1. **Believe you can do it.** You are smart, driven, and passionate. If you weren't, you wouldn't feel the pull to run your own business. I hear time and time again from my clients and colleagues that they struggle to manage their business finances because they feel they aren't a numbers person. I want to bust this myth! No one is born a numbers person. It's a skill and something that you can learn if you put your mind to it. After all, when you first went into business, did you know all that you needed to know about your area of expertise? Probably not. You likely needed to acquire some new skills. Think of your business bookkeeping in that way. Those numbers won't feel so scary once you learn what you need to know. Believe in yourself!

2. **Keep your business and personal accounts separate.** This is a practical strategy that will also create an energetic container for the money in your business. Open a checking account that you will use *only* for your business. It doesn't have to be a true business account, just one separate from your personal bank account. This will help make it easier to follow the numbers when looking at your transactions and foster the energy that your business is truly a business and deserves its own space to grow.

3. **Have a system for tracking your finances.** It's important to look at the flow of money in your business and pay attention to the ins and outs. Tracking your finances takes it one step further. When you can clearly see the revenue you're bringing in, you'll better understand which areas of your business to focus on. It's also important to know what you're spending money on to manage that appropriately. When deciding on a tracking system, the most important thing to consider is *to choose one that you will feel comfortable using.* It's no help to have a complex and intimidating system. For most solopreneurs, fancy accounting software is more than they need; using a simple tool, like a well designed spreadsheet, is usually sufficient.

4. **Make a date with your money.** As I mentioned earlier in this chapter, where your attention goes, energy flows. Becoming comfortable with your money requires regular attention. Set aside a recurring appointment in your calendar (weekly, monthly, etc.), where you review your business accounts and add the information to your tracking tool. Be sure to set the tone for this money date so that you feel at ease. Put on some music, pour a cup of tea, and get comfortable. Then dive in! It might feel stressful at first and take you more time than you think it will, but like any practice, the more you do it, the more natural it will become. Over time, you will gain the clarity and confidence to truly manage your finances.

5. **Ask for help.** Are you unsure of where to begin? Do you feel confused about an investment you want to make in your business? Get support. I would bet that you learned most of the new skills you have gained in your life more easily with a guide. Finances are no different. There is so much helpful information available at no cost, and coaches, accountants, and other professionals can help you on your way. Don't be shy. Ask for help if you need it. You will be glad you did.

I hope that these suggestions give you some ideas and action steps for how to get started managing your business finances. If you're looking for more tools and tips, visit www.sarafins.com/soulbusiness.

As we close this chapter, I will leave you with this takeaway. Regularly paying attention to your business finances may feel daunting at first, and it will likely bring up a variety of emotions. However, working through these emotions and taking the time to get clear on how to manage this area of your business will provide you with the information you need to grow your earnings *and* your impact. You will be able to serve more clients when you're financially supported. The work is worth it, I promise!

**Sara Fins** is an expert Financial and Certified Health Coach who spent over a decade as an accountant in the corporate world and a decade running her own health coaching practice. Now she blends her accounting background and entrepreneurial experience to help other solopreneurs manage and master their business finances with ease.

Through her private coaching programs, workshops, and signature course, Easy Business Bookkeeping, Sara helps small business owners feel confident, take their businesses to the next level, and earn money and freedom they desire.

When Sara isn't working with clients, you'll find her hanging out with friends and family or curling up with a good book in her Long Island, New York home. She loves to travel and see the world, and her favorite place to relax and recharge is at the beach.

Connect with Sara:

On her website: www.sarafins.com
On Facebook: https://www.facebook.com/easybusinessbookkeeping
On Instagram: https://www.instagram.com/easybusinessbookkeeping/
In her Free Facebook Community,
The Easy Business Bookkeeping Community:
https://www.facebook.com/groups/easybusinessbookkeeping.

# CHAPTER 8

# A JOURNEY FROM PANIC TO PROFIT

## THE POWER OF LEVERAGING RETREATS

Amy Flores-Young, Travel Planning Specialist

# MY STORY

### CAREER HIGH TO UNEMPLOYED CAREGIVER

I was a public speaker and national trainer for many years. One of my opening lines was, "I have seen more shit than a stable hand in Kentucky." It always got a giggle. I didn't use it as a pity approach but to set the tone that I have "been there, done that" and moved on. My whole life was built on that "move on," and "move forward" mindset.

We all have our craptastic moments, and dark baggage we cover with rainbow patches, to make it easier to carry. I get that. But my bags are oversized, and I've paid a fortune in baggage fees.

I've yet to meet a therapist who isn't taken aback by the frequent flyer rewards I've received for my *shit happens* miles. My attitude is, it happened, so don't sit in it. Learn from it, look for the meaning and positives, and get on with it.

That perspective helped in the creation of my twenty-plus-year career in nonprofit work, involving building programs, and teams to increase service to those less fortunate, with disabilities, or in crisis. I also had personal experience with many of these issues, and that allowed me to be a leader in service to others.

Years ago, my teenage disabled daughter experienced complications from surgery, and for six months I lived between Children's Hospital Boston, and Spaulding Rehabilitation Center. One typical autumn rainy day in the northeast, while the wind and leaves danced in the rain, I sat crying uncontrollably in my Dodge Caravan—me, the stoic, no-nonsense pillar of strength. On that day, I found out I lost my job, career, support network, and my community. I didn't know it yet, but I'd also lost my identity.

As I took the phone call from my previous employer, I started walking. I moved out of the claustrophobic, very public, in-patient hospital room. I was purposefully walking hard to feel my steps and keep myself grounded while feeling out-of-body.

Upon hanging up the call, I found myself soaking wet in the parking garage. Subconsciously, I headed towards private cover. I found my van and got in. Then I turned on the heat, and the sobbing hit like a nor'easter storm. You know it's coming, but the storm's force is still surprising when you feel it.

So many sobs came in and out like ocean waves, with small moments to catch my breath before getting slammed again. I felt fear, shame, regret, sadness, betrayal, loss, guilt, and grief. Yet, I also felt relief. Yes, there was a large sense of lightness, openness, and relief at the end. I was relieved of the pressure of a career that no longer fulfilled me, and I could then concentrate 100% on my child's recovery. I felt so much relief that I hadn't even been aware of the strain I was under. While I still remember that day as my 'who I thought I was' reality-shattering low point, it's also where my deepest healing started, and my true potential was unleashed.

As I mentioned, I was built from an "it's beyond your control, take it in, shake it off, and move on," model. I took the upside of all that relief and got to work. In focusing only on my daughter's recovery, I was in pure amazement at how I'd done it while I was working. It was exhausting and woke up parts of me I didn't know were there. We returned home and got into our new normal routine. Without the crisis mode of recovery, the sheer panic of being unemployed and still having a family and household to support set in—hard.

I did temp work that allowed me the flexibility I needed to be home for my care duties. But it was lifeless, and I was lifeless as well. I was in the deepest depression I'd ever had. Thoughts were getting darker, and that lightness of relief turned into constant panic and anxiety. *There has to be a better way.* I traded in the panic of scarcity and took on the "now what?" mode.

Instead of focusing on all I had lost, and the panic in the future, I focused on the possibilities and opportunities all this change created. In that thinking, I became clear in knowing I needed to take my leadership, planning, facilitation, and communication skills to build something for myself—something in my control. That clarity in intuition (*knowing*) made it easier to take the steps to move forward in creating my own business.

## BUT WHY TRAVEL?

It takes an extraordinary effort to have an ordinary day when you live in a family that includes a person with a disability. Understandably, most people don't think of trying to do something extra-extraordinary. Not me! Getting out of the heavy ordinary daily needs is what lightened and enriched my family. Travel was the glue that kept our family together. I know that my husband and I would not still be together, and my children would be very different if we had not prioritized travel when they were toddlers. Living in a medically complex household means therapists, nurses, and aides in and out of your life and house.

Most of my attention was given to my daughter's care and managing her schedule while my husband did the sports aspects with our son. While we are one family unit and function as a winning team, our interactions are not conducive to creating traditional parental/sibling bonds. When we travel, all the stress of our day-to-day fades, and we can focus on each other. While the disabilities don't disappear, they are not the main characters during our travels like they are in our usual days.

Our trips strengthened our familial relationships and brought us to understand each other as individuals and our family roles. The first stories my children, now adults, share when someone new enters the house are about our travel memories. Photo albums come out, and the kitchen fills with laughter. Our dinner conversations often reflect our travel and where we will go next, cueing into what we want to experience together.

I am one of those Disney people. Yes, my house is filled with mouse-shaped art, my dogs are named after lesser-known characters, and I have Pixar soundtracks on my iTunes. I have traveled to Disney Parks and cruises dozens of times. As a result, I quickly became the friendly neighborhood house of mouse expert. Traveling with medically complex needs is not easy. So, I also became a go-to advisor for others looking to make accessible travel happen. "Why don't you do this for a living?" was a constant question. Well, talking about trips for the fun of it is very different from being responsible for someone else's vacation. Travel was important in my life, and I wanted others to be able to have magical memories. So, I shared my tips and tricks as often as possible, for free.

It took a few more knocks from the universe for my thick skull to hear the message—*this is what I am built for.* What most people struggled with or had worries about were easy issues for me to solve or workaround. Feeling hopeful, I experienced the *now what!*

The process of figuring out this next phase was messy and in no way linear. Thank you to all my intuitive healers, human design, and spiritual mentor friends for helping me make sense of my gifts and showing me that my fast-paced yet creative thought processes are magical. And that being able to trust my understanding of big picture plans while handling intricate details is a fairly unique balance. I love that I can embrace and harness both of those sides well.

A new exciting panic joined my emotional range. Putting aside all the *what if's* and *can I really,* I researched agencies and the ins and outs of building a travel business. I'd started nonprofits, supervised dozens of staff members, and spoken on stages. But this was a whole new world for me (cue the magic carpet ride). Social media for the win! After reaching out to a few agencies and looking into owning my own, a non-related post in a health group led to a chat that made the travel business dream a reality. I founded my home agency with the flexibility to build my own business while still handling caregiver duties.

## UP, UP, AND AWAY

There are many travel advisors that are part-time hobbyists, and there are also full-time travel professionals. Since I have played both sides, I feel I am in a unique position to state that there is a difference. After keeping side gigs and temp work while starting my hobby travel business, I decided to go full-time travel specialist. That was the fall of 2019. Referrals were growing, and revenue was turning steady. It was time! I knew outside accountability with a trusted mentor or partner was imperative to succeed as a nonprofit professional. If you think you can do it all, you're wrong.

If you take nothing else from this whole book, please reflect on that.

I didn't want a business partner but knew I needed unbiased input and tough love to keep moving forward. I had little profit margin at this point, so where do you go for free support? The internet!

I started following a few business/entrepreneurship groups. It quickly became apparent that I had too many ideas and questions, and my "why" and goals were not as clear as I thought. The term business coach was in these groups, and I started booking calls with anyone who used this title. Those few months were interesting, and I think I heard every sales pitch you could imagine. My intuition said *meh* to them all. Interviewing business coaches to find a good match is grueling. That is a topic for a whole other chapter.

There was one last call, and I was about to cancel it as I was headed on a road trip to New Jersey. At least the call would pass the time. I took the call and met my dream coach, Ms. Jessica Miller. She was no-nonsense with a sense of compassion that I immediately felt.

Determining my ideal client audience and gaining clarity on what made me stand out in the field was the starting work. I finally felt there was direction and a foundation to build a business.

Was I freaked out to invest in a business that was not profitable yet? Was I second-guessing this choice for weeks? Did I lose sleep and not tell my husband? Yes, yes, yes, and panic, panic, panic. But there was an even bigger "hell yes" in knowing I could not reach my potential and see past my roadblocks without an outside partner!

The panic started to subside, and the numbers started making sense and seemed achievable. I felt alive and relevant again. Revenue and referrals were coming in. Followers and networks were growing. All things seemed possible again. Do you recall the timing of when the "fully-in" started? Working with Jessica started late in 2019 into the shiny new year full of opportunity, 2020. Whoomp—whoomp! Do you hear the *Jaws* theme music coming in? Talk about panic!

I cannot imagine what I would have done without the support of Jessica and her curated community of solopreneurs. As travel shut down all over the globe, Jessica and I started trying to figure out how to keep revenue coming in. Some ideas included virtual travel tours online, guide books, how to plan your bucket list trips workbooks, virtual retreat support, and so many more. Again, my intuition said, *meh.* I could no longer see a future for my travel business. Then came another day in another parking lot.

It was one of our last scheduled one-on-one coaching phone sessions. Many other travel friends were dropping out of the business. Jessica usually got right into the meat of things, and "I don't know" is never an acceptable answer. I am paraphrasing, but it went something like this:

"You have turned your nose at every suggestion. What doesn't work with those things?" Jessica asked.

After a long pause, taking a breath and tuning in, I realized. "I can't imagine having to sell 100 things for $100 over and over again."

"Okay, so you want an offer that creates a recurring client base. Fewer clients at a higher price point." Jessica summarized matter of factly.

"Yup. I want long-term relationships." I knew I would not be happy without a connection to my clients.

"What is something that people can work on now without committing to dates and deposits in the future?" Jessica probed, wondering how it works.

"Um, groups. Groups always take a long time to coordinate and need budgets and research before offering. I did tons of groups." I could feel this was going somewhere.

There was a small silence, and Jessica said, "There you go! Retreat plans that coaches or leaders can implement in the future. How does that feel?"

My chest, heart, throat, and head filled with light, and I almost felt like I was floating as soon as she said it. Tears were streaming, and a wave of calm washed any leftover panic away. I could see it all clearly in front of me. I had roles as a group leader, budget strategist, facilitator, event planner, stage speaker, and conference director in my previous career. As a travel professional, I'd assisted groups of all kinds in getting free perks and taking advantage of traveling as a larger booking. Why had I never merged the two? In that parking lot, my two professional identities merged, and Retreat Concierge Services was born.

## KNOW YOUR ZONE

If you're not familiar with the phrase "zone of genius," I highly suggest you read *The Big Leap* by Gay Hendricks. Basically, all we do falls into four zones: incompetence, competence, excellence, and genius. Starting my travel business, I was competent in messaging, marketing, media, and office tasks. I was excellent in determining the right locations to meet my client's needs and in finding the best prices and customer service. I thought I was in my zone of genius at that time. I didn't understand the nuance in the difference between the zone of excellence and genius until offering retreat services as the core of my business. Working in the zone of genius is using innate skills so tasks flow, rather than learned skills, which do not result in abundance.

Outsourcing tasks from my zone of competence and some from my zone of excellence has allowed my genius zone to evolve. Investing in that outsourcing may seem counterintuitive but delegating those items to a team of consultants granted me the time to thrive in my genius. As I passed along each task, the joy in my business and life leveled up. During a global pandemic, I have doubled my revenue from my best previous year in a travel-based business.

Read that again. My travel-based business has never been more profitable! During a catastrophic time with unprecedented shut-downs, political strife, and unknowns, people awoke to the need for community and connection in a more meaningful way. Staying in the flow of my intuition, leading with my zone of genius, and holding firm to my calling of in-person travel relationships created the business model I had been dreaming of.

# THE STRATEGY

That was the journey of how my panic was transformed into the profitable business I have by leveraging retreats. Did you keep track of the stops along the way that made my immense and rapid growth possible?

1. **Look back but move forward.** There is value in feeling the feelings and working through the darkest patches in life. But don't live in those patches or blame them for your situation. Reflect on the gifts they bring and use the lessons to move forward.

2. **Build up your outside support.** You will never see your own roadblocks. That is why they are also called blindspots. Be sure you take the time to interview coaches to ensure a quality, trusting relationship.

3. **Slow down to speed up.** Step back to take the time to differentiate your *zone of excellence* from your *zone of genius.* Then delegate things outside of your genius. This awareness will catapult your growth timeline.

My zone of genius is the back-end business of leveraging retreats. Retreats and in-person events shine even more for the front-end business offering them. Here are four ways you can leverage retreats to grow your business bottom line:

- Retreats allow you to introduce yourself to many potential clients at one time. The fastest way to build relationships, trust, and loyalty is with an in-person shared experience.

- The retreat itself needs to be priced realistically for profit, including paying yourself for the transformation or service you're providing. On top of that, offering VIP experiences and other add-ons increase revenue.

- Co-lead a retreat with complimenting services to build cross-community awareness like a graphic designer and copywriter leading an experience to create an opt-in and email sequence all programmed by the end of the event.

- Small and local offers allow you to practice your delivery flow and management of your energy. Understand your leadership style before making financial commitments and grand plans.

The first step in successful retreat planning is knowing your numbers. It's also the step I see most leaders skim over. They either start with a price in mind, "I want to charge $4000 for this experience." Then they try to find a location and agenda that fits into that predetermined fee. Or, find a place, take the cost of those base expenses and divide by the number of participants. Either way, they do not account for their time or value what they offer. In creating a budget, pay yourself first! Retreats are not a regular group travel experience and should not be priced like one.

Think of all the hours spent researching locations, creating the content and materials, developing marketing and timelines; all of these need to be added to the actual cost of an event. Then there are always the small amounts that add up quickly that decrease the profit—things like gratuities, credit card processing fees, and taxes.

It's not worth spending energy and time to end with a loss. I have created a Retreat Profit Calculator to assist you in this first step. You can access it here: https://www.floyotravel.com/retreat-calculator.

Look over these locations and itineraries for inspiration: https://www.floyotravel.com/retreat-sampler.

Review the top pitfalls to avoid before you dive into a plan: https://www.floyotravel.com/retreat-pitfalls.

I hope my story and these resources have you thinking creatively about incorporating retreats into your business. Let me help you bring all the adventures to life. Go to:
https://calendly.com/amy_t-travels/retreat to book a free strategy call.

*We travel, initially, to lose ourselves; and we travel,
next to find ourselves.*

~Pico Iyer

**Amy Flores-Young,** known as Flo-Yo, is all about transformational destinations and reclaiming the joy in travel. A full-time travel professional and retreat concierge, she specializes in helping coaches and leaders host profitable retreat experiences for their communities. When clients hire her, they get to enjoy their travel too—because Amy takes care of all the details required to wow retreat participants—from start to finish. Coaches and leaders profit more, stress less, and deepen client relationships when they work with Amy.

A former facilitator herself, she knows how difficult it's to manage the endless logistics while being the face of the room. Amy has perfected the art of weaving together the ultimate location and itinerary that both engages and energizes your guests. She is a sought-after speaker in the world of travel planning and retreats business strategy, and when she is not planning and traveling, she is petting every puppy she meets, DJing kitchen dance parties, and shopping for new hoodies.

Connect with Amy:

On her website: https://www.floyotravel.com/
On Facebook: https://www.facebook.com/amy.floyo
On LinkedIn: https://www.linkedin.com/in/amy-floyo/
In her Free Facebook Community, Transformational Travels:
https://www.facebook.com/groups/amyttravels

# CHAPTER 9

# CONQUERING MENTAL AND DIGITAL CLUTTER

## THE SUCCESS FORMULA FOR CALMING THE CHAOS

Sydney Tyler Thomas, MCP

## MY STORY

*God, please don't ask me to do this right now. Make him stop talking!*

I was surprised I could still hear him over the sounds of my sobs. I could barely see through the tears cascading in waves down my cheeks. I clutched my chest to stop the pain from stabbing me each time I tried to take a breath.

*I hate Zoom right now. I'm having a total meltdown in front of my spiritual advisor/friend and his wife. They're watching me do it. I'm watching me do it. I look like shit!*

"Sydney, do you believe God's given you a purpose and that all you've been through has led you to this point?"

"Yes."

*He's going there.*

"Do you know in your heart that God wouldn't have called you to this work if He wasn't going to provide all you need to do it?

"Yes." *Please stop talking now. I know where you're going with this, and I can't do it right now. You know I can't do it now.*

"So, what are you waiting for?" *I can't believe he just asked me that.*

"You know what I'm waiting for!" *Now I'm getting pissed and scared.*

"I can't afford to leave my job right now. I have a mortgage, bills, and nowhere near enough money saved. I need the health insurance I have, and can't afford to pay for it on my own. You know I can't just quit my job right now!"

"So, you're telling me that you don't trust God to provide you with what you need to do what He's asking you to do?"

"No, I do trust Him, but . . ."

*Shit!* The minute the words left my lips, I knew how lame they sounded. *I'm screwed.*

"For months, you've been telling me how God's been sending signs that tell you it's time to move. We've watched you struggle as the lessons get more frequent and more painful. What more will it take for God to get your attention?"

*He just dropped the mic.*

The truth was I'd been living on autopilot for a long time, firmly planted in a comfort zone that stopped being comfortable years ago. I'd lost all joy and passion, was suffering from frequent migraines and other health issues, and knew I wasn't using the gifts and talents God gave me to make a difference in the world.

Yet there I stood.

That was the precise moment I realized my fear of *not* answering God's call was stronger than my fear of answering it.

It was time to move. So, I did. I left my job to start my coaching practice.

The first several weeks weren't easy. I didn't realize how much I didn't know about starting a coaching practice. I'd just gotten started and was already drowning in to-dos. I didn't know where to start.

Sure, I'd been coaching informally for as long as I could remember. I had several coaching certifications hanging on my newly-built backyard home office walls to prove it.

I was confident I would be a great coach. But what suddenly scared me to death was having no idea how I was going to build a practice with no social media followers, email list, or advertising budget.

I know now that God wanted me to say "Yes" to Him based on faith, not because I could find a new freelance gig that would deposit a fat paycheck into my bank account every other Thursday.

German Author Goethe was right when he said, "At the moment of commitment, the entire Universe conspires to assist you."

My version of *A Course in Miracles* began about a month later. There were countless synchronicities, what I like to call God Winks, and the undeniable miracles I experienced in the first five months of my new journey were life-changing, both professionally and personally.

Unsolicited grant and scholarship opportunities suddenly started showing up. They offered professional education programs I couldn't resist, including Positive Intelligence training and a certificate in Women's Entrepreneurship from Cornell University. And, at the time of this writing, I'm on my way to receiving a Ph.D. in Conscious Business Ethics!

*I sure didn't see that last one coming!*

Each unexpected opportunity was aligned with where my new practice was headed. I just didn't know it yet.

The other amazing thing that happened during that time was that I finally found my tribe online, and it was the last place I would've thought to look.

Don't get me wrong; I don't have hundreds of faux friends that I follow or that follow me. I'm talking about genuine and authentic friendships with women from various parts of the world that I engage with regularly. We laugh together, cry together, share disappointments, and celebrate successes. We've created small sacred circles where we unconditionally love and support each other. We're planning to meet in person someday.

For soul-aligned entrepreneurs, it would be impossible for me to overestimate the value of connecting with your tribe.

I had no idea where they would lead me when I took my first steps on this journey of creating a soul-aligned business. But I know that where I am now is where I'm supposed to be.

And I'm just getting started.

# THE STRATEGY

## CREATING AND INTEGRATING HEART SMART GOALS

My name is Sydney, and I'm a recovering high-achiever with perfectionist tendencies.

That's probably why it didn't take long for me to feel so overwhelmed, stressed, and exhausted by all the things I believed I needed to do to get my business up and running.

Eventually, I realized that the "If I think I need to do it (or if an expert tells me I need to do it), that means I have to do it" approach to identifying and prioritizing my action items was the cause of my distress.

My to-do lists were all over the place. They were in my digital planner, my printed planner, on my wall calendar, in my inbox, under those cute magnets on my refrigerator, and of course, in my head.

Sound familiar?

I'm here to tell you that the need to implement every idea you come up with or hear about isn't a great business strategy. Neither is feeling compelled to follow the exact steps in the exact order an *expert* swears you need to follow to guarantee success. That's especially true if those steps don't feel right to you. The obsession with doing things perfectly or at least better than everybody else isn't helpful either. The pressures created by these common but misguided ways of thinking amount to a series of self-inflicted wounds.

It's virtually impossible to figure out what's truly important among a mountain of action items without having a basis for discernment because if everything is important, nothing is important.

I believe lack of clarity about our core values and vision, both personally and professionally, is the root cause of many of our struggles. Our difficulty letting go of limiting beliefs and the inefficient task management habits they create make things so much more challenging than they need to be.

I call this invisible suffocating heaviness Mental and Digital Clutter.

The chaos that results from not being intentional and consistent about aligning our core values and goals stifles our creativity, zaps our energy, and causes sleepless nights. On some days it may even make us wonder if we're cut out to be entrepreneurs at all.

Are you ready for a simple yet profound shift in perspective that's the first and most important step in overcoming the mental and digital clutter that's keeping you from reaching your fullest potential?

If so, the challenge, and the solution, are elegantly simple.

## STEP 1: DEFINING SUCCESS

As an entrepreneur, I'm sure we can agree that you want to be successful, right?

But what does success look like to you? Not to your family, friends you grew up with, colleagues, neighbors, or culture. How do you define success?

Merriam-Webster defines success as "The attainment of wealth, position, honors, or the like."

Really?

I wonder if Anthony Bourdain, Kate Spade, or Robin Williams would agree.

Probably not.

I've fallen in love with and embraced what the author of *Wabi-Sabi Wisdom* calls "Soulful Success." Andrea Jacques defines it as "The state of vitality, abundance, confidence, and commitment that results when you trust in your ability to achieve goals that are intrinsically meaningful to you."

Now that one makes my heart smile.

So, whether you adopt Andrea Jacques' definition like I have or come up with your own, take the time to decide how you define success and then visualize what it looks like for you in as much detail as you can. Write it down.

Then continue to visualize it. Daily.

What are you doing?

Where do you live?

Where do you work?

What brings you joy?

What do your workdays look like?

The more you visualize your success, the more likely you'll be to achieve it. Visualization creates clarity, supports intention, combats negativity, reduces stress, boosts confidence, enhances motivation, sparks inspiration, expands creativity, gathers energies, optimizes performance, and fosters purpose.

All that and it's free!

## STEP 2: GOALS ALIGNMENT

After you've truly internalized your definition of success and can visualize how you look when wearing it, the next step is to create meaningful goals to serve as guideposts to get you from where you are to where you want to be.

You probably know that to be meaningful, goals need to be SMART (Specific, Measurable, Achievable, Relevant, and Time-Bound.) However, even the smartest of SMART goals lack a critical component for soul-aligned entrepreneurs.

They address the mind but leave the heart and soul hanging.

The essence of a soul-aligned business is the alignment of purpose with core values and goals. This alignment is the invisible thread weaving Divine connection between mind, body, and spirit. When we're in alignment, we operate in flow, feeling the love over worry.

We're able to make decisions more quickly and confidently. Time expands as we lose track of it when we're doing the work we enjoy, synchronicities abound, and the magic happens.

You probably don't want to hear this, but if you've adopted a set of SMART goals for your business and you're still dreading the start of each workday and feeling even worse as the day wears on, as SMART as they may be, the goals you've set have probably missed the mark.

If you're serious about being a soul-aligned entrepreneur, clearly and consistently commit to a set of goals that align with your purpose and your authentic definition of success. I promise that once you do, things will get a lot easier.

Am I saying that clarity and alignment are magic potions that will suddenly make all your business challenges disappear?

Of course not!

But what I am saying is that once you know where you're headed, it's a hell of a lot easier to program your internal GPS to get you there following the path of least resistance. And of course, as Goethe said (sort of), once you're clear on where you're going, the Universe will kick in to turbo-charge the journey.

So, set new goals that align with your definition of success by making them HEART (Holistic, Energetic, Aligned, Realistic, and Transformative) SMART. I've created a simple HEART SMART Goals cheat sheet you can find on my Resources Page to help.

Write your new goals down and put them where you can see them daily.

## STEP 3: COLLECT AND CURATE ACTION ITEMS

The information overload that causes mental and digital clutter grows like weeds in many different places.

Action items that make their way directly to our to-do lists are easiest to see. But using our email inboxes, smartphone apps, and digital bookmarks as ticklers to remind us of things we want to revisit later compound the clutter.

I've created a checklist to help you scout out the additional to-dos hiding in places you might not think to look. You can download the checklist on the resources page of my website.

Once you've gone through the checklist and know what areas you need to tackle, it's time to grant yourself some grace. It'll be easy to become overwhelmed by the number of action items and reminders you're going to find. So, you'll need to accept upfront that it's going to take some time to deal with them all.

Start with your paper clutter because it's the easiest to see and manage.

Grab a box and then go through your office and anywhere else you put to-do items. Collect all the notebooks, Post-Its, magazine articles, and scraps of paper that serve as reminders of something you think you need to do.

Put them all in the box. Yes, all of them. Be sure to put any that are urgent or time-sensitive on top.

You may want to set aside a weekend to gather everything at one time. Or you may want to set aside an hour each day or a few hours each week. Either way, once you commit to the process, don't stop until you're done.

Next is the part where the rubber meets the road.

Grab your new HEART SMART goals and keep them front and center because now you're going to ruthlessly apply what I call the 4D Principle to your box of papers:

1. **Delete** – Let go of anything that no longer aligns with and supports your goals, which means send it to the trashcan, shredder, or recycle bin.

2. **Do** – Take care of any tasks that still need to be done and can be completed in 5-10 minutes or less.

3. **Delegate** – Acknowledge that you can't and shouldn't have to do everything yourself, and when possible, start delegating those remaining tasks so you can focus on the things only you can do. (Note: I know this one gets tricky for entrepreneurs with limited funds for outsourcing, but here's where you get to be creative and resourceful. I can help. Trust me, that's how I roll!)

4. **Defer** – Give yourself some breathing space by accepting that anything still supportive of your goals that isn't time-sensitive can wait.

The transformational shift you'll experience is created by viewing your action items through the lens of your HEART SMART goals. When you do this, it'll become clear that many of the things you thought you needed to do no longer have the same sense of priority or urgency. Even better, you'll find that a lot of your to-dos don't need to be done at all!

Great job!

Now that you've had lots of practice on your paper-based items, repeat steps one through three for every other place where digital clutter hides. Continue to be fearless in letting go of anything that no longer aligns with your goals.

If you've made it this far, you're probably wondering where to store, organize, prioritize and retrieve your new streamlined set of action items.

Great question! That's the next step on the journey.

I support my clients that want to dig deeper into this work by helping them identify and reject limiting beliefs about entrepreneurial success that might be keeping them stuck.

Then we work together to identify the unproductive habits that have contributed to the chaos. We replace them with simple daily and weekly routines to maintain the new workflows and minimize the chances of clutter and overwhelm creeping back in.

Creating a holistic business model that integrates alignment with your values and HEART SMART goals into every part of your business makes things so much easier for soul-aligned entrepreneurs. And it's just good business.

This alignment provides the confidence to make choices that are right for you and your business more easily. It significantly reduces overwhelm and stress attached to soul-sucking and unnecessary action items, whether you're doing them or avoiding them. And it creates more space and energy for the things that support your goals and empowers you to unapologetically live a life that honors who you truly are.

**Sydney Tyler Thomas** is a certified Goal Success Life Coach and has a certification in Women's Entrepreneurship from Cornell University. She is committed to working with female soul-aligned solopreneurs and small business owners to create elegantly simple strategies to reduce mental and digital clutter that enable them to work smarter, not harder. She spent nearly 40 years in market research, business development, and strategic planning for corporate, consulting, and nonprofit organizations, learning more than she ever cared to know about how conventional business organizations are managed.

After witnessing the transformations of so many women she supported through the years as they attained goals they didn't believe were possible, Sydney finally answered the call to devote her energy to support as many women as she could through her coaching practice and writing. She found the courage to follow her heart and share lessons learned from her wildly unconventional journey. She now gracefully but unabashedly challenges other women to do the same. She's a kind-hearted but no-nonsense coach who commits fully to supporting her clients, but only if they're willing to commit fully to supporting themselves.

When Sydney relaxes, she can usually be found in her veggie and flower gardens, reading, writing, exploring new creative hobbies, or enjoying her puzzling out-of-character guilty pleasure of watching WWE wrestling with pizza and a great bottle of sweet and fruity Moscato. She loves jazz, cowboy boots with blue jeans, fresh-cut flowers, photography, and creating cool designs in Canva.

You can find Sydney's private resources page for readers of this book here: https://sydneytylerthomas.com/resources_ugsb_private_access.html

Connect with Sydney:

On her website: www.sydneytylerthomas.com
On Facebook: https://www.facebook.com/coachsydney
On LinkedIn: https://www.linkedin.com/in/sydneytylerthomas/

# CHAPTER 10

# SMALL BUSINESS MARKETING SECRETS

## SIMPLY CRUSHING YOUR ONLINE PRESENCE

Desirae Haluk, Chief Queen Bee at Clairant Services, LLC

# MY STORY

Two days before Christmas. 6:30am. I lay in bed in the dark, in denial, squinting my eyes, reading the words on my phone that felt too bright for that time in the morning. I read the email over and over again and tried with every ounce of my body not to believe what I was reading. How could this be true? It's impossible. Could it be a mistake? So many things ran through my mind and finally I read it out loud. "We regret to inform you that our beloved CEO has passed away."

Fifty-eight years old! How could this be?

I had no idea what to do. I sat up on the bed and felt the blood draining from my face.

Thoughts sped through my brain. *His wife. His poor daughters who adored him. What are they going through right now? I just saw him! He was fine!*

After a few days of allowing the tragic news to set in I started pondering what would happen next. Normally a tragedy like this wouldn't automatically make you worry about your job but my situation was different. In a company with 70 brands, the brand I was working on was the CEO's baby that exactly three people believed in out of thousands - the CEO, me, and one other person. I knew without him backing this venture, all momentum would be lost and naturally my job would be at stake.

Here we go again.

The funeral was about a week later. For some reason, even though he was just a boss, it was one of the most difficult funerals I had ever been to.

He was too young. There was so much life left to live. I sat there with a colleague of mine in a sea of dark suits. There must have been 1500 people in that room.

My colleague held our boss in the same regard as I did. I could tell he was hurting too. Just like me. We were a great team. We were handpicked from hundreds of employees to promote the CEO's dream product and we were as dedicated and committed to it as he was. The three of us had a connection that was unstoppable and now it was broken forever.

The permanence of death is just awful. There is no turning back. Nothing you can ever do to undo it. It was so hard for me to accept and as I sat there drowning out the speeches, thinking of my future, the tears began to stream down my cheeks. I tried so hard to hold them in but they kept on pouring out.

After the funeral, I drove for hours - my mind swirling with so many thoughts. Not only was his death beyond sad but I have to be honest, I was worried for my future as well. I thought about what I would do if I lost my job. I knew my boss dying would mean big changes at the company which was publicly traded and handed over to the board of directors who were not forward thinking individuals. What would I do? I was so sick of being tossed around in an industry that valued the old ways and stature over performance and vision. I knew that it was only a matter of time before I was pulled into the boardroom, yet again, and told that I needed to collect my things and go.

I wasn't ready for that!

This was supposed to be my chance to land my dream position in corporate America. But I knew it wouldn't happen without my boss. At least not at this company now. He was the missing piece to the puzzle, and it was permanent. I had to think of my next step.

After three excruciating months full of budget freezes, employees worried for their jobs, and rumors, my worries became reality. I was pulled into the boardroom, told my brand was being shut down, and was handed my severance package. It felt like I had dunked my head in water and the words were all muffled. I was numb to the process to a certain degree but it still never got easier being on that side of the table. The HR director immediately took my computer and my phone, handed me a box, and told me to clean out my office and they would direct me out of the building. How demeaning after all the dedication I poured into this company.

I filled my box, smiled at all the employees as I made my walk of shame, and opened the doors into the sunshine-filled parking lot. I stood there for a second taking it all in. *What the fuck am I going to do?*

I sat in my car dreading the phone call to my husband. But instead of dialing his number, I thought of an old colleague who had approached me with a new opportunity a few weeks ago. He wanted me to lead their marketing team but I said I was happy where I was at the time, still having hope they would keep me around.

I wasted no time and made the call.

"Hey! Remember that position you asked me to fill? Is it still available?"

"Yes, why?" He said.

"Well I'm all yours!" I said with a smile and told him the short version of what had just happened.

By two o'clock I had an offer letter for VP of Marketing in my inbox and all of a sudden our family dinner conversation would get much more interesting and positive that night.

The new position was amazing. I worked as if I were growing my own startup and made it my baby. I was dealing with a much smaller company where decisions were made fast. I helped the company establish a strong marketing strategy and implementation plan. I hired more team members and we went from two million the previous year to 17 million in the next 12 months. What a success!

One morning, about a year into the position, I walked happily into the office to start my day and I sensed a somber tone amongst the owner and other employees.

I put my computer on my desk and walked over to my boss to see what was going on.

"Hey good morning! What's up?"

There was a long sigh and a pause before learning that our largest client was way over budget and they were slashing their external agencies.

My stomach immediately dropped to the floor and I leaned against the door jam.

"Well, I guess that means we have to get some new clients!" I said the words with fake positivity but knowing full well our days were numbered.

I drove home that evening thinking of what it would be like to run my own business. I told my husband my thoughts and we discussed how great it would be to have control over my career, dig my heels in, and start my own agency.

"You should have done that a long time ago," he said.

Over the next few weeks I lost many nights of sleep running over strategies and ideas for my own company. The excitement was invigorating as I explored the idea of controlling my own destiny.

While still working at my current job, I started to build my business. I listed services I would offer my clients and created Standard Operating Procedures after work each day. I purchased the LLC, and bought the domain name. In a few months I built a website and took my networking to another level. I called all my old contacts, joined as many networking groups as I could, and went to a conference for the company I worked for, but pitched my own business and got my first client!

Meanwhile, each week would bring another employee being let go. I knew I was somewhere in that queue and each day I expected the worst as I walked into the office.

Sure enough, one early Friday morning in December with Christmas quickly approaching, I was asked to meet in the infamous boardroom.

As I sat there, anticipating my boss' words, words that would normally break a person, a big smile appeared on my face. The feeling of relief and pure joy came to my heart as I knew I was about to begin the greatest adventure of my life...and that is how Clairant was born.

# THE STRATEGY

Many small business owners shove marketing in the back corner of their brains, and try for as long as they can to avoid it like the plague. They may not know where to start, they may not have a budget for it, or they may not think it's important. I am here to tell you that marketing doesn't have to be complicated or expensive and should always be a priority for every business.

All you need is to build a foundation using a list of priorities. Be an 'Essentialist' as Gregory McEwan teaches in his book, *Essentialism*. That's exactly how you need to think of marketing. Whether you have been in business for one day or fifty years, you have one employee or three hundred, ask yourself *what is most important for your business right this moment,* and create your priorities based on that. The best part is that you don't need to guess! I am going to provide the list you need to start here in this chapter.

You can find effective marketing strategies that can be implemented without a million-dollar budget. The most important thing in marketing is to understand your brand, learn how to best describe the products or services you offer, know your differentiators, and be aware of exactly who your target market is. Once you know this information you can craft a message that will speak to the pain points of your audience by telling them why your product or service will solve their problems better than your competitors. It's all about the messaging, dedication, consistency, persistence and patience.

So let's get started!

Here are some items on the list of marketing priorities every business needs:

**Brand guide** - A brand guide is a document that provides specific information about the branding, logo, color palette, messaging, target audience, differentiators and other important information about your brand. It should be shared with all employees and agencies working with your company in order to have a successful marketing plan. This guide is typically used when creating any type of marketing or sales material so that consistency and clarity is top priority for your brand.

**Target Audience** - Having as much information as possible about your target audience is crucial to the success of any marketing plan. A very common phrase that I hear from potential clients when describing their target audience is, "everyone!" This is every marketer's nightmare. Describing exactly who your target audience is helps you understand their pain points (their frustrations and what keeps them up at night). Once you know this you can craft a clear and effective message that will capture their attention.

**Messaging** - Once you are an expert in knowing your target audience and you can recite their pain points, you are ready to craft the perfect message. Ask yourself, how is your product or service a solution to easing those pain points? Why would a prospect choose your company over a competitor? Note those differentiators clearly in your messaging and convince them to pick up the phone and call your business. Your messaging should be driven by emotion and speak to the benefits of your product or service rather than the features. And don't forget about a call to action (CTA). A strong call to action like "call now" or "click here" should be stated clearly on all your messaging - you need to strike while the iron is hot!

**Website** - Now that you have crafted the perfect language for your brand's message you are ready to showcase your business. In a world heading in a mostly virtual direction, having an effective website is imperative to growing a brand. You don't need to spend tens of thousands of dollars on a great website. You can build one yourself or you can hire an agency to build an affordable one. Here are a few components that need to be present in every successful website.

- Clear messaging. Read the messaging section above and apply it to your website. Now that you have a brand guide you can use that to start! Visit websites you like and don't like, and ask yourself why? Chances are, they are simple and easy to follow - borrow inspiration from them! A website with poor messaging will equate to losing revenue. So make it concise, engaging and easy to find basic information. And leave out the technical jargon.

- Simple navigation. A great user experience on your website will determine whether someone continues on or presses the x to find a better one. Try putting yourself in the reader's seat and provide easy ways to get that information. Everybody has been on a website where you can't find something as simple as a phone number or a price, so don't be that guy. Be the one they stay on and explore because you offer them the experience they are looking for. Have menu options that are clear. Do research and learn what your visitors are looking for when they search for your brand. Give them clear access to that information so they can find it quickly.

- CTA. Call to actions are a necessity on every website. When people land on your site what do you want them to do? Fill out a form? Call you? Sign up for a program? Find what your call to action is for your product or service and place it strategically on your website so it is clear what your visitors need to do and they can do it from every page.

- Contact Information. Do you ever land on a website and all you want to do is find the company's phone number? I do, and it's frustrating. Don't let this happen to your website visitors. Have your contact information clearly displayed on all your pages. You can add it to the footer, the header, and have a dedicated contact page with address, phone numbers and emails.

- Appealing Imagery. Landing on a website full of text and limited images is very tiring. If a website isn't visually appealing it could mean losing a potential client. The majority of people make a decision to stay or leave a website in less than ten seconds (https://www.nngroup.com/articles/how-long-do-users-stay-on-web-pages/). If the imagery isn't attractive enough, no matter how great your content is, you may lose out on a potential client to a competitor with a better looking site. Think of imagery as the shiny bait that lures them in to take a closer look - then you hook 'em with your content!

- Site loading speed. There is nothing more frustrating than landing on a website you are eager to explore, and the pages take forever to load. You are guaranteed to lose customers with a slow site. So speak to a web developer or use a tool like Ubersuggest (www.ubersuggest. com) to help assess the speed of your site and fix the reasons for slow loading. Forty-seven percent of people expect a website to load within two seconds according to Website Magazine (https://www. websitemagazine.com/blog/5-reasons-visitors-leave-your-website). So get your site loading at a speed your visitors expect!

There are many other important factors to consider when building or redesigning your website, but the above are essential.

**Google Business Page -** Now that you have a kick ass website you will start being found on search engines like Google. When a website is public, Google will send bots to assess the ranking of your website on the SERP (search engine results page) and will extract information from your pages to display. You will want full control over this and there are two ways of doing it. The first is to make sure your meta tag descriptions are clear and concise on the back end of your website. But for the sake of this section I will focus on the second method, and that is claiming your Google Business page. It is free, and all you need is a gmail account to create one. You will need to have an address connected to your business and they will send you a postcard for verification. Once you have that you are all set. You can control all the information about your business including hours of operation, contact information, descriptions of your products and services, events you may be hosting or attending, and even photos and videos. It can almost be treated like a social media platform. You can post as much or as little as you want and you can offer promotions for your products or services. There is a review link you can send to your customers for 5 star reviews, and they provide analytics about all the activity for visitors clicking onto your website, viewing posts, photos or videos or calling you. If you haven't claimed your Google Business page please do so NOW!

**Social Media -** Who wants free marketing? I do! And that is why every business should be on social media along with most of the world's prospects.

Social media is the perfect place to showcase your business as much or as little as you want without the expense other than the time it takes to post and make your profiles effective. You don't have to boil the ocean and have a presence on all platforms. All you need to do is a little research to see where your target audience hangs out and choose those platforms to be on. Two or three platforms is sufficient. Post regularly, at least five times a week, and provide educational, entertaining, good beneficial content that is simple and your target audience will come back for. Keep your posts short because attention spans are short. Basically think about what you like on social media (behind-the-scenes sneak peeks, funny stuff, easy tips and tricks) and then do that. This will help you increase your followers, keep them engaged and grow a steady stream of prospects. There are many more methods using social media to promote your business, but start with the basics of posting good content five days a week.

There are plenty of other effective and affordable marketing activities that should be part of every marketing plan. But the above mentioned are critical for every business to build a strong marketing foundation. The order of the list provided above is crucial to follow if a successful marketing strategy and implementation plan is your goal. This strategy will provide you with a solid foundation and will help your company grow. For more information on other activities or help with setting up your marketing plan check out www.clairantservices.com.

**Desirae Haluk** is a neuroscientist turned marketer, born and raised in Vancouver, Canada and currently resides in New Jersey, USA. After her neuroscience career she decided to return to her original career path - marketing. She used her scientific background to create effective data-driven marketing strategies and quickly made her way up the ladder in her corporate marketing career. She went from management to director level, followed by vice president quickly and realized her calling was owning her own marketing agency in the startup and small business world, where decisions are made fast and creative freedom is encouraged. She then launched Clairant Services LLC, named after her two children Claire and Anthony, in 2019, and used the honeybee as her company logo after her love of beekeeping and fascination with the efficiency of her worker bees. She now has four employees, has helped over 40 clients with their marketing plans, has won a few awards, and continues to grow rapidly offering digital marketing services to her happy clients all over the USA and Canada.

# CHAPTER 11

# HOW TO SHUT DOWN YOUR INNER CRITIC

## LEARN HOW TO STOP SELF-SABOTAGE SO YOU HAVE MORE CLIENTS AND MONEY

Meryl Hayton, Accredited Certified EFT Practitioner,
Law of Attraction Guide

## MY STORY

I went from needing food stamps to making a consistent high four-figure income just two years into my business. But that's not really where my story starts.

Let's go back to 2017, when I decided it was time to leave my first career. I realized it was time to move on from operating the small high-end nail salon I'd owned for almost thirty years.

I'd already been a 500-hour registered yoga teacher for five years and was into holistic and alternative health and wellness. So, becoming a life coach was calling me. Although I didn't know what that looked like as a business, I searched and found my first mentor, Dr. Kim D'eramo, who practices conscious medicine. I took her class in MindBody Medicine, where I was introduced to EFT. (Emotional Freedom Technique; aka tapping)

The biggest A-ha I had was learning the root of what's underneath most limitations of unworthiness; that damn inner critic! So, I started offering workshops called I Am Enough to help others manage stress and emotions and accept all of their not enough-nesses, fears, and doubts. I loved it and saw the quick results people were getting.

In 2018 I sold what salon supplies I had, brought home my nail station and clientele so I could still make money, and kept building my coaching business at the same time. I thought I'd be an overnight success.

Well, the universe had a different plan for me because one month later, I fell and fractured my wrist. I remember sitting on the floor whaling like a baby with snot dripping down my face. I was so mad at the world, myself, and I couldn't even imagine how I was going to support myself. I felt worthless. Ah, there it is, that inner critic.

I didn't financially plan for moving on, so I had little money in the bank, and I felt so alone and defeated. One great lesson from this is that I learned my worth is not contingent upon how much money I have, though I am still working on this one.

After two days, I realized all this happened for a reason because that is my belief in life. It's happening for me, not to me. I had so much fear around letting go of doing nails I couldn't completely move on. And even though I wasn't sure about anything, I was somewhat happy and relieved. I knew it wasn't fulfilling anymore, and my body hurt from all the years of sitting and the repetitive motions. So, needless to say, having the fractured wrist on top of it all was tough.

I was yet again being led on my path, or I should say I was bulldozed off a ledge without a safety net. Truthfully, it was the only way for me to let it go because I thought *I don't know who I am without doing nails.*

*Hmmm, what am I going to do with all this free time?*

Well, I decided to record videos and post them on my YouTube channel to help stretch the body, for people with hand, wrist, or arm limitations. But I had this deep desire to transform who I was, shut down my inner critic, love myself more, and show others how they can do this too.

You see, my whole life, from about age three, I carried around what I call emotional clutter. Lots of self-judgment, negative thoughts, and anxiety were constantly swirling in my mind, body, and energy. I was always seeking inner peace, to love and accept myself and feel happier inside. Because of this, I knew I wanted to join my mentor's six-month training called Be the Medicine, but felt I couldn't afford it. *Yet, I thought I've got all this time, and my intuition is pulling me like a magnet. This is the next right step, so I'm doing it.* So, I did!

Over the following two years, I worked with Dr. Kim and other marketing and mindset coaches, including Danielle Marggraf, a Wealth Consciousness Creator and Somatic Coach teaching Law of Attraction. I learned that I was self-sabotaging my life because I had, and still have, layers to heal. I found that I connected the root cause to an event from my past of feeling forgotten as a child. These stories stay in our subconscious energy until brought up and healed.

I got into a routine of journaling, meditation, and tapping every day. I checked in with how I felt and learned (I am still learning) to accept my limitations and remove what was in my way. I understood that I had to take action steps in my business because my passion for helping others was paramount. With consistency in my daily routine, I was rewiring my brain and downregulating my nervous system. I was also self-regulating my frustration, anxiety, and overthinking, which helped me embody more inner peace, acceptance, and clarity.

I finally had real results. After decades of reading self-help books, trying to work it out on my own, and working with therapists, I still hadn't found the results I have now.

Over time, I found EFT to be the best modality to manage my emotions, stress and heal some of the deep hidden layers. Anytime I felt anxious about not making enough money, I'd tap. Comparing myself to others who had more than me, I'd tap. I'd call a friend to vent or cry. I did whatever I could to accept where I was and stay hopeful.

I even went to a rage room twice to smash some glasses and bottles to help get rid of some pent-up frustration—really powerful and cathartic stuff! After only 15 minutes, I'd feel exhausted because I had cleared out so much stuck energy.

I shut out the naysayers who said, "Enough already, maybe it's time to get a real job." *No, No, No!* I felt the time for my business to take off was near. *Just stay the course, Meryl. You know this is your calling. You must keep wiping out your doubt and follow your intuition.*

Back in 1988, a year after I graduated high school, I was working in a corporate accounting position and going to college at night. I followed my family's corporate business mindset but doing nails was a calling, so I quit college and went to cosmetology school.

I remember my mother saying, "What Jewish white girl is going to make money doing nails." Four years later, in 1994, I decided to leave corporate, the steadiness of my job and all the paid benefits to work full time doing nails. Within a year, I was working for myself and making more money than I had been before.

My point is that *this is for me* feeling of knowing I had back then, is the same feeling I had when it came to becoming a coach. So no, there was no other option. Do you know what I mean? You've got to trust yourself. I feel blessed that I've had two career callings in my life.

So, I just kept following the breadcrumbs. I continue to invest in myself (over 60K to date), market my business, heal from my past, and accept more of my limitations. I continued (and still continue) to work with a coach, practice self-care, network with others, and stay focused on my mission to help keep as many people as I can from suffering in their own mental warfare.

I thought *EFT could help everyone,* so I didn't buy into having a niche for a while. But honestly, that didn't work because I was all over the place marketing to everyone and no one. Creating a niche might scare you, but it does create the know, like, and trust factor with your potential clients because they will know exactly what you do. You can still help other clients as well. It's your business, and you make the rules.

In 2020, I became certified in EFT and mentored privately for eight months to receive my accreditation. Wow, what a game-changer. I thought I guided people through transformations before, but I had no idea what was possible. It's so powerful, and I feel grateful I get to do this work.

I also realized my evolution wasn't complete without studying and practicing the Law of Attraction. This has been a daily practice in my life for about three years now. It is the practice of envisioning what you want in life and anchoring into the emotion of what it would be like to already have it. This has allowed more abundance in my life than I could have ever imagined. I followed another passion of mine and moved to the beach. I felt I couldn't be the light and inspiration for others if I wasn't fully living out my dreams. I'm telling you, this stuff works. I transformed my thoughts from disbelieving to believing that I, too, can have what I want. It's not just for other people.

I've joined this and EFT together in my coaching programs and created my signature five-step process, The Emotional Clearing Method.

I found myself again. I transformed into a new confidence and am calmer, centered, grounded, and happier than ever. I've paid off my debt, and my business has been steady ever since.

A fun fact is I've been using my fingers in my career all along for data entry, nails, and now tapping.

My story has only just begun, and I'm grateful for the support I've gotten and am excited to see what's next. If I can do it, you can too. It's my mission to help you stay focused and continue to take the action steps to build your soul-aligned business. So, let's get you started with how this works.

# THE STRATEGY

So, what is EFT anyway?

EFT (Emotional Freedom Technique; aka tapping), is an evidence-based holistic healing method designed to dismantle your emotional attachment to events, memories, and daily experiences keeping you feeling stuck, frustrated, and second guessing yourself.

EFT reduces cortisol, a stress hormone produced in your body when you have chronic negative thoughts and emotional highs and lows. (Studies show EFT lowers cortisol by about 24% in individual sessions and 43% in group sessions.)

When cortisol is reduced, it allows your body to return to homeostasis (a balanced state), where you can repair yourself naturally from within. So, when you let go of overthinking and negative emotions and learn how to manage your stress, you immediately calm your nervous system, and your body and mind relax.

We tap on the 12 main Chinese meridian points while saying psychological phrases about your issue. It's similar to acupuncture by targeting these energy points but is non-invasive, as it only requires you to use your fingertips.

This rewires your energy system and neutralizes your thoughts, which disrupts the attachment to your issues, leaving you hopeful, clear, alert, focused, energized, and more confident than ever.

The results are profound!

You can watch a tapping video on YouTube on any subject for short-term results, but when you work with a qualified practitioner, the words and phrases are customized and personalized to fit your exact needs. That's what gives you fast and even permanent results, which is the impact you really want.

One thing tapping has been proven very effective in is helping you revisit past events that could be impacting your current state of mind, but without re-traumatizing yourself. This is done by utilizing special clearing tools that work without you having to explain the details. I do this with my clients. Awesome, right?

EFT helps quell emotions in the moment, but it also helps produce long-lasting results by getting to the root cause of what's stopping you from being your best self.

Sometimes, but not always, there is childhood or adult trauma or an unpleasant memory you've experienced that you have internalized and have not fully addressed because it keeps you safe from feeling sad, hurt, or even angry. It's not uncommon as we all protect ourselves from feeling pain in some way.

If you avoid your feelings and not say what's on your mind, or distract yourself just to keep from having these uncomfortable feelings, then you are just stuffing them down into your subconscious energy. This behavior only perpetuates the same reality you already have. So, I invite you to learn to be okay with what you are feeling so you align yourself with a higher vibe. Using EFT helps you do just that. This is where you need to be to allow in more clients and money.

Mindset is a daily practice, and it takes time to rewire your brain. This, along with continuous EFT sessions, which can take about eight weeks or might even take months, to truly change your behaviors and attitude, so you keep moving forward with your life, dreams, and goals. And trust me, it never ends, but it does get easier!

What's more, it's known to shorten traditional therapy from years to months to even minutes! I've experienced it, and so have my clients.

Okay, here we go.

I want you to get comfortable, in a seated position, with your journal, pen, and maybe some water or tea. Give yourself about 20 minutes of uninterrupted time.

Close your eyes and inhale through your nose to the count of three or four and exhale out your mouth the same or longer. Do this about three times. Feel your feet on the floor and let your jaw, shoulders, belly, and legs relax. Let your body settle into your seat and let it be for a moment.

Ask yourself what is the biggest challenge in your business right now? Let your wisdom guide you to the answer, which is usually your first thought. Don't try to force the answer.

Now write down what it's like for you. How does it feel in your body? What emotions are coming up? Does it feel big, heavy, tense? Are you anxious, feel judged, overwhelmed, sad, or angry? Do you notice where in your body you might have these feelings? And, don't worry if you don't. You might not until you're more familiar with connecting your mind and body, or when you've cleared out some emotional clutter, it might become more apparent to you. Sit with what is coming up and do your best to pick out the most intense word.

Now create a testable goal. How would you rather this situation be? How would you like to feel? What would you like to accomplish? For example, feel neutral, have inner peace, more confidence, take action to market your business, raise your prices, say what's really on your mind to others, trust your intuition? This is what you will test back to time and time again to check in with your growth and acceptance of how you're self-sabotaging yourself in your business less and less.

Go back to your word to tap on. I want you to rate it on a scale of zero-to-ten. Zero for me is neutral, and ten means I'd be crying or screaming mad. So do the best you can.

If your number is above seven, then please tap and take a deep breath on each point in the basic recipe (see below) until it's seven or lower. You might do many rounds, and that's okay. I do this whenever I feel off, out of alignment, triggered, or emotional about anything. The whole idea of tapping is to lower your intensity, so if you're tapping with words on your issue with an intensity above seven, you will probably increase your intensity and feel worse. Using EFT this way is best and will give you the fastest results.

Here are the tapping points for the basic recipe: (see below for a link to a live video discussing the points.)

1. Karate Chop (side of the hand)
2. Top of Head
3. Inner Eyebrow
4. Outer Eye (temple)
5. Under Eye (top of cheekbone)
6. Under Nose
7. On Chin
8. Under Collar Bone (find the center and then down two inches on an angle)
9. Under Armpit (where it meets the side of your ribs)

Once you have your number to seven or lower, you're ready to add words. When ready, use the karate chop point and create your setup statement and acceptance phrase. Repeat this three times aloud, so you set this into your subconscious, and your body knows exactly what you're working on.

Say, "even though I feel (fill in the blank) I love and accept myself, even though I feel (fill in your word) I honor how I'm feeling, and even though I feel (fill in your word), I just acknowledge what's happening right now."

Then go to the top of the head point and say your word. "I'm just feeling (fill in the blank)," next point all this (fill in the blank), and so on till you're done. Gently tap about 7-20 times on each point. Follow your intuition.

Check-in afterward and rate your word on the numbers scale zero-to-ten, and notice what's coming up for you. Say your issue out loud and test it. Hopefully, the number went down. If not, keep tapping until it does. This neutralizes your issue at hand while loving and accepting yourself in the process.

Take cleansing breaths as you go through this process. Breathe in slowly and deeply through your nose and exhale big sighs out your mouth. This helps to move your stuck energy and issue out more quickly.

While practicing with any energy work, drink plenty of water, take good care of yourself physically and emotionally. Eat well and get plenty of rest. Listen to what your body needs—sending you healing, hope, and happiness.

For those of you who are not familiar with tapping, please click the link below to see a video of me showing you how to do it. This mini masterclass is designed to harness your full potential by increasing your sense of worthiness. You can come back to this strategy time and time again for great lasting results. https://mailchi.mp/5590cb270a86/tappingintoworthiness

**Meryl** is an accredited certified EFT Practitioner and Law of Attraction Guide. She helps others heal from past situations, silence their inner critic, self-sabotage, and what holds them from achieving their true potential to boldly build the life and career/business they love.

She believes the relationship we have with ourselves is more important than any other. She's spent her life working on her relationship within and healing her chronic negativity. Five years ago, she decided to follow her calling to be a coach so women wouldn't suffer as she did.

Clients work with her to accomplish their best health in years because they've resolved underlying emotional issues, like anxiety, overthinking, doubt, and fear. They feel empowered and stand up for themselves, honoring who they are, their values, beliefs, and dreams. They make more money in their business, have more loving, supportive relationships, and trust that life is going as planned.

Meryl lives at the beach in New Jersey and is a mom to her cat Sammie. She loves to cook healthy gluten and dairy-free meals and desserts. You might find her at a yoga class, dancing, singing karaoke, lying on the beach, or entertaining friends.

# CHAPTER 12

# MAKING SOUL-CENTERED CHOICES

## TOOLS FOR DIMENSIONAL LIVING

Dr. Sonia Luckey, DNP, MA, FNP-BC, PMHNP-BC

## MY STORY

"I feel like maybe you'd make a better academic."

My vision blurred, and I couldn't get a breath in.

I got up and navigated in slow-motion, on auto-pilot, from my boss's office to my own. The floor-to-ceiling windows beckoned me over, inviting me to gaze down 15 floors. It would be a long way down.

I looked down, wondering how many more hits I could take and how much more inner work I had to do to get through this crap and retain some dignity. I pressed my face against the glass, and the heat fogged up the window as the anger came like a tidal wave. The next wave washed over me, and depression threatened to take over. *Again.*

*I'm so sick of this. No matter what I do, I can't win.*

I'd just completed a very large and successful project, so I knew that being fired was personal. I worked my butt off, pretending I didn't hear the gossip about the disintegration of my 20-year marriage and my involuntary transfer to a different part of the company because some people had some thinly-veiled issues with divorce.

I worked hard to establish my own identity and be my authentic self instead of just putting my head down and staying out of sight so I could keep earning a paycheck.

*I'm not about to get beaten down now, not like this.*

Anger flared again. I stepped back and sank into my chair, spinning it around so the busybodies sitting outside my office door couldn't see me contemplating my options. The office was buzzing with news of restructuring. I could feel their eyes burning with curiosity.

*Should I make a break for the elevator? Maybe I should make it good, like a movie scene. Storm out with some flair*—something befitting a loyal executive who deserved better. Some fireworks could make a point. *They can't embarrass me like this and get away with it!* My ego-mind was jumping up and down in outrage. *Some door-slamming would show what a huge mistake they were making.* I could hear background music playing with clapping and voices cheering me on in my private movie.

And then I heard a voice coming from another part of my brain—one of my spiritual mentors. *What was he doing here in my triumphant fantasy?*

*I have a question for you,* he said. *What if all this was for you instead of against you? What if it was all set up as a lesson in your life curriculum to give you an opportunity for spiritual growth? What would your response be then?*

Well, crap. And now, a second spiritual mentor shows up in my head, twirling her long, curly red hair. *It's not so hard to stay aligned when things are going well. I'm curious, where are you in your emotional landscape? I noticed your inner conversation changed when you got angry. Authenticity and dignity are important to you. How is this in alignment with your core values?*

I was way too wound up to think about accessing authenticity, dignity, and core values. Maybe I could process that later in a session. Right now, I could hardly think straight. I was immersed in this *real-life* 3-D humiliation going on. Being fired was definitely screwing up the career plans on my life goal line.

But moving up the soul line would be a movement toward authentic self-realization and honoring my purpose in this world. If this was the universe giving me a test in my overall life curriculum, could I use this experience for my soul's growth? Instead of letting my 3-D ego-mind take over and pitch a royal fit, what would a heart-centered, soul-aligned 4-D or even 5-D reaction look like?

*Not nearly so movie-scene worthy. But why create another scene to support the fake illusions that I've been fighting against all along at this job?* Going further into non-productive emotions might be satisfying at the moment but could ultimately be counterproductive.

On the other hand, if I could tap into authenticity, maybe I could pull out of this emotional soup of righteous anger, embarrassment, and, yes, fear. I could lock into a higher vibrational state of renewing emotions that would feel more positive and productive. I might even tell this story someday to help show how good can come out of big challenges. It certainly resonated with my core values. I could become a better human and stay balanced in emotional equanimity. It was much closer to embodying the authentic self that I set out to be.

I had all the tools to do it.

So I put them to work. Three minutes later, I spun my chair back around. I grabbed my purse and casually walked out for nice lunch at my favorite Greek restaurant.

# THE STRATEGY

As we hurtle through the universe on our 3-D Planet, Earth, many of us tend to think of ourselves as human beings who are having a spiritual experience. In Spiritual Psychology, when life challenges come our way, our perspective shifts to who we really are: spiritual beings who are having a human experience. This opens another world of possibility to us. In this world, some of us are marching to the beat and the frequency of a different drummer.

I'm sure you knew that. And that's the point.

As heart-centered entrepreneurs, we want to show up differently in the world. We are soul-centered, we want life to be meaningful, we want to make a difference, and we want to be better humans. We want experiences that help our spiritual growth at that moment and build our spiritual muscles over the long term. Then the experiences come, and what happens? Often, we go right back to being our fully human selves, warts and all.

But this is where the rubber meets the road. This is the opportunity for a shift in dimensional living—living in harmony with something greater than ourselves.

Spiritual psychology invites us to take a learning orientation to life, and it follows that everything that happens to us is for our benefit and learning. Each experience we have in business, relationships, and life situations are potential lessons set up in this curriculum we call life. As we mature, grow, and increase our awareness and consciousness, we can look at our experiences through a different lens and use each in service to our spiritual growth. The trick is to stay present and aware enough to do that.

Most people look at life from the usual 3-D perspective of duality, meaning good-bad, happy-sad, up-down, etc. Your challenge, should you choose to accept it, is to decide how you will view those situations and decide what action to take.

Most reactions are automatic, without thinking. People don't take the time to think about how to handle situations differently for a better outcome. We know that we want things to go well for us so we can be happier, have great relationships, successful jobs, make more money, etc. This is the goal line perspective of life. Not good or bad, just 3-D life on Earth.

Looking at it from a spiritual perspective, you apply a filter that looks at an additional viewpoint. This is where our core values come in, the higher principles and universal laws of 4-D and higher that we aspire to live in our lives. Through this filter, our choices are different as we try to discern what is the best and highest good for our well-being and everyone concerned, in alignment with our core values, mission, and life purpose.

These physical and spiritual dimensions have different energy frequencies that influence how we think, feel, and react. Sometimes we even physically feel it. It's the difference between yelling at the fool who just cut you off in traffic or keeping your cool and sending them a blessing because they are obviously having a bad day.

Our perceptions, priorities, and actions are based on how we process information. You can integrate a spiritual perspective into your experience and raise it to a higher level. The good news is, there are skills and strategies for that!

I begin with an emotional assessment based on the Mood Meter, which was developed by the Yale Center for Emotional Intelligence as part of the RULER approach for tools and instructional strategies to teach emotional intelligence (To learn more, see resources at the end of this chapter). First, I figure out just where I am, and then I decide where I would like to be.

Then I bring in more spiritual psychological principles by setting intentions: first to let go of the mind chatter or story that I'm running in my mind about the situation, and an intention to choose a new way of thinking to put me on the right side of my own Mood Meter. Recommended strategies to go with the use of the Mood Meter include taking deep breaths. There are many ways to do that. In this final step, I bring in the Quick Coherence® Technique developed and researched by HeartMath®, which has been shown to actually interrupt the body's stress response, and help you go from anger, anxiety, and overwhelm to feeling focused, alert and calm.

This is how you begin to transform your 3-D thinking.

## THE MOOD METER

A foundational key to making soul-centered choices is to first become aware of your current emotional thinking. Emotions contain information, and they impact your energy and frequency levels. You can decide what needs to be changed or added to raise the vibrational frequency of your emotions and moods.

The Mood Meter is a tool that focuses on being aware of the emotions we experience in our everyday 3-D lives on Earth. After all, you can't adjust and improve what you aren't aware of! The Mood Meter is personalized and populated by the emotions you may have in daily life and emotions you would like to have more often. You can download a ready-to-use Mood

Meter from the resources link at the end of this chapter. If you want the fun of making your own, read on.

To create your Mood Meter, start with a blank sheet of paper. Draw a line from left to right and then an intersecting line from top to bottom. The line from left to right is the x-axis. Starting from the left, number it from -5 to 0 at the center, and continue from 0 to +5.

The line from top to bottom is the y-axis. Starting at the top, number it from +5 to 0, where it intersects with the x-axis. Then continue the numbering down from 0 to -5.

To label your Mood Meter, focus first on the x-axis going from left to right. Label this Personal Experience. This is your subjective experience. It's how pleasant you feel in your mind with whatever is happening. It's measured from a -5 to a +5, based on how pleasant your emotion is. A -5 would mean the lowest pleasantness or negative feelings you've ever had. A +5 would be the highest amount of pleasant or positive emotions you could feel.

Now label the y-axis (the line from top to bottom) Energy. The y-axis focuses on how much energy your body uses when you're experiencing an emotion. A +5 (at the top) would be the highest energy you could feel, the most energy you've ever had when you experience an emotion. A -5 (at the bottom) would mean you feel the lowest energy level you've ever had when you experience an emotion.

When your Mood Meter is drawn, you should have four quadrants. Each of the four quadrants is based on your level of energy and the level of pleasantness you're feeling.

The top right quadrant is feeling the happiest of pleasant feelings, with high energy. Examples of feeling words that would fall into this dimension on the high end are ecstatic, excited, or elated. Words that might be more in the mid-range are happy, optimistic, or joyful. Visible signs you might notice in this top right quadrant are physical ones you can see, such as happy and cheerful expressions, jumping or dancing, clapping, and cheering. Fill in some feeling words in this top right quadrant for positive, energetic emotions you have or would like to experience more often.

In the top left quadrant, the feeling words that might fit here can still have a high amount of energy, but they are less pleasant. Examples of this might be stress, panic, or fury. You might find words like worry, anxiety, anger, nervousness, or overwhelm in the middle range. A slightly lower energy range of emotions in this quadrant, closer to the x-axis midline, might be uneasy, stressed, distrustful, or feeling on edge. Physical signs you might notice with these kinds of feelings are frowning, a furrowed brow, biting your lip, a clenched jaw, or making fists. In the top left quadrant, write in some of the less pleasant or negative emotions you might experience, with higher energy ones near the top and middle energy level ones near the x-axis line.

When looking at the lower left quadrant, the feelings are still unpleasant and occur with lower energy levels. The negative words with middle-level energy would be near the x-axis and the lowest energy around the level -5. Examples of feeling words that might appear here range from disappointment, worry, lonely, despair, depression, helplessness, or hopelessness at the lowest end. Physical signs you might notice are moving slowly, slumped shoulders, avoiding eye contact, being disengaged or distant, or poor sleep. In the lower-left quadrant, write in some low energy, unpleasant or negative emotions you might experience.

Moving over to the lower right-side quadrant, feelings in this section are quieter and lower energy but becoming more pleasant. Examples of feeling words that would fit here are calm, content, love, peaceful, and serene. Other words with a little more energy (but not as much as the top right quadrant) might be optimism, joy, or appreciation. Physical signs here might be smiling, calm movements, good eye contact, and speaking in a quiet, calm voice. In the lower right quadrant, write quieter, calmer emotions you might experience or would like to experience more often.

Now, take a look at your Mood Meter in the context of your life. What are you feeling right now? Where does it land on your map? What other emotions have you experienced in the last day or two? This can show you a bigger picture of where you are emotionally and how often you're there. It also helps you to decide where you want to be.

Where do you have more emotions? On the left side of your Mood Meter, where they can sap your energy and ruin your day? Or are you having more emotional experiences on the right that build your energy and put you in a positive mood?

You can implement strategies and skills to help you be more soul-centered, so you can have more feeling experiences that are more pleasant, build your energy, and help you be more resilient. Of course, we are all still human and will have bad days. The goal is to spend a greater proportion of time on the right side of your Mood Meter.

## MOVING TO THE RIGHT SIDE

Think about the last time you made a good decision. How were you feeling at that time? The chances are that you felt balanced, positive, in a good mood, and in your power. This is the state you want to create again if you find yourself feeling some unpleasant emotions or negativity. Let's do it!

1. Awareness. Acknowledge the situation that has you feeling off-balance. Pull out your Mood Meter and pinpoint where you are.

2. Choice. Choose a place on your Mood Meter where you would prefer to be.

3. Set an intention to let go of whatever mind chatter or story is keeping you on the left side and an intention to choose a different way of thinking or outcome to put you on the right side.

4. Now bring in the HeartMath® Quick Coherence® Technique:

   Step 1: Focus your attention on the area of the heart. Imagine your breath is flowing in and out of your heart or chest area, breathing a little slower and deeper than usual. Suggestion: Inhale for five seconds, exhale for five seconds (or whatever rhythm is comfortable.)

   Step 2: As you continue heart-focused breathing, make a sincere attempt to experience a regenerative feeling such as appreciation or care for someone or something in your life, and breathe that feeling through the heart area.

## TIP:

When I practice The Quick Coherence® Technique, I also choose other renewing feelings from my Mood Meter. I do this for a few minutes, which can make a huge difference in how I feel.

Spiritual Psychology tools give me a solid foundation for my approach and philosophy, the Mood Meter helps me get clear on where I am and what I want, and HeartMath® skills bring my physical, mental, emotional, and spiritual systems all into alignment.

Remember, your heart intention + mind effort + soul alignment = change in emotion and frequency.

Allow change to happen in the moment. Ask your heart and your soul for the appropriate attitude and frequency. It's a conscious adjustment, and it becomes easier to make. Each time, it's a step into a new dimension of living aligned with your heart and your soul.

## RESOURCES:

1. To learn more about incorporating skills and tools of Spiritual Psychology, HeartMath®, and the Mood Meter for a soul-centered life, visit:
   https://sonialuckey.coachesconsole.com/resource-request--the-ultimate-guide-to-spiritual-living.html

2. To view a Mood Meter sample, go to
   https://www.ps120q.org/mood-meter (used with permission).

3. To learn more about the Mood Meter and the full RULER model, visit the Yale Center for Emotional Intelligence website at
   http://ei.yale.edu/ruler/

4. To learn more about HeartMath® tools, visit
   https://www.heartmath.com/. HeartMath® is a registered trademark of Quantum Intech, Inc.

**Dr. Sonia Luckey** is a holistic nurse practitioner with over 25 years of experience, board-certified in Family Practice and Psychiatric Mental Health. She is the president of The Nightingale Way, a nurse-owned education and consulting company.

Sonia has been following a breadcrumb trail of learning about holistic healing modalities her entire career, including Reiki, shamanic training, energy medicine, and HeartMath. She then took everything up a notch by earning a Master's in Spiritual Psychology and a Doctorate in nursing and applying principles and evidence-based research into these healing modalities. This created an amazing toolkit that she has used to help her patients and clients be more in control of their well-being and health care. Through her workshops and coaching, she teaches them how to shift their thinking, connect with their inner guidance, and then apply spiritual principles and universal laws to their personal lives, business, and relationships to live authentic, heart and soul-centered lives.

For fun, Sonia loves to write, read, and meditate. She loves connecting with water and nature spirits, taking it all in with a tall glass of water garnished with mint and cucumber while working poolside when possible. Her ideal getaway always involves beaches and the ocean, and she loves enjoying a little bit of heaven with dark chocolate and a nice glass of wine.

One of Sonia's greatest pleasures is seeing each person's full potential. Her goal is to help them tap into it and make sure everyone else sees it.

Connect with Sonia at:
www.sonialuckey.com
Facebook: DrSoniaLuckey
Instagram: @sonialuckey
LinkedIn: www.linkedin.com/in/sonia-luckey-dnp-285b019

# CHAPTER 13

# VALUE, HONOR, RESPECT

## CHANGE YOUR MONEY HABITS BY CHANGING YOURSELF

Lisa E. Gibbs, Ed.D.

## MY STORY

It's another day of dressing like a man. My shoes, socks, and trousers are *all black*. My hair is in a low ponytail, and I am wearing a freshly ironed white button-down with a white undershirt. At work, I add a black apron and vest, a name tag with black letters, and a black book with a black pen to write guest orders. (Not customers; we call them guests.) Thank God the tie doesn't have to be black!

With welcoming eyes and a smile, I explain how the aged steaks are seasoned and broiled and that the side dishes are large enough to share. "A bottle of Opus One would go perfectly with that!"

*Leave your troubled eyes and tense face at the door, and put on a grand façade because you need the money. This is just a means to an end.* I tell myself as I enter the guest's order in the Micros. *What end? I don't know. Surely something will come.*

During a lull in guest arrivals, a co-worker, fresh out of college with the whole world in front of him, asks me, "If you could do anything you wanted, what would that be?"

*Huh.* I take a minute to answer. "I don't know right now because I've already done the thing I always wanted to do—be a professional dancer in a small dance company."

In the spring of 2013, I was 47, working two full-time jobs, attending classes in graduate school, and writing a dissertation. I had two boys in middle and high school and was in a decent marriage. My young co-worker hit me with that question, and it completely threw me for a loop. Well, what *would* I do if I could do anything I wanted?

*What is my dream job other than the one I already achieved? And what the heck am I doing right now to get me to where I want to be? Where do I even want to be? I have no clue.*

That question, though; My heart feels it.

Later that summer I met one of my best friends for lunch. She was managing her husband's booming visual art career. He was a biochemist turned self-taught folk artist, touring the country to present at art festivals, and he sold art in several southeast galleries. She said she was overwhelmed with the required paperwork and logistics. She knew that I was very organized and said, "I need a *Lisa* in my life." I smiled and felt honored. "I'm just too busy right now," I reply. My head reminds me, *I am the one with a steady job that provides benefits. I can't leave that. My family needs the money.*

In my mind, I was doing the things to progress in a career I thought I wanted. I was a full-time secretary with part-time faculty duties in a university theater department, and I enjoyed it, except for the pay. My responsibilities also included managing the box office, directing the summer theater camps, overseeing and teaching for the dance minor program—on a secretary's salary. The only way to increase my salary was to have the proper letters after my name so that I could be full-time faculty. "It will be great to have another doctor in the department," I was told in 2010 when I decided to go back to school. In 2011, I added job number two, bartending and waiting tables at a high-end restaurant, to help pay for tuition.

That question, though; My heart still feels it, and I start seeking answers. However, my head has erected sturdy walls to manage my daily life. What my head says to do is now quietly but insistently being questioned by my soul. By the end of summer in 2013, my heart told me to leave the university job. My head reminded me: *I have a steady job that provides benefits. I can't leave that. How would we pay for everything?*

When you don't do what your soul tells you to do, the universe manages it for you, and not in a good way. One hour after being introduced, along with the rest of the faculty and staff of the performing arts division, to the majors and minors at an assembly on the second day of fall classes, I was unceremoniously fired.

My once sturdy walls of defense that said "life is all butterflies and unicorns" as I managed school, work, and family suddenly had giant holes. Darkness fell. Dark because my head tried hard to quiet my heart, and my heart said, *Enough! It's time to live.* I don't know how to do that. Dark because my heart told my head that I am very much out of alignment, and I am afraid to accept that.

My body told me as well. I couldn't reach down past my knees or sit for more than five minutes without intense tightness and tingling down the back of my right leg. I was a ballet dancer and teacher, for gosh sake, with limited mobility, and I didn't know why. My head tried to hold onto what seemed on the surface to be a great life, but my heart and then my body showed me it wasn't so great.

I met my friend again for lunch and told her what'd happened. She beamed. "Oh, good! You can come work with me now!" I think she saw through my walls.

I began spending my work hours in the presence of two people who constantly talked about dreaming, purpose, joy, love, and spirituality. They balanced the material world with the spiritual world, their heads and hearts with openness to both. My journey began.

I searched for podcasts and books focused on topics like purpose, alignment, and abundance. I filled notebooks with notes and references to anything written or spoken that stirred something in my soul. I filled sticky notes with quotes and reminders and placed them on my mirror, computer, and workspace.

Todd Henry, the host of *The Accidental Creative*, says, "To be prolific, brilliant, and healthy, you must be purposeful about how you structure your life. It happens by design, not default." I typed that quote in large letters and taped it to my refrigerator.

*I must be purposeful about how I structure my life. It happens by design—that means it's up to me. By default, it means it's up to other people.*

This quote by Anais Nin was on my cellphone home screen, "And the day came when the risk to remain tight in a bud was more painful than the risk it took to bloom." The more I uncovered by allowing my heart to speak instead of my head, the more I knew I was on the path, albeit slowly, to bloom.

Realizing that mentally, spiritually, and physically I was in the wrong place took lots of soul-searching and crying. I didn't know how much I'd closed off my soul, but there were so many walls hiding it! My work to self-heal led me to discover I did not value myself.

Why did I not value myself? I'm still not completely clear on that, but it definitely had to do with the relationships I've had over time. What matters is I discovered the thing in my heart that needed to heal so I could be my true self.

So, where does money fit into all this?

When I did not value myself, I did not truly value money either. I've always earned money and, at the same time, was nervous about not having enough. Even in a two-income, middle-class household, I felt scarcity around money. I would say shopping is not buying and then go for some good old retail therapy. Why in the world did I go shopping when I was nervous about having enough money?

I know now that the feeling of monetary scarcity was a coverup for a lack within myself. My soul behind all those walls was wasting away. The walls came down as I worked with my artist friends, read books about women who uncovered themselves and found their purpose, and listened to diverse voices discuss how they discovered their spiritual truth. I let go of feeling like money was never enough, committed to believing in abundance, and bloomed.

That question, though.

*If I could do anything I wanted, what would that be?*

How did I answer it?

In 2014, I wrote down the things I was good at and enjoyed doing—a vital distinction for making a new life decision. For example, I was good at waiting tables and bartending, but it did nothing to feed my soul. I was good at teaching ballet, and it made my spirit soar. I wrote down what I liked and disliked about my four part-time jobs. Yes, four jobs: restaurant, dance studio, artist studio, and assistant to the director of a non-profit. I determined I did not want a full-time university position. I wrote down what I did want from a new career.

I started searching for an industry that connected the dots, where my skills, talents, and spirit could make a difference in someone else's life. I asked people who knew me well what they would suggest. Rather than taking their advice immediately, I listened to what my soul said about their suggestions.

Several people said, "What about financial services?" and something in me liked that. I researched several companies to see which area of financial services appealed most to me. Banks? No. Office full of suits and ties? Ew, no. Cold-calling? No. Then I got a quarterly statement in the mail and realized I was a client of one of the largest financial services companies in North America. I called my agent, and we met three different times before I decided to join her agency.

When I began to value myself through those years of self-discovery, my money habits changed. I began to treat money like it was to be valued, honored, and used with respect instead of treating money like it wasn't enough, almost literally throwing it away like trash. I began to be open to people who considered me valuable, honored me, and treated me with respect. This, in turn, led me to choose work where I am valued, honored, and respected and where the work I do values, honors, and respects other people.

It's been said, "Purpose leaves clues." When you listen to your heart, you can feel the clues. I get as excited about helping people understand the time value of money as I do teaching a ballet or modern dance class. Researching an investment strategy and analyzing a fact sheet for a mutual fund is just as interesting to me as creating and teaching a new combination for my dance students. My head is still surprised at how much I enjoy my new career in personal finance, and my heart sits and smiles.

# THE STRATEGY

## FIVE CORE STANDARDS FOR YOUR RELATIONSHIP WITH MONEY

A few months after the effort to stop the spread of Covid-19 resulted in lockdowns, I had a discussion with a friend in the cruise ship industry. What a pivot she had to undertake! My business, personal financial services, was considered essential—not so for those in the entertainment and hospitality fields.

We talked about some of the mindsets and shifts we had put in place over the years as we let our hearts speak more loudly than our heads. For my friend, she had become more physically healthy and financially secure. For me, I'd released the feeling of scarcity of self and became more open to abundance in all areas of life. We agreed; our hearts know what is best for us. We just have to get out of the way and listen.

Not only listen, but we must also act on and be intentional with our choices. The soul-aligned business only works if you act upon what your heart tells you, and your actions must align with your core values. These values are reflected in your relationship with yourself, your family, friends, business, food, clothing, money, pets—you name it, there is a relationship.

My friend and I brainstormed our core standards for relationships and the non-negotiable traits our spirits demand to live our most purposeful, soul-aligned lives. I left that conversation feeling invigorated and clearer about my work in the world.

How to determine your five core standards:

1. Write down what you value/what is meaningful to you.
2. Write down what you seek out of a relationship.
3. Identify the top five core standards, based on your values, that are non-negotiable when it comes to relationships.
4. List the standard and describe how that standard relates to your values.

5. Apply those standards to any and all areas of your life, including how you choose to earn money.

Here's how I discovered my list. I framed the question this way: If money were a man, what would be my non-negotiable traits for us to have a relationship?

1. Generous - Be generous to yourself and other people. Give from a place of genuine intention to uplift, whether it be a warm smile or an unexpected gift.

2. Teachable - Your soul teaches you how to live, and there is always more to learn. You also draw to yourself other people who are your teachers.

3. Valuable - Understand the value you bring to the world by living your true self. Value what others bring to the world as well.

4. Honorable - Honor the divine uniqueness that is you, and honor the uniqueness others bring to this world.

5. Respectful - Treat yourself and those around you with respect, even when it seems challenging.

Today, my relationship with money reflects my relationship with myself—I am valuable, honorable, and respectable. Now my mantra is, "Earning money is a paycheck. Having money is a behavior."

Value money - don't spend more than you earn.

Honor money - use it for good.

Respect money - give it a place to grow and flourish.

As I continue to practice being free from scarcity of self and money, I more deeply understand the power of relationships. I understand now the most important relationship you have is the one with yourself. A soul-aligned business can only be that way when you live what your spirit tells you. Value, honor, and respect yourself enough to let yourself listen and act. Let your soul be open to receiving the tiny clues that will lead you to do the things that make you feel like yourself. Happy blooming!

**Lisa E. Gibbs,** Ed.D. is a passionate money mindset coach who will transform the way you think about and manage your personal finances to live a healthy money life. With help from friends, family and by listening to her heart, she discovered how to blend her diverse range of work experiences into a career that aligns with her heart. Her background includes numerous years of waiting tables and bartending, administrative assisting at several non-profit dance-related businesses and a university, a 13-year performance career, and teaching ballet and modern dance. Now living a healthy money life herself, she helps people learn to become financially secure through conversation and action steps regarding mindset and behavior around money.

You can find her taking a ballet class on Saturday mornings, as she has nearly every Saturday of her life since age 10.

Connect with Lisa:

On Instagram: https://www.instagram.com/healthy.money.life/
On Alignable:
https://www.alignable.com/birmingham-al/healthy-money-life
On LinkedIn: https://www.linkedin.com/in/lisaegibbs/
On Facebook: https://www.facebook.com/lisagibbsprimerica
On her website: https://www.primerica.com/lisaegibbs

# CHAPTER 14

# BRING MORE SOUL TO YOUR ROLE

## FROM CORPORATE BURNOUT TO CONSCIOUS LEADER

Erica Zygelman, Integrative Leadership Coach

## MY STORY

"Hello? Erica, are you still there?"

I rolled from my back to my right side so I could rest my phone on my ear without having to hold it up as I lay on my couch. *Ugh. I don't have the energy to be coached tonight.*

"Yeah, I'm still here. I'm just so tired I can't even sit up right now."

"I know, honey. You're completely burnt out! What do you have planned outside of work for the next two weeks?"

"Um, I have a few business dinners, and my friend's birthday is on Saturday. I'm supposed to meet an old coworker for drinks on Wednesday," I trailed off.

My life coach, Julie, proceeded to give me the most radical and unexpected assignment I'd ever received, "Yeah, you're gonna be canceling *all* of those."

I'd been hired by a prominent music company two years earlier, in the summer of 2015. This would have been a dream job for anyone with my background: the director of a national client services team for the biggest music platform in the world. Except I could never really enjoy it because I was perpetually exhausted.

I remember my very first day at that job. My boss called me into The Blue Note, one of the music-venue-themed meeting rooms.

"Welcome, Erica! We're excited you're here. I know you asked how many people were on your team during your interview, and I told you 12," he dove right in.

I swallowed hard and felt my neck stiffen as I exhaled all the air from my lungs. *Where is he going with this?*

"Well, we realized we'd under-counted the client service managers and also decided to add Canada to your remit."

Did you know it's possible to scream inside your head without emitting any sound or making a facial expression? Because that's what I was doing.

"The final count is 20." He said flatly.

A smirk crept across my face. *I had 20 direct reports? Surely, he was joking.*

"Hmm, that's a pretty big difference from what we discussed in the interviews."

"I suggest you spend your first six weeks on a listening tour. Talk to everyone you can and get a lay of the land. Start with Kal, Lisa, Maureen. I'll give you a list, and you can schedule time with them."

*Cool, so no actual onboarding plan. This is going to be chaos.*

And off I went, feeling totally out of my depth.

The next six months were a blur of panic and anxiety. I scheduled 20 introductory meetings with my direct reports, spanning ten cities and two countries, while also learning what the heck everyone did. That varied across the board, as it turned out. I worked 12+ hours a day and on many weekends to wrangle all the people, processes, and projects that needed my attention.

Managing 20 people became predictably unsustainable, so I identified the strongest client service managers and promoted them into an intermediary management tier for our team.

I made it my mission to ensure my new managers felt supported, confident, and prepared for the roles they were stepping into. It was my earnest attempt to disrupt the pattern I'd experienced where I felt abandoned and left to wing it on my own when I most needed support.

Fast forward two years, and I got into a steady rhythm overseeing the team, which had grown to 45 members strong and included Latin America. My seven first-time managers were confidently running their local regions' business.

But the path to get there had taken its toll. The fast-growing company, aggressive sales goals, constant business travel, and my New York City social life were demanding.

My Hashimoto's thyroiditis started flaring, requiring adjustments to the dosage of my medication. I developed insomnia, with ruminating thoughts waking me up almost every weeknight, itchy skin patches on my elbows, gained and lost weight—all physical manifestations of chronic stress.

I was burned out. My body had nothing left and was begging for my attention.

All of which led me to that moment lying on my couch, in a puddle of exhaustion, during my coaching session with Julie that night.

"I hate this assignment. But I'll try it."

I canceled all of my social plans for the next two weeks, and it sucked.

It seems obvious now, but my nervous system was addicted to the adrenaline of go-go-going all the time. It was hard for me to stop, painfully hard. All of these fears and judgments came up.

*Am I a bad friend because I am missing her birthday dinner?*

*Will I miss out on a big business decision at happy hour?*

*What if everyone stops inviting me to stuff?*

I continued receiving coaching for the next two years, and my patterns and mindset slowly shifted. I started prioritizing downtime and saying no to plans that didn't excite me. I went to more yoga instead of boxing classes, listened to soothing music, and dabbled in meditation. I started hearing the voice of my intuition, getting clearer and louder as it guided my decisions.

Through this slow recovery process, I tapped into a spiritual part of myself that was deeply connected to the essence of my soul and the nature of everything around me. This part of me was always there, but it was a parched, fragile seedling in a dark corner that was only watered in rare spaces and in company that felt extremely safe.

So I started feeding and nourishing my soul with space, slowness, rest, and deep care.

Then Julie said something that stuck with me during one of our last sessions, "Your work is only 30% about what you *do*. The other 70% is who you *are*."

I took in a full breath of air as I felt the truth and ease in that statement. My jaw unclenched, and my shoulders relaxed.

I released some of the pressure from the productivity I was fixated on and allowed myself to focus more on being present. I knew one of my deepest gifts was how much I cared about people and how I created safe spaces for them to grow. I also knew I was highly skilled at my job and could trust my experience rather than feeling the need to prove myself all the time.

I began listening to my seven managers intently during our status meetings, asking them more questions with curiosity than offering solutions from my expertise. I mindfully practiced box-breathing to calm my nerves before big presentations. I remained present to what was happening in meetings rather than anxiously rehearsing responses in my head to unasked questions.

I was becoming a *conscious leader*.

As much as I was evolving in this role, I knew something felt off. I still wasn't fully in alignment. And, as it does, the universe soon brought me what I needed. I was laid off during a department reorganization, and I took that opportunity to lean way out on doing and focus on cultivating my being.

I traveled to India for two months and studied yoga, meditation, and breathwork. When I got back, I found my way into Functional Medicine and got my health coaching certification. This unexpected sabbatical and holistic training reinforced the importance of integrating the physical, mental, emotional, and spiritual sides of myself so that I could bring my whole self into my work.

It gave me the freedom to *choose* how I want to lead and live with a more conscious mindset. It also revealed the value of guiding others to cultivate this approach for themselves, which I had rarely seen in the corporate world.

Ultimately, I decided to dedicate my career focus on supporting new and rising leaders as an integrative leadership coach. Inspired by my personal healing journey and the junior managers I guided in my corporate roles, I finally feel aligned in my mission to serve this often neglected yet highly formative window of the early leadership journey.

As an entrepreneur, I continue to integrate all that I have healed and learned within myself into my leadership. I am passionate about elevating leaders to thrive with their well-being as the cornerstone, not an afterthought.

I am leading from my soul and encourage you to lead from yours. It's the secret to transforming your career into your calling so that you, too, can achieve success with greater well-being, freedom, and ease.

# THE STRATEGY

## HOW TO RISE FROM CORPORATE BURNOUT TO CONSCIOUS LEADER

The corporate world has become consumed by outcomes and outputs, quotas, and metrics. In this paradigm, productivity, hustle, and sacrifice are the table stakes of success. Yes, hard work is important. You are a leader because you care. You have a mission to serve your people and make your corner of the world a better place. But you, your people, and the world do not benefit from your suffering.

You can breathe now. There is an easier way.

At its core, conscious leadership is about raising your glance from what you are *doing* to who you are *being*.

Becoming a conscious leader requires us to *un*learn what has indoctrinated us to believe is the truth about success. It requires a reprioritization from how it *appears* outside to how it *feels* on the inside.

Here are **three powerful paradigm shifts** with simple embodiment practices you can apply to begin rising into conscious leadership.

# 1. CONNECTION OVER PERFECTION

The pursuit of perfection is a trap. It's a constant uphill battle to keep up the appearance of having it all together, maintaining composure, and knowing all the answers. It's also a sneaky cover-up for some deeply rooted fears. It often stems from fear of failure, judgment, or even worse, rejection. It tends to have the opposite result of what we want. Rather than winning the admiration and respect of our colleagues and peers, it isolates us on an imaginary pedestal. Perfectionism makes us rigid and protective rather than curious and open to the people and opportunities around us.

As a conscious leader, choose to prioritize connection over perfection. There is nothing more human than imperfection, so when you approach a conversation or business challenge with the intent to connect with your employee or teammate rather than have the perfect solution, your whole perspective will shift. You can be more curious about their perspectives and seek *understanding* rather than being *right*. Your success metric becomes how connected you feel rather than how perfect the outcome is. The funny thing is, your intention to connect and collaborate will likely yield even better results than if you had tried to solve the problem perfectly yourself.

**Embodiment Practice**

1. Free write ten reasons why connecting with others is important to you.

   a. *For example: 1) Connection builds trust 2) It makes my relationships stronger 3) I appreciate others' perspectives.*

2. Now choose your favorite reason that connection matters, and create a mantra or affirmation that you can repeat in your mind.

   a. *Favorite reason: I appreciate others' perspectives.*

   b. *Affirmation: I let go of perfection and am open to others' perspectives.*

3. Write your affirmation on a post-it and place it by your computer or on a mirror. Repeat it regularly when you catch yourself in perfectionist mode and remind yourself to connect instead.

## 2. PRESENCE OVER PRODUCTIVITY

Do you find it hard to relax in the evenings or on weekends, constantly refreshing your email or ruminating on your to-do list? Maybe thinking about a challenge at work while talking to a friend over dinner? We become addicted to the constant adrenaline rush of achieving goals, completing tasks, and checking off our to-do lists. So much so that it's hard to unhook ourselves from the dopamine hits our brains get from feeling productive, even in our downtime.

One antidote to this is prioritizing more presence over productivity. When we're in productivity mode, we are future-focused on anticipating the endless things that need to get done. Presence brings us back into the moment and reconnects us to the people and environment around us.

The simplest way to cultivate presence is by connecting to your body and, more simply, your breath. Your breath is always happening in the present moment, 100% of the time. The key is to recognize when you are future-tripping on the productivity hamster wheel and gently guide yourself back into the present through mindful breathing.

**Embodiment Practice**

1. When you catch your mind racing and hyper-focusing on all that needs to get done, pause and simply notice this is happening.

2. Find yourself a comfortable seat, close your eyes, and take five mindful breaths, elongating your exhales so they are twice as long as your inhales.

    a. *For example: Inhale for a count of two, exhale for a count of four. Repeat for five breath cycles.*

3. Open your eyes and take a moment to notice any shifts in your mental state as you land back in the present moment.

## 3. BODY OVER BRAIN

As busy, intelligent, hard-working leaders, we tend to live in our heads. We rely on our knowledge, experience, and cognitive power as our main access to solutions. But we can't discount the information we get from the neck down. We are accustomed to the familiar cues that let us know what we most need on a physiological level. Hunger, sleepiness, or chills let us know when we need to eat, rest, or put on a sweater.

Our bodies are also the vehicle by which our intuition communicates with us through feelings, sensations, and gut instincts. Trusting our body wisdom is an incredibly powerful tool for conscious leaders. Our bodies are the most sensitive radars to provide highly reliable feedback and information. We can easily dismiss these signals as fleeting, but honoring them and leveraging them to make decisions, in addition to our brilliant thoughts and ideas, is where our superpower lies.

**Embodiment Practice**

1. To practice mindfully connecting to your body, first locate yourself by noticing where you are physically, and place your hands somewhere on your body that feels safe.

2. Begin cycling through each of your primary senses through the 5-4-3-2-1 method:

    5 - Observe five things you see around you.

    4 - Listen for four things you hear in your environment.

    3 - Feel three things that you sense touching your body.

    2 - Smell two things that you can identify in the air.

    1 - Taste one thing that you can detect in your mouth.

3. Play with layering these sensations and practice sensing multiple things at once.

Making these intentional shifts in your awareness is the very first step. I am here to support you along your journey to conscious leadership and integrating your whole self at work. If you'd like to connect or explore the various ways we can work together, please come on over to www.ericazygelman.com. I would love to hear from you!

**Erica Zygelman** is an Integrative Leadership Coach committed to supporting the next generation of leaders to achieve sustainable success by integrating conscious leadership and holistic wellness principles.

Erica has a 15+ year track record of leading high-performing corporate managers and teams at world-class tech organizations including Apple and Spotify. She is also well versed in overcoming the pitfalls of self-sacrifice and burnout from her personal experience and observing these patterns throughout her corporate career.

Her superpower is equipping leaders with the tools to source their energy from a balanced, intuitive, and mindful lifestyle to thrive and shift the paradigm of what success looks and feels like. She supports her clients through private and group coaching, management training, and corporate workshops.

On a personal level, Erica loves to geek out about functional medicine, personal development, yoga, and mindfulness. She feels most inspired by international travel adventures, immersing herself in live music, and being outdoors exploring nature. After a decade-and-a-half love affair with New York City, she is smitten with her new hometown of San Diego.

Connect with Erica:

On her website: https://www.ericazygelman.com
On LinkedIn: https://www.linkedin.com/in/ericazygelman/
On Instagram: https://www.instagram.com/ericazygelman/
Erica's gift to you: The 3 Secrets to Being a Successful Leader and How to Embody Them
https://www.ericazygelman.com/opt-in-free-guide
Additional Resources: https://www.ericazygelman.com/resources

# CHAPTER 15

# MERGING BUSINESS AND SPIRITUALITY

## HOW TO ACTIVATE PROSPERITY AND FREEDOM WITH EASE

Susan Prescott, MA, Transformational Business, Spiritual Coach

## MY STORY

I was sitting in the back seat of a car directly behind the driver. There was no headrest, so I was looking at the back of the driver's head, which was long-haired and shaggy. I realized the driver was a wolf, whom I consider to be my spirit animal. He is my protector. I felt comfortable and safe as I snuggled up in the back seat and allowed him to drive the car. I woke up from my dream with a sensation there was a message for me. *I better pay attention!*

As I meditated on what this dream meant, a shivering horror swept through me: *Oh my gosh! My wolf wasn't protecting me! There was no protection of my authentic self, who I am at soul level, or my unlimited divine self. He was protecting my false-self ego. I'm being manipulated and controlled by things and people outside of me.*

My ego fed me external messages to support a business structure based on competition and scarcity. The idea is that there is only so much to go around. The belief is that the only way to win is to crush the competition, and success requires sacrifice and working long, hard hours.

In addition, I received messages that supported my false limiting self-beliefs keeping me separated from my divine self.

I was hiding the part of me that was very spiritual from the outside world. Being a chameleon adapting to the expectations of others kept me safe in the back seat of the car.

My heart started racing. *I've always wanted to merge the part of me that is very spiritual with the part that is driven and wants to create abundance.*

I drew in a deep breath, and my entire body froze as a sinking feeling crept through me.

*My family will think I have gone off the deep end. Will I be disconnected from those in my professional circle? Do my clients believe being spiritual in the business world is woo-woo? Will I lose them?*

I could hear my ego taunting me as if tugging at the wheel. "Why do you want control of the wheel? Don't you know I'm keeping you safe? You don't have to be responsible for your life. Just play the victim game."

After a long pause, I declare: "I want freedom."

"I want freedom from the negative beliefs that hold me hostage. Since I was a little girl, others made me feel insignificant. I want to be significant."

"I want the freedom to pursue my dreams, live the life I know I am destined for, and experience the highest expression of myself."

"I want the freedom to be my authentic self in all areas of my life, including my business."

"I want to create my business using my soul gifts and talents, but you keep telling me the shoulds of running my business. I'm not even sure what my soul gifts are."

A quote by Maria Robinson flashed through my mind. "Nobody can go back and start a new beginning, but anyone can start today and make a new ending."

Finding freedom was so simple but, at the same time, so difficult. The answer is to align my personality with my true self, my divine self, and merge my spiritual self with my business.

The words of one of my favorite authors, Gary Zukav, came to mind. "When the personality comes fully to serve the energy of its soul, that is authentic empowerment."

There is no better way to serve the energy of my soul and expand the consciousness in the world than through my business!

The paradigms no longer support who I am at a soul level. Developing a new and expanded mindset that supports new ways of approaching business emerged.

I took a long deep breath embracing the truth that there is no separation between my spirituality, business, and life. It's all one!

The inner hunger gnaws in my stomach and will not go away. *Is this inner hunger, my soul, calling to me to wake up to my authentic power—to my spiritual self?*

Spiritually has nothing to do with religious dogma or ideology. It's heart-centered. I'm to connect my logical, analytical, rational left brain with my spiritual heart center.

My heart quickened. *Yes, this is mine to do. I hear you calling me. I will merge what I know at the core of my heart into the business community.*

- The Universe is abundant, and there is more than enough to go around.

- I am an energy being living in a vibrational universe. The higher my vibration, the greater connection I have with Divine Source.

- I am a creative being, and my reality is co-created with my guides, angels, and Divine Source.

- Everything I create or manifest begins with a thought.

- I am living in a duality world—a world of opposites. When my thoughts are focused on the negative, I produce negative results. When my thoughts are focused on the positive, I produce positive results.

- I always have a choice—it's called free will.

The key is in knowing that the Universe has my back.

The energy bubbles up in my body. I am making the conscious choice to align myself to a presence some call God, Divine Source, Christ Consciousness, or some call it intuition. I choose to be in the driver's seat of the car.

Driving my car means I must be who I am at a soul level. Not just thinking it, not just doing it, but being it.

The Law of Being states: "Who you are being is based on your level of conscious awareness of who you really are. This determines what and who you are going to attract and what type of life you will live. It's a formula that determines your reality. It's how you create your world."

Relief overcame me. I knew that once I mastered this law, I would no longer have to monitor what I think and do. I am attracting what I truly desire and doing it without effort to activate prosperity with freedom and ease. A knowingness swelled in my heart. "I am safe, and I love driving the car as my authentic self."

I breathed deeply, focusing on my spiritual heart. *Thank you for your guidance and your wisdom. Thank you for guiding me to experience my purpose, passion, and principles through my business. Thank you for bringing goodness, beauty, love, and compassion into all areas of my life.*

# THE STRATEGY

## TIPS ON GAINING CONTROL OF THE WHEEL

Merging spirituality with business is an inside-out process. We are creatures of habit, and the outside influences continue to try to take over the wheel. Be gentle with yourself as you awaken to your full potential and the unlimited opportunities awaiting you.

## 1. START EACH DAY CREATING A BEINGNESS LIST

I am a firm believer in the daily to-do list. I live by it. However, there is a much more important list that I create daily. It's my being list.

Michael Beckwith said, "In a society where doingness is more encouraged and awarded than beingness, it can be challenging to grasp that 'in inaction' there is a great deal of action taking place."

Set your intentions daily. Choose two or three words that will support you during your day. I am:

Accepting, happy, trusting, centered, peaceful, focused, generous, self-confident, reliable, compassionate, non-judgmental, forgiving, tolerant, understanding. Add your ways of being to this list.

Over time it makes a difference. Focusing on who you want to become will raise your vibrational frequency and align you with your higher self—your authentic self. You will find yourself moving from thinking positive to being positive. You will not only change your thoughts and action, but you will change at the very core.

## 2. EMBRACE THE POWER OF GRATITUDE

Being in a state of gratitude vibrates at the same level of abundance.

Gratitude will keep you from the mindset that supply is limited.

"If the only prayer you ever say in your entire life is thank you, it will be enough." - Meister Eckhardt

Gratitude is the key that unlocks the door to your abundance on all levels—physically, emotionally, mentally, spiritually. Being grateful to everyone and everything in your life is the first step in gaining control of the wheel.

Notice the sensations you feel in your physical body when you're in a state of gratitude. It's more than just saying the words or writing in a journal, but feeling the energy of gratitude move through you. The energy of gratitude is like a magnet drawing to you more to feel gratitude.

Develop your gratitude muscles through daily practices. Practice gratitude every moment of the day. There are multiple ways to do this.

- Before going to sleep at night, express gratitude for ten things that occurred during the day.

- Take a walk and breathe in gratitude as you commune with nature.

- When you're faced with a challenge during the day, pause, breathe deeply, and express gratitude for the positive outcome that will emerge.

- Keep a gratitude journal. It will make you increasingly aware of your many blessings. Writing down what you're grateful for causes you to be more present, more aware.

- Embrace and be grateful for what you consider to be the bad, unfair, unjust things that happened in your life and recognize they have helped shape you into who you are today.

## 3. THE POWER OF THE BREATH

How many times have you been told to "just breathe" when under stress or overwhelmed?

Your breath is your direct connection to Divine Source. You breathe in the breath of Divine Source. When you breathe out, you breathe out the toxins of the body and the mind.

Stretton Smith tells the story of three little fish in Monterey Bay. These three little fish were going to fish school, and one day their professor told them about water. He told them that water was present at every point in space at the same time. So, after school that day, the three little fish talked and wondered where the water was. One of the little fish understood the concept. He knew he was already in the water. With great excitement, the other two said, "Let's go find the water." And so, they swam the seven seas, and finally, years later, they returned to Monterey Bay, old, decrepit, impoverished, and at home to die. They looked up their old fish school chum, who was still looking young, had a whole string of condominiums in the reef, and a fine family with several generations of grand fish. And the two fish asked, "How did you ever find the water?"

Your connection to the Source, like water for the fish, is everywhere. It's present all the time. It flows through you with every breath as the water flows through the fish's gills.

Become conscious about your breath. We tend to breathe shallowly or even hold our breath when feeling anxious. Sometimes we are not even aware of it. Shallow breathing limits oxygen intake and adds further stress to your body, creating a vicious cycle.

Breathing exercises can break this cycle. You can feel the love, light, and wisdom coming in.

Experiment with breathing exercises and find what works for you. Use the following as a starting point.

- Sit up straight. (Do not arch your back.)
- Place your hands on your stomach. Breathe in slowly through your nose, pushing your hands out with your stomach. This ensures that you're breathing deeply. Imagine that you're filling your body with air from the bottom up.
- Hold your breath to a count of five or six, or whatever you can handle. Slowly and steadily breathe out through your mouth, feeling your hands move back in as you slowly contract your stomach until most of the air is out.

Follow the breath with this simple mantra to return you to the present moment.

Breathing in: I calm my body. (Think this as you breathe in.)
Breathing out: I smile. (Think this as you breathe out.)

Dwelling in the present moment (Think this as you breathe in.)
I know this is a wonderful moment! (Think this as you breathe out.)

Every day I remind myself I have the choice to be the driver of my car or slip into the back seat. Some days are easier than others. The paradox is we are already what we seek to find. Freedom is in our everyday lives.

We are beings of energy. Your business has its own unique energy. Are you interested in learning how aligned your energy is with the energy of your business? Check out how to receive a free energetic analysis of your business at https://activatingprosperity.com/energetic-analysis/.

**Susan Prescott** is an expert certified coach and Akashic Records reader who helps business owners identify their soul talents and energetic gifts to align with the energy of their business and experience profound shifts for success.

As a former high school teacher, she co-authored a series of business textbooks used at the secondary level. She loved working with her students but always knew there was more to do. Entering the corporate world allowed her to learn the pitfalls of being a manager and the necessity of self-leadership before leading others.

After experiencing the pain of being downsized and wondering what will I be when I grow up, she developed a passion for helping others in the business community. Susan founded Optimal Outcomes in 2001, where she partnered with independent professionals and business owners as a coach, mentor, guide, and facilitator.

An inner hunger led her on a deeper spiritual journey. Susan found herself walking two paths, keeping one foot in spirituality, and the other in business. She realized others also had this inner hunger and yearned for something more in their lives; something meaningful and fulfilling. She had this inner calling. It was time to merge the two paths and share with others what she wished she had known at a much earlier age.

Activating Prosperity became an extended branch of Optimal Outcomes in 2021, where Susan works directly with business owners ready to align their gifts and create soul-centered success.

Connect with Susan:

On her website: www.activatingprosperity.com
On LinkedIn: https://www.linkedin.com/in/susan-prescott-1629271
On Facebook: https://www.facebook.com/susan.prescott44/

# CHAPTER 16

# ACCESSING THE SOUL OF YOUR BUSINESS

## REVENUE WITH PURPOSE

Linda Berger, International Akashic Record Teacher, Consultant, Strategic Business Coach

## MY STORY

*What have you done, Linda?*

Suddenly overwhelmed with self-doubt and fixated on what I could have done to make a client leave her coaching program so suddenly. Then, in a panic, I kept thinking, *this is my only client left because of Covid. What did I do wrong? I don't have any more revenue.*

It was a Wednesday in February at 5 p.m. sharp. The moment that changed the trajectory of my business as I knew it. Pulling my car into my parking space, I heard a text ding from inside my purse. As I got out of my car, I grabbed my phone to see who had texted me.

*It's Jen. OMG, I can't wait to hear what she says about her trip.*

I was so happy to hear from her, as she'd been in California for a month. I started reading her text, "Linda, I write this to you sitting on the beach in such a space of love and gratitude, knowing this is the right decision for me at this time. . ."

*Stop reading,* now!

I couldn't go on, knowing it would send me into, *oh no, here it comes,* immediately, the pit of my stomach clenched, my heart started pounding, my eyes teared up.

I heard myself say: *shit, shit, shit, shit! Jen is my last business client. What am I going to do? I'm out of business. It's over.*

Until that day, I'd painstakingly separated *my* two businesses, strategic coaching and Akashic Record consulting/teaching. One I kept in the metaphorical closet (the spiritual one), the other, front and center (coaching). My coaching clients knew me as Coach Linda Berger, strategic business coach. My Akashic clients knew me as the heart-centered spiritual consultant/teacher who gave them the soul guidance they wanted and needed to change their lives.

I knew for some time that combining my two businesses was essential. So my next steps were to create Akashic Record Business Coaching/Training. But in taking my sweet time, the two souls of my businesses intervened. Enough. The time is now. You're ready.

Was I ready?

Knowing both of my businesses picked me, as they do for all of us, and were helping me face my old fears, I distracted myself to escape the inevitable. My students and clients faced those blocks I was evading. They know their businesses highlight what needs to change to experience untapped potential. But I didn't want to meet my deepest fears. I was afraid of being that vulnerable.

I didn't dare trust the soul of my Akashic business to show up for me.

*So who do you think you are, Linda? You aren't unique. Don't trust anyone other than yourself.*

I never had anyone or anything I could trust unconditionally to support me in building my dreams. And here was the soul of my business which I couldn't see or touch, wanted me, flaws and all. All I needed to do was trust it to show up so we could build my dream business.

Easy peasy, right? Nope.

It took my dear brave friend and client, Jen, to act for me. She stepped in as the ignitor, obviously having a soul contract with my business, lovingly forcing me to change the trajectory of my life's work. After the shock wore off, I realized I was acting like a spoiled child who had her blankie taken away.

Too distracted, I hadn't noticed I'd outgrown my need for a safe place to hide. So after putting on my big girl panties, I went to have a heart-to-soul talk with my Akashic business, patiently waiting for me to trust its guidance and become my most loyal adviser.

The business soul and I had a lot to talk about during our time together. There were many questions, doubts, and a lot of fear—all on my part.

And then so lovingly, my heart burst open, tears ran down my cheeks as I said out loud my fear of all fears, "What if I fail to complete the contracts we have with our people? I'm only a human being, so small compared to your mission. What if I die and leave those soul contracts unfulfilled?"

I gave myself a few days to think about our conversation and the changes I would have to make in myself. The information was profound and felt true at my deepest sense of self.

I knew I could trust what I heard, but could I trust myself? Could I become vulnerable enough to clothe myself in the expectations of others no longer? Was I ready to show up, dressed like me, flaws and all?

There would be no more becoming a basket case woven in old memories of loneliness and abandonment when I couldn't control the outcome.

My life and business would have to follow the new business paradigm, Revenue with Purpose. It was the soul's way to focus on how many other souls could become empowered. I felt a newness about myself and my work, an unburdening of sorts, a lightening of the load I'd carried for so long.

Maybe this is trust.

We are in business to serve our segment of life that has created a resource to fulfill its needs, dreams, and wants with services, tools, products, courses, etc. We start our businesses driven by the passion for sharing our special sauce, and we want to make money.

Whether we admit it or not, we all need money to pay our bills, go on vacations, support our families, live the life we dreamed of when we were kids, and on and on.

But the truth is, we hide it by saying we want to help others, serve others, heal others. Yes, that is true. But when we burn the candle at both ends, and the bills are coming in without revenue, we are broke, tired, and burnt out. In that reality, we either give up or change to build a sustainable and profitable business.

Revenue with Purpose works with the company's soul to be the trusted advisor to stop wasting our time, money, and energy guessing the right path to take.

The soul also shared that every business' soul picks the most likely human to ensure success.

So did it mean my business saw my brilliance and had the confidence in me, clothed as me, flaws and all, way before I believed in myself? If so, that has to be true for you, also.

Our business's purpose is to service soul contracts with the segment of humanity with needs, wants, desires that only the business can fulfill. That's its only mission. So we need to show up to follow its blueprint in reaching those people. When we follow the plan, we reap the rewards.

Also, it needs us because we each have the right stuff to fulfill the soul's objectives successfully. So, yes, you, like myself, were picked because the soul saw our expertise, experiences, training, and knowledge before we did to ensure its success.

After all, that is why it chose us as ambassadors and partners.

Okay, I know that is a bit woo-woo, but bear with me.

I saw a vision of a business as an energetic orb. It was a beautiful animation of hundreds of lines moving back and forth, in and out, circling each other. I was mesmerized by the magnificent colors, each line representing a soul contracted with the business, clients, vendors, employees, contractors, affiliates, etc. They were dancing together, moving closer and further apart from one another. It was a sight to behold.

I'm lucky enough to see this sight often when working with my clients. However, my favorite is when they get to witness it for themselves.

I hope one day, I can assist you in seeing it for yourself—the majesty and magnificence of what you do every day just by showing up for your business.

Never again would I become distracted from the soul of my business. I often wonder why I distracted myself for so long. But whatever my excuse may have been, it no longer matters, as I am and have been following the soul of my business since shortly after that kick-in-the-ass day in February 2021.

Putting into practice, Revenue with Purpose confused my way of thinking about running a business. It was the opposite of what my business training taught me. I finally wrapped my head around the paradigm idea and committed to trusting what was showing up for me as an indicator to follow that direction. So I went without dragging my feet or asking a gazillion questions.

I know it's a mind-bender.

But think about it, doesn't changing the way we do business by focusing on the numbers of lives we can change rather than just dollars make much more sense? First, we have to change our judgments around the worth and value of our services and or products. I revisited my fees and business systems to support my desired success, including my old patterns. I made the necessary changes.

For myself, worrying about making money was fruitless; instead, I was to focus on showing up and going through the doors my business opened for me.

Before committing, I stated my guidelines, set my boundaries based on my priorities, and designated the days I could be fully present. Then, we metaphorically shook hands and started working in unison.

Jen was my last business client for my old way of doing business the hard way. She was also the starting point.

After that soul-filled day, my new Revenue with Purpose clients started showing up. I trusted the information I gave because it came from my trusted partner, and clients lined up to learn from me.

*Why did I wait so long?*

Sometimes my eyes well up in tears when I think about how lucky I am to be so blessed and loved, just for doing something that makes my heart sing. I want that for you.

If you don't have it already, know the soul of your business is patiently waiting for you to show up.

Revenue with Purpose shifted my willingness to trust, guided by something I had to believe in wholeheartedly and show up just for the clients.

As a result, my business is what I imagined but never fully believed was possible for me. I had hoped, of course, but never truly embraced the belief. So I thank the soul for helping me face my stuff that limited our work together.

The irony is, Revenue with Purpose is so much easier, with eternal rewards. The more I learn, the more I'm excited to share with others.

Joy oozes out of my pores. It's an honor to show up for clients every day to help them discover more potential and use it moving forward in their lives and businesses.

For myself, the soul had been nudging me to write a book teaching about the soul of a business and why it's essential to know and follow. Instead, I complained that there wasn't enough time because I was teaching, coaching, and showing up for summits and podcasts.

So, they created a doorway through someone else who referred me to the publisher of the book you're holding in your hands. The result? You have it in your hands right now.

Yep, it made sure I followed the blueprint to share what I know about the soul of a business by writing one chapter—baby steps, I'd say.

It's effortless once we stop fighting and start trusting. Take it from a warrior.

If you aren't ready to trust the soul of your business, trust me because I've been there, done that repeatedly. I know all you need to do is take baby steps just like me.

You will see, like I did, without a shadow of a doubt, that the soul of our businesses will always guide us and tell us the next best step to take or person to hire, or program to follow, that will lead us to more people that are waiting for our business to show up in their lives.

Our business' success depends on us because we were selected. It has the right stuff, and so do we. Together we are dynamic and unstoppable.

Revenue with Purpose teaches us to be soul-led and heart-driven in reaching the numbers of souls our companies have contracts with to assist.

And assist, we must, just by trusting enough to show up.

# THE STRATEGY

### How to Create a Partnership with the Soul of Your Business

You don't have to know how to access the Akashic Records to start a conversation with the soul of your business. Instead, have an intention and know how to ask questions to garner more information.

Your intention to connect will let the soul know you're ready. You want to be in a state of receiving.

Formulating questions is an art form. You can start with your own or go to the www.akashicrecordbusinesscoaching.com resource section to receive a free copy of the best questions to ask and a how-to video demonstrating the exercise below.

How to Prepare:

- Have a journal and pen handy.
- Set the intention for your meeting.
- Write down a few questions you would like answers to or use my questions. Be sure to have a couple of yes/no questions to get the energy flowing.
- Find a quiet, uncluttered place where you won't be disturbed.
- Turn off your phone so that you can stay focused.
- Always use the same place to consult with the soul of your business. (Consistency counts.)

You Are Now Ready:

1. Sit quietly to settle your mind and bring your breathing into a steady rhythm, in and out. As you breathe in, concentrate on a loving memory to create a space of love and connectedness. Breathe in all the love you can conjure up from your memories. As you exhale, send out your desire to connect with the soul of your business. Let go of any judgments or thoughts.

2. Call in your business by its legal name to join you.

3. Picture an infinity sign in your mind that connects your heart with your business. (You may want to use the one I give you with my questions).

4. See and feel different colors of energy flowing unobstructed, moving through the infinity sign. Watch the energies shift to business's side, then back to your side, connecting at your heart and back and forth, repeatedly.

5. Once you feel connected, start asking simple questions for yes/no answers to get the energy from the soul to flow. You're looking for clarity. Start slow. Don't judge what you hear.

6. Listen, feel, and become aware of all of your senses. If the answers aren't flowing, you're judging the outcome. You'll want to get back into your vulnerable state to receive.

7. Continue to do this process to build trust. Don't allow yourself to get frustrated if it doesn't work the first time. Some of us have more resistance than others.

8. Keep showing up, same place, same protocol.

9. Always write down what you felt, saw, and heard. You will be surprised at what you write down. You may not recognize the information, something you wouldn't have thought of or said in that way.

You have now formed your partnership. Your trusted partner is ready, willing, and waiting to assist you in creating a Revenue with Purpose business.

Reach out: linda@akashicrecordbusinesscoaching.com.

**Linda Berger** is an International Akashic Record Teacher, Consultant, and Strategic Business Coach. She is the Founder of Akashic Record Business Coaching, formerly known as Business Women Warriors. Linda's secret sauce is that she is bi-lingual, fluent in the language of business, and fluent in the language of the soul.

She leans into her 30+ years of sales, management, investment, soul work, and entrepreneurial experience to coach. She teaches business owners how to access their businesses' souls to unlock their latent potential to impact humanity in their unique way. As a result, they confidently work to fulfill more extraordinary accomplishments in their businesses and lives.

Linda's coaching clients and students credit her expertise in working in the Akashic Records and strategic coaching for her to boil down the myriad of details in their businesses. They learn to focus on identifying the most significant opportunities for growth.

She then equips them with the tools they need for developing a sustainable business. Linda helps clients strategize a practical action plan that nets positive results much faster than they imagined possible through her courses and coaching.

An expert *tough love* practitioner, Linda challenges clients—many of whom are already high-achieving standouts in various fields—to buck the status quo and grow in their capacity to be extraordinary.

Linda spends time traveling with her husband and hanging out with her grandkids in her spare time.

Connect with Linda:
On her website: https://www.akashicrecordbusinesscoaching.com/

# CHAPTER 17

# YOU BECOME
# YOUR THOUGHTS

## MINDSET MASTERY FOR ULTIMATE SUCCESS

Claudia Haller NBC-HWC, Health and Wellness Coach

## MY STORY

I don't think I'll ever forget the look in my husband's eyes the day he tried to help me get up from the bottom of the stairs in front of a beautiful Victorian house in New York. It was a perfect summer morning during track season. Saratoga Springs comes to life during that time of year. The big hats come out, and the live bands play in the streets. Everyone seems vibrant and chatty while sipping their drinks from the local coffee place.

I looked into my husband's drained eyes, and my thoughts took control. *What's wrong with me? Why can't I be like one of these vibrant people passing us? What have I done? That look in his eyes crushes me and I know it's my fault, all my fault. I hate myself. I'm worthless.* I already knew that. So, what's new? Another wave of guilt came over me.

Thoughts are powerful and can quickly and mercilessly take us to dark places. I would know.

After our move from Switzerland to the US, I'd had occasional bad days. I never quite felt like I fit in. Now and then, I would feel overwhelmed and believe the voice in my head telling me I wasn't good enough—nothing that wouldn't go away after a good night's sleep. Then, a bad day turned into an entire weekend, and before I knew it, negative thoughts were following me everywhere.

I felt like I was not up to par with the other moms living in my town. I'd painted a picture inside my mind that all these amazing women were so much smarter than me, had Ivy League educations, and most likely left behind their impressive jobs at Manhattan law firms to raise a family. It's interesting what kind of stories we tell ourselves, isn't it? Of course, none of this was helping my crippling sense of self-worth.

Back home in Switzerland, I went to the gym almost every day; it was basically my second home. But here? Anxiety overcame me the second I walked through those doors. I felt totally out of shape and was convinced I was wearing the wrong outfit.

Is it even possible to wear the wrong outfit to a gym?

I made a big detour around the treadmills remembering that I couldn't run. Why? I felt like I was too slow. I wouldn't even dare to run around my neighborhood.

*What would my neighbors think if they looked out of their windows to see me struggling to maintain an acceptable pace?*

With a gym *full* of people watching me, how was running on a treadmill any different?

In Switzerland, I was a decent cook, adventurous even. My mother would always tell me, "If you don't put something in the food that tastes bad, the meal won't taste bad." So, I was never afraid to try new combinations. Despite my best efforts to convert cooking temperatures from celsius to fahrenheit and grams to ounces, things didn't go as well in the United States. Keep in mind that this was before the time of "There is an app for everything." I decided that I sucked at cooking—period.

Slowly my negative thoughts eroded my self-esteem. I got good at it too. I believed every negative word I said to myself, although I was surrounded by my husband, family, and kind, loving, and encouraging friends. None of them knew the real battle I was facing in my mind every single day.

That summer in Saratoga Springs marked that rock bottom moment people often talk about. I'd always struggled, but this summer was different; it was an *extra* shade of dark. I didn't have the energy to dust myself off and regain trust in myself. I was afraid to make a promise that it wouldn't happen anymore because deep inside, I knew I would fail *again*. Disappoint *again*. I was done. I was tired of fighting the inevitable cycles of ups and downs. Afraid of the tailspins taking me down that dark place faster than I could react to it. I wanted to sleep—forever.

After these episodes, I often felt like I'd been hit by a truck. It's fascinating how our minds can exhaust us physically, wouldn't you agree? If you've e been there, you know what I'm talking about.

After days of barely moving, my husband tried to take me for a walk, but I was too weak and collapsed. That brought me to that pivotal moment in front of the beautiful Victorian house. I was facing a choice: Do I give up or find a reason to get back up? Looking into the helpless face of the man I love, I felt crushed. *What have I done?*

The decision I made that day completely altered the course of my life. I got back up. When my husband and I returned to our condo, I was overcome by the sound of my kids' laughter. I wondered how many memories the disease robbed me of. Enough! My family deserves better. *I* deserve better.

According to a medical professional, the next logical step would be medication: anti-depressants, most likely. The accepted theory was that depression is a chemical imbalance of the brain, and there is a pill to help with that. Something about this explanation didn't feel right, but what did I know? The doctor went on to say, "If you had diabetes wouldn't you take medication? It's the same thing." *Hmmm, okay then.*

I'm not here to judge, but from where I stand today, I would argue that there is *always* more you can do other than to *just* take medication. I gave the medication a try, but I can honestly say it didn't help all that much. It most definitely didn't change my thought patterns. All it did was treat my symptoms, not the cause.

Accepting a medical professional's opinion and opting for medication is okay. But I want to challenge that thinking. What if we considered this while also educating *ourselves*? Wouldn't you feel empowered once you understood your healing journey holistically and got to the root cause of the problem?

My wellness journey started. I even went back to school for it. I knew that diet and exercise play an instrumental role in well-being, so I first improved those areas of my life. I started to feel better physically. My mindset? Not so much.

I've always been drawn to personal growth and spiritual messages. I landed on an interesting podcast during a car ride to our annual camping trip. The main message was about the power of what follows "I am . . ." I didn't immediately buy into this concept. However, I began to understand when I read through my journaling notes later that week.

*Oh, my goodness!* I had become *everything* that followed all of my *"I am's"* *I am worthless. I am weak. I am not good enough, etc.* I quickly realized that I had constantly been proving this theory.

*What if I could change these statements?*

I stood in front of the old, dirty mirror in the bathroom at the campground. I was all by myself, looking at my distorted reflection. I gently whispered, "I am confident." I stood there for a few minutes, waiting to feel empowered—nothing. I clearly needed practice, but I knew I was on to something.

Having repeated hundreds of *I am* statements since that day, I firmly believe that mindset is our superpower.

My affirmation cards tell me things like, *I am confident, I am disciplined, I am fun, I am good enough, I am organized, I am patient, I am successful.*

Actively practicing my affirmations made a significant impact on my mindset. But I also realized that there was more work to be done, and I couldn't do it alone. Have you ever noticed how many people are actually part of a successful team? It truly takes a village. I believe that life is a team sport as well. We can't succeed by ourselves. So I decided to put together my own A-team, and one of my favorite players is my spiritual guide.

"I am *trying* to get my workouts in!" I complained to her during one of our sessions.

*Trying is not a thing!* She fired back at me. I was instantly aware that she had a point, although I didn't want to admit it. You *decide* to work out. So, I *decided* to work out, eat clean, and not get as easily offended.

I kept making progress. I felt lighter, *confident* even. I slowly started to get compliments from those around me, "You're so vibrant. I love spending time with you. I always walk away energized after we hang out."

*What? Me!*

Life was better. *I* was better. But I still had trouble staying on track at times. This needed to be explored further.

For my birthday in 2021, I gifted myself a brain health evaluation. You read that right. I allowed a doctor to thoroughly evaluate each part of my brain and mind. It was scary. I walked away diagnosed with ADHD, Anxiety, Depression, OCD, Traumatic Brain Injury, and more. Yikes! "Anything else?" I asked sarcastically during our two-hour meeting.

It was a lot to take in. Yet, at the same time, it helped me gain clarity on why I am the way I am. I want things neat (OCD), yet I can't stay organized (ADHD). Talk about opposing forces, no wonder I felt like I was in a tug-a-war with myself!

*At least now I know why I do what I do,* I thought. *I am not worthless, and I'm probably not that different from most other people.*

"Do you see this area here on the scan?" The doctor continued, pointing to a bright area of my brain. "It shows that you're highly intelligent." *Really? Me? Smart?* For a split second, that *negative Nelly* wanted to have a say. Instead, I allowed this comment to raise my confidence. *I am smart!*

Looking back, it's interesting how many people told me I didn't have ADHD before my brain health evaluation. "You aren't restless, kicking your feet, or fiddling with your fingers. Therefore, you don't have ADHD." "How are you OCD? There are piles *everywhere*." Isn't it funny how freely people share their opinion on personal topics without asking permission? Ever since I *decided* not to be easily offended anymore, situations like this have become a lot easier. I also believe that people's reactions say everything about them and nothing about *me*—period.

It has been 18 months since my diagnosis, and my journey continues. Through meditation, I have created a vision of my highest self: She's fun, smart, confident, and loving. In business, she is resourceful, curious, and fearless. She enjoys family time and knows when to let stuff go. She lives in a condo, maybe even a penthouse, with a big terrace where she enjoys the view of the lake. Her home is clean, free of clutter. Her early morning workouts include a nice balance of yoga, cardio, and strength exercises. She eats clean and shows up fully for her clients and her community. She travels with her husband often to visit family and friends. She always has the answer when I struggle. She is the best!

A vision is like a destination. Are you familiar with Waze? It's a navigation app that gets you from where you are to where you want to go, no matter the roadblocks, accidents, or traffic jams. Simply enter the destination, and off you go! I found this app fascinating and wondered: *What if I programmed my vision into my own mental app? Will it take me to my higher self?* I can tell you that I'm getting closer every day. I take a few minutes in the morning to deeply connect with that best version of myself and set my route for the day accordingly. It's a work in progress.

Creating routines is important too, but ADHD makes that very challenging for me. I decided to do it anyway. See what I did there? I didn't use the word *try!*

The biggest lesson first: If you plan your day that same morning, you've already lost. That's right!

I am at my best when I close out work and anything that involves electronics before our family dinner. Then before reading a book at bedtime, my workout clothes, water, and journal are made ready for my morning routine. When I look at my desk, it's cleaned up and ready for the next day.

When you block out time once a week to plan, you set yourself up for success.

Reflecting on these past few years, I'm proud to say I did the work. What I was struggling with wasn't just depression. In my case, the depression was more like a side effect of undiagnosed ADHD, OCD, Anxiety, etc., and the fact that I had no tools to deal with it. I went from a very dark place where my only option seemed to be medication to thriving, having a career, two businesses, and being a fun wife and mom (at least for the *most* part). I have my A-team on my side, and when I get picked to join someone else's team, I show up fully.

My mantra: Food is medicine, mindset is our superpower, and guarding our time is key. What are *you* giving your time and attention to? I am not perfect—far from it—but I know for sure that I am unique, and so are you! God gave us each our very own fingerprint and DNA. I'm married to the journey to become the best version of myself. How about you?

# THE STRATEGY

## HOW TO MASTER YOUR MINDSET FOR ULTIMATE SUCCESS

You know when you hear someone say, "If I can do it, you can do it?" and then you immediately think, "Yeah, I wish." I challenge you to say, "Really? Show me how."

You can't change what you don't acknowledge. As you move through this exercise, I ask you to have an open mind and to come from a place of curiosity not judgment. Remember.

*Absorb what is useful, discard what is useless, and add what is specifically your own.*

~Bruce Lee

Ready?

What you need:

- A journal and a pen
- A few blank cards for your affirmations
- A quiet place to sit
- Time

Let's get to work. Here are the nine most important steps to master your mindset for ultimate success

- *Vision:* Take some time and ask yourself: Where would I like to be in a year from now in my business and personal life? How does it feel to have achieved your goal? Journal about it. You can keep making changes over time, but you have now created your vision. Connect with it daily.

- *Planning and routines:* Start mapping out your ideal days and weeks. Make sure to set yourself up for success—the evening before. I am a big believer in getting up early and having a morning routine, including exercise and journaling.

- *Exercise:* Decide to make exercise a priority. A combination of cardio, strength, and stretching is ideal. (I had a client once who slept in her workout clothes to get her exercise in first thing, so do *whatever* it takes!)

- *Journaling:* You can use it to vent, dream or follow a prompt. You will find my favorite prompt on my resource page. Maybe you need to meditate for a few minutes to calm down your brain? Then, read your vision and write three to five things you can do today to get one step closer to your goal.

- *Food is medicine:* It might sound a little harsh, but everything you put into your mouth is a deposit or withdrawal into your health account. *Decide* to make more deposits than withdrawals. It's just like with money. If you're struggling, consider working with a health coach.

- You become what follows your *I am:* I encourage you to pay close attention to what follows your *I am* statements. Make sure they are positive, encouraging, and aligned with your vision. Write them on blank cards and read them daily. Make the most important ones into screen savers or put them into your phone as a reminder.

- *Gratitude:* Practice gratitude and expect amazing things to happen in your life. If things don't work out the way you had hoped, assume there is a reason for it. Something even better might be waiting for you.

- *Guard your time:* Focus on tasks closely related to your big vision and watch out for time sucks like scrolling through social media.

- *Life is a team sport:* Embrace the idea that you can't do it alone. Put together your A-team. Make sure you assign your players the perfect position. Not everyone can be everything for you. The person who is your best workout partner might not be able to give you the best business advice. Also, if you're invited to someone else's team, understand what your role is and then decide to show up fully.

Mindset is everything.

*Whether you think you can or you think you can't – you're right.*

~Henry Ford

Remember, the grass is greener where you water it! Be intentional with where you spend your time and energy, and don't forget that you're unique. *Decide* to dream big. I can't wait to see where your journey takes you. Connect with me and check out my resources here. https://www.vibranthealthbyclaudia.com/resources.

**Claudia Haller** NBC-HWC is a board-certified Health and Wellness Coach and the owner of Vibrant Health by Claudia and Virtual Health Coaches.

She offers one-on-one sessions, group coaching, corporate wellness workshops, and webinars in her coaching business. She loves to meet people where they are, dream up wellness and life goals together, find out what's possible, and walk the journey with her clients. Health and wellness goals can feel overwhelming. Breaking them down into practical steps that fit into the client's day makes all the difference. She coaches to results. "There is no one-size-fits-all approach in my coaching," she says. Some clients need more than just weekly check-ins. That's why she provides support in between sessions, daily if needed. "We're a team, and we'll make it fun," she says.

Claudia is also the owner of Virtual Health Coaches LLC, an organization serving two purposes:

- Connecting health seekers with board-certified health and wellness coaches on their website www.virtualhealthcoaches.com.

- Leading a community of hundreds of amazing, certified wellness coaches where they can work on sharpening their coaching skills, find support, and learn about business growth. It's the ultimate resource for continued education.

Claudia loves connecting with people and believes family hugs are the best medicine. She annoys her family with daily doses of wisdom, whether they want to hear it or not. She now calls herself a runner and a peloton junkie. She loves organizing things. But most importantly, she believes in making the most out of the time given to us and will be the first to tell you that sleeping in is a waste of time. With Claudia by your side, get ready to meet your highest self, and build routines that work. We are given *one* life—let's make it count.

# CHAPTER 18

# SEDUCING THE
# SOULFUL TRAVELER

## MARKETING WELLNESS AUTHENTICALLY
## AND STRATEGICALLY

Jackie Roby, Chief Excellence Officer

# MY STORY

Thirteen hours of travel. That's 780 minutes of being around people, going in and out of unsatisfying sleep, watching movie after movie, and desperately pretending that I wasn't smashed up against someone I'd never met. A red-eye from Boston, a layover, and a 35-minute drive later, I'd finally arrived at my resort in Algarve, Portugal.

I was too tired to be anything but tired. *How many hours until my massage?* As usual, I was counting down until the next thing and the next thing until I could just go to sleep. *I'll be excited tomorrow, I swear. Damn it, Jackie. That's the wrong way to think. Be positive, be grateful. For crying out loud, you're here for the Healing Summit. Get it together!*

This was a business trip, so I needed to be on top of my game. But I was feeling the terror of an insecure 20-something, trembling when anyone talked to her, trying to look like she had it all together. It'd been 11 years since that first depression, and only a year since the second fall. I still felt like the floor could drop out from under me at any moment. *All this work on myself, and nothing has changed.*

My inner critic was temporarily disrupted when I heard a familiar voice brimming with excitement. "Jackie! You're here!" My colleague, Sallie, was her usual confident self with a big smile on her face and ready to take over the world. She said, "You have to meet Anne and Elisabeth." Without a chance to say no, we were walking in their direction.

First of all, I'd just landed. I was carrying luggage, hadn't looked in a mirror, and my yoga pants likely had food on them. Second, who were Anne and Elisabeth? *I am so not ready for this intro.* While Little Jackie was screaming no, my adult self couldn't find the words. I clumsily said hello, feeling completely unimportant and unworthy of being in that space. *Nobody wants to meet me, Sallie.*

I somehow managed to make a quick exit to my room, where I just concentrated on breathing. I love to travel. I do. My anxiety forgets that sometimes.

That was my first visit to Portugal, the first time I'd attended the Healing Summit, and my first year of getting to know wellness travel. It was a lot of firsts for my shaky confidence. *I hope I have packed the right clothes.*

After 17 years in the travel industry, I'd been to many shows. Just because it's wellness or healing (or whatever they're calling it) doesn't make a difference. A show is a show.

As I entered the ballroom, my eyes were drawn to a wall of floor-to-ceiling windows leading to lush greenery and a view of the limestone cliffs. There was sunlight shining into this space, making everyone look angelic, like they were all higher beings. *Do all these people know each other?*

I scanned the room for something low maintenance to drink. It's a habit at events when I'm uncomfortable. My strategy was to make the least amount of noise, and get in and out of the crowded space without making a fool of myself. I grabbed bottled water for three of us and took my seat between Sallie and our friend, Chris. It felt safe.

Anne and Elisabeth walked on stage. *Oh no. The women I met yesterday are a big deal?* I didn't remember what I'd said or if I'd looked nervous or interested. It certainly wasn't my best first impression. Butterflies were putting on a show in my stomach. *I hope I'm not breaking out in hives.* Anne walked to the microphone, and the group quickly learned that she and Elisabeth are the co-founders of Healing Hotels of the World. *I'm such an idiot. Why didn't I study this on the plane?*

After the initial introduction, a healer took the stage to guide us in a group meditation. I couldn't help but smile. While I've had my meditation practice for years, I have never been to a professional event that made this an activity; especially to kickstart our day. *This is my jam!* All the books I'd read said group meditation is extremely powerful. I hadn't experienced it yet and couldn't wait to get that energy party started.

As I closed my eyes, the healer's voice was soothing me into a peaceful place. There was a white light shimmering with flecks of gold. I could feel the smile on my face getting wider and the energy around me was buzzing with joy. The books were right; being in a space where 120 people meditate together is extremely powerful. Suddenly it hit me. *This is where I want to live.* The happiness was bubbling up inside of me. Here I was surrounded mostly by strangers, yet I felt at home. Like they understood who I am at my core.

My eyes were closed, and my heart was open. It was a vulnerable place to be. All the feelings from the past year came rushing to the surface. How the job paying my salary was tearing away at my self-worth, belittling my value, and isolating me the way an abuser does their victim. But that day, that love, care, and togetherness was what I'd been searching for. The healer brought us back into the room, and I wiped the tears from my eyes. *I wonder if anyone can see how different I am now, how our meditation has changed me?*

Next up on the stage was a neurologist speaking to the science of meditation. I had no idea it altered our brains. Throughout the summit, we heard from a psychologist about ways to find happiness, a philanthropist sharing world issues and ways we can impact change, a Nobel prize winner, a wizard, and a refugee. That was more than I'd expected or could've even imagined. It was a meeting of the minds coming together to create a kinder, emotionally intelligent world. And somehow, a hospitality company made it all happen.

Everything I'd been working on for the past 11 years had been brought to life in the industry I love. How could I have not known that was available? All those moments of struggle, the years I spent on my healing journey. I could have used that support. With each speaker, my skin tingled as if being softly caressed. Listening to my body, I knew I was sitting close to my destiny.

*This is my time to be bold. I'll approach Anne and tell her I want to bring the brand to the US.* I'd never done anything like that before. After my first hotel position, every role since had been a referral. I'd been recruited for everything, and valued for my reputation and experience. But the world of wellness travel didn't know me at all. Would this elevated woman see me or reject me? I had to take the chance, or I'd regret it.

My timing was imperfect, my delivery ineloquent, but I made the move. I walked up to a co-founder, a CEO and expressed my passion and desire to work with her company. This was a big step. I could see the shock on Anne's face. Luckily, it turned into a smile, and we set up a meeting to discuss it further. Somehow, I'd opened a new door, even if just a smidge.

Months later, I was on a call with Anne, one of many since we met. With her natural warmth, she gave me the emotional support I craved from a leader. She led me in a visualization exercise, and I unexpectedly heard my intuition. *I need to step through my fear.* Once we hung up the phone with love, I quickly walked into the living room where my husband, David, was wrapping up a work call. To his surprise and delight, I told my number one fan that I was going to quit my job and start my own business.

The Healing Summit was a pivotal moment in my professional life. Though the sparkles of destiny didn't all align the way I envisioned, it was the catalyst for change. It stirred something in me that had always been at my core—helping people.

A Reiki practitioner once told me I was a natural healer, but I didn't know what to do with that information at the time. Now it all makes sense. I will take my superpowers to help the wellness travel industry and ultimately help people like me who need support on their healing journeys. Let's be real—we could all use a helping hand.

Throughout the years, travel advisors shared with me the challenges they faced finding the wellness traveler. Considering my own experience as an industry insider, it is clear that the average consumer doesn't know about wellness or healing travel. My mission is to bridge the gap, be the connector of ideas and a trusted voice. It starts with speaking the language that sings to the ideal traveler's soul.

# THE STRATEGY

Sometimes business separates us from the depths of who we are. We've been hit over the head with expectations to fit into certain molds that are almost robotic. It can cripple creativity and reeks of revenue-focused messaging. Wellness travelers see through that. So, we must throw out the old way of thinking. It's time to expand into a deeper realm.

What is it about wellness travel that lights your soul on fire? Unlike booking a room at a hotel or planning a corporate incentive trip, this is a niche that requires a soul connection. To truly bring in the ideal traveler, surface-level communication won't cut it. Ask yourself the difficult questions.

- Where are you on your journey within?
- If this is new for you, are you ready to receive your intuition?
- Do you run from conversations about your feelings?
- Can you look yourself in the mirror and speak an affirmation?
- Is it possible for you to speak about chakras and crystals without rolling your eyes?
- Do you refer to alternative healing as woo-woo, or are you open to learning?

I'm not suggesting that you need to know it all, care about each corner of the industry, and be deep into your own healing. This is a temperature check for your accurate location. Being your authentic self is important, and we want to honor that and provide a sense of belonging. It also gives you a path forward.

Think about the type of wellness traveler you would like to attract. This might change as you change and grow. It's important to outline what this looks like today. We can't be everything to everyone, so let's not try to be. As we go through these five steps, keep this traveler in mind.

1. **Reflect on personal experiences.** Think of your path, the struggles, and successes with emotional, mental, physical, or spiritual wellness. Consider what people you love have gone through. Write down the examples. Can you remember when the problem seemed impossible? What did that feel like? If you're stuck or want more ideas, talk through this with your loved ones. Think of it as informational interviews that will enhance your business. This research is now the basis of your marketing campaign. You're uncovering the problems that the consumer needs help fixing.

2. **Speak from the heart.** Being vulnerable connects the soulful traveler with you and builds a relationship. If this is outside your comfort zone, I challenge you to stretch. When we share vulnerability, it can be very impactful and contribute to our success. If this is off the table, I respect your boundaries. Instead, reflect on the difficult emotions you just wrote down. How can you organically bring those into the conversation with the traveler? Above all, people want to feel seen and heard. Show them that you understand what they're going through and want to help.

3. **Learn the language of wellness.** Study the spa menus, watch the webinars, read the articles, take the training, and become a student in search of wellbeing. Try ways to incorporate this into your life because then the love will be real, and that shines through. The soulful traveler wants to know that you prefer the Temazcal over Reiki for deep emotional healing. That you, too, are on this journey with them. Hearts speak to hearts.

4. **Define your message and sing it for all to hear.** Look at the tone of your written content. Does it stir any emotion? Can the traveler start to think about their own life when they read it? Make sure you're bringing them into the conversation. Examine your sales and marketing avenues. How often are you sending emails to your mailing list? What webinars are you attending? Where do you show up online the most? Social media is your new best friend if you're not tight already. Like any bestie, treat it kindly. It must be used wisely, with proper strategy and positive intent. This is a tool for building relationships, not just posting pretty pictures.

5. **Work the relationships you have.** Remember that secondary wellness travelers account for 92% of wellness tourism trips taken in 2020, according to *Global Wellness Institute; The Global Wellness Economy: Looking Beyond COVID.* That means travelers add wellness to their present itinerary. If you're dipping your toes in the wellness pool, the consumer doesn't need to be someone searching for an immersive wellness experience, a retreat, or a structured program. Depending on your journey, those might not resonate with you. The client you're looking for could be the same client you've been talking to for years. Once you share your knowledge, emotional connection, and love of wellness, this could spark their internal fire and build your wellness clientele.

You're not alone on this journey. One of the greatest things about wellness is the community. Become part of the conversations in whatever way brings you the most joy. An important lesson I learned from my healing journey is the importance of asking for help. Even just bouncing ideas off someone can create clarity. I'm happy to be that person for you who holds space, then adds shimmer and strategy to brighten your already brilliant message.

**Jackie Roby** is Chief Excellence Officer of Inspired Journey Consulting. As a sales and marketing solution strategist and brand ambassador for healing and wellness resorts, she helps clients stand out as authentic wellness to reach their ideal guests. In addition, she coaches wellness travel designers on communicating the magic of their vision and mission. Jackie brings 19 years of travel and hospitality sales experience along with an empathetic perspective and tools learned from her healing journey.

If you were to ask Jackie what she's most proud of, it would be having a strong, healthy marriage based on consistent communication, raising an emotionally intelligent daughter, and creating a business that aligns with her authentic self. She advocates for diversity equity inclusion, domestic violence awareness, and body acceptance. She can't get enough of street art, chocolate, or candles. Ever since she was nine, she's been devouring books. These days it's a balance of reading books on mental wellness, inclusion, and business. While she can celebrate in groups with the best of them, her people know that QT (quality time) is everything. Every week she and her husband, David, go out on a date to tour museums, try new restaurants, sip creative hand-crafted cocktails, and talk about the week's accomplishments, challenges, and gratitude.

Jackie hosts the podcast Through Inspired Eyes, where the message of #TravelCanHeal is shared across the globe. Her vision is to encourage healing through travel for a kinder, more inclusive world.

Ways to Engage with Jackie:

Through her website https://inspiredjourneyconsulting.com/
Learn More
https://inspiredjourneyconsulting.com/seducing-the-soulful-traveler/
Follow on Instagram
https://www.instagram.com/inspiredjourneyconsulting/
Listen to her podcast https://inspiredjourneyconsulting.com/podcast/
Connect on LinkedIn https://www.linkedin.com/in/jackie-roby/
Friend on Facebook https://www.facebook.com/IJCpresents
Follow on Twitter https://twitter.com/IJCpresents
Subscribe to her channel on YouTube
https://www.youtube.com/channel/UCyKLXBbqHkHISv9Zs8Hcyog

# CHAPTER 19

# THE REWILDING RESET

## THREE MINUTES TO REACH HEART-HEAD COHERENCE

Nicole Parker, Growth Consultant,
Business Strategist, Soul Activator

# MY STORY

Most of my life up to this point has been about learning, planning, growing, seeking, achieving, and doing. *What's my next move? Career goal? Purchase? Trip? Adventure? Course? How am I expanding and growing?* What next became my default mantra for over a decade, and I let it dictate my every waking move. Addicted to progress and needing to stay in motion, I got off on the adrenaline of racing to a deadline, not having enough hours in the day, and feeling like a freaking Superhero when I somehow managed to make it all happen.

You could say I was born this way, and I'm sure my parents could provide ample evidence to support the theory. But we also enforce and strengthen the parts of ourselves we most resonate with. As a picture-perfect doer from an early age, I loved the titles and ego-stroking identities people projected onto me. I welcomed them with open arms.

Teachers would call me advanced and ask me to be their aid. Friends would tell me I was a force to be reckoned with, strangers complimented my infectious aliveness, bosses praised my tenacity, and family members called me reckless or brave, depending on the day. The more they said it, the more I enacted it. The more I enacted it, the stronger the identity became. Mostly it served me well, motivating me to level up regularly, progress at work quickly, and find the courage to take big risks. It sculpted and shaped me, offering strength, pride, and joy.

When I was thrown into single motherhood at the age of 23, I was even more grateful to be wired this way because I knew it would provide the inner strength and ferocity necessary to get me through.

There's nothing wrong with strengthening the parts of ourselves required for various chapters of our lives. We're resilient beings meant to grow through what we go through. The problem I later discovered was that I'd gotten so caught up in survival mode, in confirming and adhering to those labels, I could no longer remember who I was without them. This unknowing of myself, this deep-rooted misalignment, this uncertainty about who I was or what I was meant to do in this world led to over a decade of anxiety, restlessness, substance abuse, and occasional bouts of depression.

I started living fully from my head and hushing my heart. A constant need to fix, coach, judge, and control caused issues in my personal relationships. I had a big fallout with my mom.

In moments of stillness, my heart would whisper, *Be nice, call her; she loves you, step outside of yourself and see things from her point of view. It's not about fault—it's about love. Plus, you miss her. She's your mom.*

But instead of listening to that voice, my mean and stubborn head would overpower, time and time again.

*She's the mother, and she should fix this. Plus, she's being too sensitive and too nosy—too many opinions about my life, so selfish. And she says I have no compassion? Pssh. Compassion is my middle name. Just look at all the animals I save; I'm like a straight Mother Theresa over here! How is it at all my fault that she gets her feelings hurt too easily?*

Our vacations were planned down to the minute, and the free-loving spontaneity that once exhilarated me had all but disappeared. One day, I had the guilty revelation that I was only ever half-listening at best when people spoke to me. Even the most important people.

"Mommy, did you hear me?"

"Mmm, I heard you, honey. Wow, that's so awesome!"

But my son Caden was too smart for that. He always knew when I was distracted or somewhere else. He'd shoot me a sideways glance and a sigh, then give me a supportive hug or bring me his special homemade lemonade to make me smile. The sweetest kid you'd ever meet in your life.

He'd walk away each time, and I'd kick myself, thinking, *How could I be such an awful mother? How could I ignore him like that? Why can't I shut the damn laptop and pay attention?*

I'd become more concerned with sucking my stomach in to look thinner than breathing deeply to my core. I couldn't sleep without assistance, couldn't meet deadlines without an Adderall, and couldn't sit still long enough to make it through a hair appointment or a TV show without wanting to explode inside.

My life was evolving beautifully on the outside, but I'd left a lot of the inner work to the wayside. Nothing flowed naturally for me anymore. It was all forced and forged. Uppers to get up, downers to get down. Support outside of myself, always, because I was no longer enough. I couldn't keep up with the level of me that the world expected, and that bar continued to rise.

I would still check all my spiritual boxes as this was happening, but compartmentalize rather than integrate the lessons and insights. I would understand the concepts taught intellectually but fail to embody them again and again. I'd never explored those scary depths of truths beneath the surface of who I wanted to be. Beautiful lessons and wise words of truth would surface regularly in my breathwork sessions and yoga classes.

"Stress is the overachiever's word for fear." *Hell yes! Except for mine of course. Mine truly is just stress, I'm not scared of anything.*

"Everything will flow as soon as you stop trying to force it." *I don't force, right? No, I just gently help things go in the direction of my choosing!*

"See the difference between passion and addiction, and be honest with yourself about which one is true for you." *I definitely do not have a problem with addiction, I claim passion all the way!*

But rather than apply any of these to my *actual* life; I'd jot them down in a notepad and think:

*This is a good one I should send to so and so. It could help them with their problems!*

Or worse: *Oh yeah baby, marketing gold, going to repost this nugget on Instagram and get all the applause!*

I wasn't honest with myself or others. My laptop owned me, and I'd justified all the unsteady energy levels, insomnia, anxiety, and guilt as par for the course on the road to success. When I'd miss a deadline, fall short of an expectation, or stop moving and sit still for a while, a non-stop loop of melancholy and obsessively unhelpful thoughts would crawl their way into my headspace.

*Do I work too much? Maybe. But who am I outside of my ability to hustle?*

*What am I going to do when Caden grows up and moves out? Am I a good mother?*

*Did that girl at yoga think I was conceited because I did a handstand when she called child's pose? I felt weird vibes from her, but I wanted to get upside down! What happened to women supporting women?*

*I think my boss was giving me the side-eye today. Better set the coffee pot now. Have to burn that midnight oil to stay ahead!*

I continued to trudge, and my life continued to expand. My son got older, and I married the man of my dreams. Everything was going according to plan, kind of.

Life was better than I could have ever dreamed or imagined. After all the hustling and strong-arming, seeking, and pushing, it was at last okay to lean on someone. I had a partner in this life. Caden had the daddy he deserved, and I could finally exhale and take a beat after all those years.

You'd think that'd be my cue to settle down and settle in, relax and unclench, and maybe take a second to celebrate all the things I have to be insanely grateful for in this life, right? Keep dreaming! Instead, I found new things to stress about. The underlying craziness persisted with force.

*What's wrong with me? Everything I've ever dreamed of has come true. What is it that is stopping me from feeling content? Why can't I be happy?*

*What's my purpose on earth, now that my son is almost ten and doesn't need me for every little thing anymore?*

*Who am I now that I'm a wife, and have dropped the identity of fiercely independent single mama? What do I have to be proud of? I have an awesome partner, a beautiful family, and I'm just like everybody else. Am I letting down the hustling females of the world by finding happiness?*

I began to journey inward. I tried a ton of things to understand myself better and quiet the neverending joy thief within. Including:

- Working 1:1 with a Peruvian Shaman, life coach, and psychiatrist;
- Diving deep into breathwork, energy medicine, NLP, acupuncture, and reiki healing;
- Opting for four months of intensive Network Spinal Care to unwind my nervous system;
- Filling our home with crystals, essential oils, Palo Santo, and tuning forks;
- Traveling to find myself in the jungles of Bali and meditate with monks at various Art of Happiness retreats;
- Certifying in Transcendental Meditation;
- Rapidly consuming every digital course, mindset app, reset program, and Spiritual book I could get my hands on;
- Investing in a sauna and cold plunge to add hot-cold work into my daily wellness routine.

Guess what? None of it worked!

I'm a huge fan of all the above-mentioned modalities, but still, I carried this darkness within myself. I changed my diet, consulted with doctors, and had my hormones tested. It wasn't until my husband and I attended Tony Robbins 2022 UPW retreat in West Palm Beach that something deep finally struck me. When I remembered who I was before I adopted all the labels.

As a kid, I was just a wide eyed curious girl—a free bird with big dreams. I loved to dance, gallop on horseback, feel the wind in my hair and the dirt between my barefoot toes. I loved to connect, to listen to others, to heal. I loved to laugh, to joke, to play. I was light, uninhibited, and unstructured.

Fast forward to my grownup self and this new person I'd become. I'd discarded anything and everything that didn't help me progress toward my goals. I realized with regret that I no longer danced in the shower or sang in the car and couldn't remember the last time I sat on a park bench or walked on the beach and called my girlfriends to chat.

Most of my off-time was spent dreaming up new business ideas, so I rarely got silly or played with Caden. Tension had built in my body, and creativity had been harder and harder to come by.

I told myself that I was just better at business, and creativity wasn't my thing, but that was a cover story. The truth was, I knew I could control my performance and most desired outcomes when building a marketing strategy, a product launch campaign, or a Hubspot workflow, so I kept doing that. Success guaranteed! It was a lot riskier, more unknown, and scarier to step outside the box and create art or try something new that I might not be good at. I called myself brave and strong, fearless and fierce, but the truth was I'd forgotten the very things that made me feel most alive. I'd stopped trying new things, stopped letting loose, and had taken the path of certainty and security.

My breathing was shallow, my brain was on overdrive, and my ability to relax and connect with others weakened.

I didn't need a recharge. I needed a reset. It was time to stop trying, thinking, and controlling. And learn instead to surrender, relax and breathe. It was time to reactivate my softest and purest feminine energies. To remember what mattered when I was young. It was time to rewild my heart.

# THE STRATEGY

REWILD = To revert to a natural, uncultivated, and untamed state. To undo modern conditioning and rekindle a connection to a truer, wilder, more holistic way of being.

Rewilding can take many shapes and forms. You can travel, dance, meditate, paint, get into nature, play with animals, anything that drops you into an optimal flow state where heart, mind, and body are connected. By practicing rituals that rewild the spirit, head, and heart to become coherent, self-talk quiets down, intuition strengthens, and a sense of deep clarity and calm can be found.

For years, the vigorous movement was my favorite way of dropping in, but I've since discovered the gentler magic of breathwork. A key power habit and master reprogramming tool, conscious breathing can shift our attention inward and help us tap into fresh perspectives while surrendering to the present moment.

I will teach you a quick and easy three-minute breathwork practice you can do every morning upon waking or whenever you need a little Rewild Reset.

Safety disclosure: Breathwork activates the parasympathetic nervous system, telling your blood pressure, heart rate, and muscles to settle down. You may experience light-headedness and tingling sensations in your fingers and feet, which are completely harmless. This practice is safe as long as you're normally healthy, but if you're pregnant or have a history of high blood pressure, strokes or seizures, stick to the box breathing technique. Lastly, always go at your own pace and remember to listen to your body!

## THE REWILD RESET

Music can enhance your practice and help you drop in quicker, plus there's nothing like losing yourself to electrifying tribal rhythmic beats! Head to my website rewildproject.net for a guided experience and full Spotify playlist, or google one of these gems and see what vibes with you:

- Different Heroes by The Halluci Nation
- Nahimana by Reya and Kjavik
- Let It In by Ayla Nereo

We're going to do three sets of ten fast power breaths inspired by Tony Robbins priming technique, ten slow and deep box breaths, and finishing up with ten humming bee breaths to activate the vagus nerve. You may want to blow your nose, wiggle out your body, and take a few deep sighs before settling in. Start by sitting up tall, lengthening your spine, rolling your shoulders back, and softening any tension within the body. Place your hands on your thighs, palms up for energizing or down for grounding. Take a moment to arrive in the space, align your attention with intention, curve the corner of your lips up into a smile, and begin.

## THREE SETS OF TEN NASAL POWER BREATHS TO AWAKEN AND ENERGIZE

With eyes closed, extend your arms straight out in front of you, bend your elbows to a 90-degree angle and point your fingers up to the sky with palms facing away from you. As you inhale, reach your arms overhead, and as you exhale, pull your elbows down towards the sides of your ribcage. You want to do this breath vigorously with a bit of power and force, about a second or two in and a second or two out.

When you're ready to begin, inhale deeply through your nostrils while simultaneously lifting your arms overhead, then exhale forcefully while pulling your arms back towards your body. *Repeat ten times.*

After your first round, bring your hands to your heart and take a second to pause. Notice any tingles or sensations in the body, feel your heart beating beneath your hands, and begin your second round. *Repeat ten times.*

Take one more moment to pause with your hands on your heart, then begin your third and final set. *Repeat ten times.*

Anchoring your mind and energy into your body, use the rhythmic beat of the music alongside this power breath to inspire and return you to a place of energized awareness. When you've completed your final breath, we'll transition into a minute of box breathing.

## TEN BOX BREATHS FOR CENTEREDNESS

Return your hands to your thighs and roll your shoulders back. You can set a timer for a minute or count out ten rounds.

**Step 1 Inhale:** Breathe in slowly through your nose for at least four seconds, filling your lungs completely. Feel the energy coming in, expanding your lungs and the sides of your waist, massaging out any tension that exists in the emotional or physical body.

**Step 2 Pause:** Hold your breath for at least four seconds, focusing between your eyebrows and relaxing into the stillness.

**Step 3 Exhale:** Let go completely, exhaling through pursed lips as if sipping through a straw, slowly for at least four seconds. Feel the tension melting away as your stomach gently contracts, relaxing reactivity, letting go, surrendering.

**Step 4 Pause:** Hold at the bottom for at least four seconds, relaxing your shoulders and jaw, softening the whole body, allowing the finest version of yourself to come forward.

Repeat ten times or until your one-minute timer is complete.

## TEN HUMMING BEE BREATHS TO DROP-IN

The final minute of this practice is known as Brahmari or The Humming Bee Breath. It's one of my favorites and a great way to wrap up this gentle reset and deliver you back to yourself to the wildest, most authentic, and truest version of you.

Place one hand on your belly and one hand on your chest. As you breathe in through your nose, practice breathing out with an *Mmmmm* sound. Relax your face and jaw, keeping the lips gently closed while allowing your teeth to remain separated.

Once you're ready to begin, you may keep your hands where they are or increase the power of the vibrations by moving them up to cover your ears gently like earmuffs and close your eyes yet again. Keep shoulders relaxed down away from the ears, breathe in through your nose, and exhale again with the *Mmmmm* bee breath. It should sound like a soft humming, and your exhalation should be longer than your inhalation.

Keeping your ears blocked, continue to take deep breaths in through your nose, and exhale as you make the gentle buzzing sound.

Repeat for ten slow cycles, or until your one-minute timer rings that you're complete.

Finish by taking a few moments to sit in silence and breathe naturally.

You can practice this Rewild Reset breathing sequence anytime you're feeling off, facing an internal war within, or need to drop into your body and gain heart-head coherence. If you'd like to dive deeper into breathwork and access a library of free guided practices and Rewilding techniques, visit rewildproject.net and stay wild!

**Nicole Parker** is a growth consultant, business strategist, and soul activator helping people re-imagine what's possible for their companies, spirits, and lives. Her mission in life is to help all beings everywhere feel alive, empowered, and free. She leans on her yoga, spin, Reiki, and shamanic healing background to help seekers and doers slow down to heal, uncover traumas, and rewild their hearts. On the corporate side, Nicole works with business leaders to help them get unstuck, fine-tune impact strategies, optimize funnels, and implement transformational systems and processes. She's known as the driver, big picture strategist, and executor but prefers smile generator, growth supporter, and energy infuser.

Connect with Nicole at:

Website: Rewildproject.net
Wellness retreats coming soon!
LinkedIn: https://www.linkedin.com/in/nicolemdewey/
Instagram: https://www.instagram.com/nicolemarie_parker/
Facebook: https://www.facebook.com/nicole.marie.dewey/

# CHAPTER 20

# UNLEASH YOUR AUTHENTIC SELF

## HOW TO GROW A THRIVING SOUL-ALIGNED BUSINESS WITHOUT COMPROMISE

Hala Dagher Chibani, Alignment Coach,
Soulful Business Strategist

## MY STORY

I sat there on the coaching call of a high-ticket program I'd tapped into my savings account, once again, to invest in. I gazed at the screen listening to their words, watching the excitement from the coaches as they celebrated big wins others shared.

*I could share some of the stuff I'm working on?!*

*No, I don't want to. It feels minuscule compared to what others are celebrating.*

*I could share about the challenge launch I ran last month?*

*Hmm, yeah. But only three people signed up.*

Sadness came over me—extreme sadness. I felt my body shrink and tried to think of something else to shake it off. But I couldn't. I closed my laptop and walked out of the office. Then my daughter saw me in the hallway.

*Oh no! This kid notices everything.*

"Mom, are you okay?

I faked a smile. "Yes, honey, I'm just tired. It's been a long day."

I rushed to my room, lay on my side, and my arms fell to the ground. I lay there on my bed, eyes wide open, looking at the sky outside my window.

Numb.

Disappointed.

Helpless.

*Why is it so hard to grow my business when all I want to do is serve people with all my heart? Why am I not making a shitload of money like everyone around me seems to be?*

I felt like a fraud, an imposter.

*Who am I kidding? I can't do this! Maybe I don't have what it takes to be a successful entrepreneur.*

Warm tears rolled down my cheeks. Then I closed my eyes and sobbed in despair. A few minutes later, I heard a soft, comforting whisper.

*You have what it takes. I created you for a purpose.*

I opened my eyes quickly, trying to make sense of what was happening. There was no one in my room. Suddenly, a bright light came out of the blue skies and shone straight on my face. I smiled, and felt a shimmer of hope.

*I can do this.*

Until that point, which was my second year as an entrepreneur, I'd followed all the guru's advice. I invested tens of thousands of dollars in high-end coaching programs to learn all I could about growing a digital business from well-known experts. And I did. I applied most of everything I've learned too.

I was on every social media platform marketing my programs, engaging with others, sending emails, launching—all of it!

Yes, I was getting some clients and making some impact. But they were not my dream clients, and that was not the big impact I knew I was capable of. Besides, I was exhausted. Most days, I was depleted, with nothing left in me to give. What was more discouraging to me was that I wasn't even new to growing businesses.

I have a BA, an MBA, well, not fully completed, but I've built an 18-year career growing brands, and leading large teams to achieve outstanding results. My experience included leading major change with top fortune 100 companies from international expansions, downsizing, restructuring, and according to my bosses and the awards hanging on the wall, I was damn good at it. I left all that behind!

I left a thriving corporate career to follow a calling I had ignored for years. It felt amazing to honor myself and do what I felt called to do, not what I should do for the first time in a long time.

I remember how excited I was that my dreams can finally top my list of priorities. I can use the skills I've developed at last and the hard lessons I learned to empower women I feel called to serve. The women who feel at a disadvantage for so many reasons, their gender, ethnicity, religious beliefs, immigration status—all and any of it. They are women who have a unique point of view to share but choose not to, to fit in, be accepted, validated, and to move up their career ladder.

I remember how I thought that building and growing my business would be a smooth sail with all I bring to the table. Heck, every program made it sound so easy. Just follow this step-by-step process, and Bam! Six figures in your bank account!

Two long years later, it still hasn't happened.

*So, where did I go wrong?*

And it hit me right there and then. My business lacks soul. My soul!

I was so focused on checking all the boxes that I forgot about the most important thing—me! In my attempts to play it safe, I stayed away from anything that could ruffle some feathers or might be considered remotely controversial—and sadly, I became my worst nightmare—a watered-down version of myself. I assumed I'd be judged and rejected for talking about my spirituality, faith in God, and how He fuels me. Unknowingly, I was the one judging myself the hardest. I assumed that a *Business Strategist* couldn't also be a *Spiritual Mentor.*

*Why not?*

I feel sick to my stomach just thinking of how I betrayed myself to fit in. No wonder I feel like I am swimming upstream. No wonder my business doesn't fully represent who I am and the magnitude of the transformation I bring.

*This changes now!*

I opened my journal and started writing. I let my soul take the lead. I poured my heart's desires. The big dreams that light me up. The potential I am filled with and the impact I feel called to make.

*I can no longer ignore this!*

I had an inspiring vision of my client's exceptional transformation. I saw how happy they were to finally embody their most authentic self. I saw them empowered, aligned, boldly taking charge of their business, unapologetically sharing their beliefs, courageously owning who they are and what makes them unique.

I felt their excitement showing up to inspire, change lives, and elevate the world's consciousness. I felt their expansion and the natural evolution of impact, influence, and revenues that followed. The magnitude of my soul's purpose is enormous.

*I can no longer play small! I am called to awaken women to live out their God-given purpose, so they—so we all catalyze a shift that is desperately needed in the world. I am born to do this!*

I felt the Divine work through me. I listened, surrendered, and allowed His Spirit to flow into everything I'm bringing to life.

*Oh, this feels so good!*

I was overfilled with gratitude for the person I'm courageously stepping into. I am no longer the immigrant girl trying to fit in. I am the woman standing out on my terms and without compromise. That's me. And that will be unapologetically you.

So many women struggle to cut through the noise and grow their businesses. They burn out, remain unfulfilled, and sadly give up on their dreams. No more!

Our awakening adds nothing to the world if it doesn't lead us to share our authentic voice, unique views, and what we believe. It doesn't happen by accident. Learning to show up as our authentic self is a journey on its own, marked by vulnerability and courage. The only journey that will help you feel at home within yourself.

As a result of this awakening, the SAGA framework was born. (SAGA: Soul-Aligned Growth Acceleration) It fueled the pivot in my business and completely shifted the direction of those who embodied it—going from overwhelmed and confused to boldly and intentionally achieving their purpose, attracting soul-mate clients, and turning unbelievable dreams into reality.

I cherish and hold on to their feedback as a reminder of why I do what I do. It's proof that you can craft your own path to more impact, more freedom, and more income by being seen, heard, and valued for who you are. I hear their words every day, and they touch my heart. I feel their gratitude and love wrap around me like a warm blanket.

"You've helped me understand what is meaningful to me after 40 years of living and breathing. I can't thank you enough."

"I no longer feel behind in life or rushed in my business. I trust my plan and execute it with so much joy. I know I'm on track."

"I feel total ownership over my dream. There is no shame now. I want it, and I'm going to get it."

"Your belief in God and Jesus has been such a blessing. I can't imagine doing it with someone who didn't share this now. You're awesome, and you're an inspiration to me."

"I removed the mask, and I am in awe of the deep, powerful connections I am forming!"

"I'm doing incredible things that are truly changing the world. I am so proud of myself for showing up for myself!"

"I feel so aligned after my recent pivot. Everything I want is falling in place so magically."

My friends, your business is the tool and the catalyst to make the impact you're born to make, achieve your soul's purpose, and live your best, most fulfilled life. Design it, shape it, and mold it into what you need it to be. Infuse your unique magic in it, and trust that God's hand will be in everything you do.

He won't let you fail. He created you for it.

When you find that your life has become so busy, your days are consumed by endless actions, and you've somehow veered off from the original intention you had for starting your business; I invite you to tune out all the noise, the distraction, and tune into your soul's calling.

Uncover, own, and unleash your authentic self. This is what differentiates you from all others, and it's where you'll experience the biggest growth and joy. Allow your soul and intuition to guide you to an unconventional yet very intentional path to living your purpose, building a business that represents all of you, and leading you to make the exact impact you're craving today.

Give yourself permission to throw the one-size-fits-all strategies out the window, and dive within.

God has created you so you can do the great things He planned for you, and He has to put things in place for that to happen. The challenges you've experienced are meant to stretch you, to elevate you into becoming the person you need to be to achieve that purpose.

To prove nothing to anyone but, to be of service by doing what inspires you, makes you come alive, and satisfy the world's most pressing needs. Wow, what a difference that has made in my life. And I can't wait to see how it will shift yours. If you're here, then you're called to activate your authentic purpose. That lingering knock at your heart's door signifies that you're ready to uncover your next-level path.

Pull out your notebook. It's time to step into who you're born to be and share the truest version of yourself with the world.

# THE STRATEGY

## THE SAGA FRAMEWORK FOR GROWING A THRIVING SOUL-ALIGNED BUSINESS

The Soul-Aligned Growth Acceleration framework has five phases—four phases loop around *you* in the center.

It's designed to help you:

1. *Awaken* your soul's purpose and embody your authentic self.

2. *Align* your vision, goals, and business plan to the purpose and impact you're called for.

3. *Connect* emotionally with dream audiences and build your community through magnetic messaging and content creation strategies.

4. *Captivate* your aligned niche of clients with your superpower through offers, services, and values they long for.

5. *Convert* dream clients authentically and consistently through leveraged marketing and visibility strategies.

Today I share the first two phases of my framework to help you align to your soul's purpose, embody your authentic self, and craft a vision and an aligned action plan to grow a business that fully represents you-without compromise.

## PHASE 1-SOUL ALIGNMENT

Trust and follow your soul; it knows the way.

### Step 1 - Awaken Your Soul's Purpose

Each one of us is born with a unique soul's purpose. For some, it's clear. For others, it's hidden underneath acquired limiting beliefs and conditioning we have lived through.

Awakening and honoring your purpose is probably the most important factor to living a fulfilling life and achieving meaningful success.

Grab your journal, and get comfortable in a place that sparks your creativity. Light a candle or put on some meditative music in the background.

Take a deep breath, open your heart, and get ready to dive within to uncover your soul's deepest needs.

It's important that the answers you're writing feel good to you. Write from the heart.

- What makes you feel alive, joyful, and playful?
- What do you endlessly love sharing about?
- What advice, insights, and tips are you often asked about? Around which topics?
- What revelations and new daring ideas have been coming to you lately?

Reflect on the skills, passion, and innate abilities you enjoy expressing the most.

- If you could wave a magic wand and have the life and business of your dreams, what would that look like?
- What would that life feel like?

Let's fast forward to three years from now. You have built a thriving brand, and you recently got told that you won the Woman of the Year Award in recognition of the transformative impact you're making.

Play out the full scenario.

- How do you feel?
- What legacy are you leaving behind?
- How did they introduce you?
- What words resonated with you the most?

Drop into your heart and journal the emotions that fill you up.

- Name the top three emotions you're feeling.

These are the deepest emotions you're craving today.

### Step 2 - Uncover What Will Bring You Those Emotions

Reflect on your top emotions and sit with the vision each one brings.

- What opportunities are you seeking to have that you know will give you the emotions you're looking for?
- Reflect on previous life experiences where you have felt those joyful emotions. What was special about them?
- What needs have you ignored for so long that you can no longer neglect?
- What is the one thing you want to look back to say, "I did it!"

  Reflect on your biggest desires.

- Why is it so important that you bring them to reality?
- How will it impact your life? The world?

## PHASE 2-YOUR SOUL-ALIGNED VISION AND PLAN

'Where there is no vision, the people perish.

### Step 1 - Visualizing Your Dream Future

Now that your future destination is clear, reflect on the answers you've uncovered so far to craft a vision for how you want it to manifest in your life.

- Close your eyes and imagine—in vivid detail, the life you're living when your biggest dreams are your reality.

  Let your imagination go wild. No dream is too big!

  Engage all your senses and allow your visualization to transition to feelings.

  Reflect and journal on your vision.

  From today and on, dedicate time weekly to visualize how your business is growing so you can craft long-term and short terms goals that align with your vision and take inspired action with your desired future in mind.

- For my guided visualization exercise, head over to:
https://www.nextlevelimpact.co/FreeResources

- Bonus action! Create a vision board on Canva and display it in your creative space as a daily reminder of what you're bringing to life.

Now, what if every decision you make going forward is led by your vision, what you love, and what feels effortless to you?

Make a commitment to yourself to release control and allow yourself to create magic in your life and business uninhibitedly.

## Step 2 - Embody Your Next Level Identity and Authentic Self
'Be authentically, vulnerably, and courageously you.'

Now that you have identified the dream life, business and impact you're called to have, reflect on your vision.

- Who do you need to be to have it and reach your soul's purpose?
- What personal values motivate you and drive your actions?
- Who were you in your vision?

A few examples to ignite your thoughts: confident, self-assured, consistent, courageous, anchored in your faith, unapologetic about who you are, happy, etc.

## Step 3 - Letting Go
Reflect on what has held you back in the past from reaching bigger goals and doing big things.

- What do you need to let go of to be the person who turns your big vision into reality?

Raise your awareness to identify what no longer serves you or aligns with your new mission.

A few examples to ignite your thoughts: comparison, perfectionism, self-judgment, procrastination, toxic friends, pessimism, self-sabotage, etc.

Decide right now to let go of it all. Let go of anything that limits you from growing and becoming everything, you have the potential to be.

Congrats, you have uncovered and clarified the purpose you're born to actualize!

You have also identified who you need to be to achieve this purpose, build your dream business, and live the life you desire.

Your next step is to uncover what you need to do to bring all you want to have to reality.

Reverse engineer starting from the vision you created to design the most aligned path to reach it, grow your dream business, elevate your impact, and live your most fulfilled life.

That is the missing piece to actualize your soul's purpose.

And that is the work we support women to do in our group coaching program—*elevate*. We help you close the gap between where you are today and where you want to be so you reach your big vision, make your dream impact, and achieve your soul's purpose.

Having this foundation will help you design a path that creates ease, flow, and fulfillment and generates dream opportunities, financial wealth, and abundance beyond what you could imagine today.

And when you have wealth, it ripples out to support your family, the people you love, your community and the world as a whole.

It all begins with you and your inner alignment.

Your soul-aligned business is simply the tool you will leverage to achieve your life's purpose and fill the biggest need the world has today.

**What's next?**

- Access your chapter's free resources and visualization here: https://www.nextlevelimpact.co/FreeResources.

- Book a complimentary strategy call to discuss your purpose, vision and clarify the plan to reach it.

I'd love to hear from you, please share your feedback in a review on Amazon!

**Hala Dagher Chibani** is an award-winning leader and soulful business strategist who empowers female entrepreneurs and thought leaders to uncover their soul's purpose and embody their authentic selves, so they can grow their brand with ease and make a massive impact in the world in a way that represents them, and aligns with who they are.

Hala's coaching framework combines soulful guidance with strategy. It has empowered women worldwide to grow their influence, reach their biggest dreams, revenue goals, and live their most fulfilled life on their terms–without compromise!

Previously, Hala held various leadership roles with fortune 100 corporations, ranging from the Middle East to North America, where she received several awards for outstanding leadership, top business, and team results achieved.

Hala's work has been featured in Authority Magazine, Medium, Brainz, and Thrive Global publications. She has been interviewed on The Faith-Filled Entrepreneur podcast, Buzz Worthy podcast, Unscrew You podcast, and many more.

When she's not advocating for women's empowerment, bringing visions to life, coaching and mentoring leaders, Hala enjoys the precious moments in life, indulging in culture and food with her husband and two girls.

Connect with Hala and Next Level Impact through their website or social media.

Website: https://www.nextlevelimpact.co/
LinkedIn: https://www.linkedin.com/in/hala-dagher-chibani/
Instagram: https://www.instagram.com/halachibani_/
Facebook: https://www.facebook.com/HalaDChibani

# CHAPTER 21

# PASSION PAYS

## IT'S ALL ON YOUR BUSINESS CARD!

Michelle Clifton, Master Sound Healer, Teacher, LMT

## MY STORY

*I thought I'd died and gone to heaven.*

I was lying on the floor with an eye pillow over my eyes as though in total darkness. A large bronze metal Tibetan Singing Bowl sat on my chest—vibrating. The weight of the bowl was surprisingly comforting. I held a wooden mallet with a felt tip in my left hand. Every few minutes, I struck the bowl. Each strike released a vibrational wave of energy into my chest. It continued to resonate throughout my entire body. *Oh, my God! I am in Heaven.* I felt so calm and relaxed. The bowl and I merged. My soul sang, and I felt connected to the cosmos. I was hugged by the Earth, and began breathing more deeply. My lungs slowly expanded, filling with air as if being blown up like a balloon.

The bowl had embodied me. I'd never felt anything like that before in my 69 years of life. I was hooked! I wanted everyone to have this same experience. Of course, I bought this Unique Meditation Bowl (and three others) and signed up for the certification course to learn all I could about sound healing.

As soon as I completed my first certification training, I started to take my singing bowls everywhere I went. I walked down the street with a bowl in my right hand and I struck it as I skipped down the street. "Can I play my bowl for you?" I asked the mailman. Yes, he nodded and I tapped the bowl. As it continued to vibrate with the most beautiful tone, I brought it to his left ear and then to his right. A big grin came across his face, and he nodded with approval. Next, I approached a total stranger who broke into a big smile as I held the bowl next to her ear. I continued skipping down the street, feeling just like a little kid.

Ever since the life-changing experience with my singing bowl on my chest, I start every introduction into a conversation with a friend or newly introduced individual with a hug or handshake. "Hi. I'm Michelle Clifton. I play Tibetan Singing Bowls." If they respond favorably and show true excitement, I'll say, "I have a bowl in my car. I'll go get it so you can hear how glorious it sounds." Every now and then, their interest will peak, and they want to know more. If time is tight, we'll say a quick goodbye, and I hope I've gotten them to think about singing bowls.

I didn't have anyone who was excited and brave enough to risk a sound therapy private session. I did have one wonderful client who loved my first four bronze bowls. She consistently booked a combo massage and sound healing appointment. Her words, "It's the deepest relaxation I have ever felt."

I wish I could remember who it was so I could thank them, but one day someone said to me, "If you want clients specifically for sound healing, put it at the top of your business card." *Ah-ha! I'll try that.* I asked my business card creator to put my name, Michelle Clifton, LMT, at the top of the card and underneath Sound Healing in big letters.

I was surprised when I got that first phone call! "I picked up your card at a yoga studio in Cold Spring, NY. It says you do Sound Healing, and I'd like to make an appointment." It took my breath away. I had a flutter of *Oh, God, what have I gotten myself into?* I'd never done a total sound healing session before. *This is what I asked for, and it's coming true.* My heart is going pitter-patter. "Of course, how's Monday at 2 p.m.?"

Now I was faced with a paying client who wanted a private sound healing session. I immediately felt like a fraud. What was I going to do? I had four Tibetan Singing Bowls, one crystal bowl, a Koshi chime, 'C' and 'G' tuning forks (the sound of the nervous system), and that was it.

I remembered something my tuning fork teacher John Beaulieu said, "You can use anything that makes a sound for sound therapy." He demonstrated with a long flexible plastic tube waving it in the air. "Listen to the swooshing sound it makes." Swoosh- swoosh! I wanted to create a unique and healing sound meditation experience. So, I started going through my house looking for meaningful pieces I'd collected from my life's journey. I came across a bell my mom gave me, a gourd I had purchased from my African safari trip, and a large bean pod filled with dried beans that made noise when you waved it in the air. I filled an empty deli container with water recreating the sounds of the sea.

I brought all my new homemade sound tools into my bodywork room and surrounded the massage table with them, my traditional Tibetan Singing Bowls, and other sound instruments. When my client arrived, I was pretty nervous—butterflies fluttered in my tummy. I hoped my outward presentation was calm and collected. Who knows what I projected?

My quiet massage studio is in the middle of the woods. The small black space heater in the corner of the tiny room makes it warm and cozy, and the smell of incense wafts through the air. Light enters the room through the tree branches outside.

My client's head rested on a pillow with love written across it. The soft white cotton blanket my mother gave me covered her body. It kept her comfortable as her body temperature cooled down. She relaxed as I began to play three singing bowls around her head and then placed the meditation bowl on her chest. Once the session started, my intuitive senses took over. I struck each bowl. The soothing sounds filled the room. My client drifted off into a deep meditative state. My heart was soaring. As the hour came to an end, she slowly awakened. "I'm a yoga teacher, and I'd like you to come and play your singing bowls in my yoga class." We made a date, and I was on cloud nine.

"Ring! Ring! Ring!" "Hi. I'm staying in Cold Spring for the weekend, and I spotted your card at Ascend Yoga Studio. Is it possible to make a sound healing appointment tomorrow, Sunday, before I get on the train back to New York City?"

*I can't believe I've received another call just a week after my first sound healing client.* "Yes, can you make it at 4 p.m. Sunday?" She replies, "Oh, I don't have a car. Maybe I can get a cab or Uber to your place." I think about what to do, and then I offer, "I am free beforehand and would be happy to pick you up in Cold Spring and then take you to the train station afterward." Excitedly she declares, "That would be great!"

It was a beautiful sunny spring day, so I took her down to Garrison Landing and pointed out The Military Academy at West Point across the Hudson River. High on a hilltop, overlooking the valley, Castle Rock has always attracted tourists' curiosity. I love sharing fun historical facts about the Hudson River Valley that I learned while producing the documentary *Henry Hudson's River: A Biography,* narrated by Orson Welles. So, I shared with her as we drove. She was amazed to learn that the hills surrounding us on our route were once as high as the Himalayan Mountains.

As our sound healing session ended, I held my Koshi water chime next to each of her ears, moving it oh so slowly. I followed with a figure-eight pattern over her entire body. The sounds allow the body to take a dive into the subconscious mind helping the body to heal on a deep level. "Take a few minutes to rest. When you're ready, wiggle your fingers and your toes. Be sure to keep your eyes closed as I slowly raise your eye pillow off your eyes. Count to ten, and then when you're ready, blink your eyes open."

While we were driving to the Peekskill train station, my new sound patron said, "You don't know much about me. I'm a singer. I'm also a yoga teacher, and I have a studio in New York City. I'd like you to come and do a Chakra Sound Healing Workshop with Tibetan Singing Bowls." *I can't believe my ears. How exciting. I have a gig in New York City.*

I heard the train's whistle in the distance as we arrived. I gave her a hug, and she skipped up the steps after the train pulled in. I yelled out to her, "Bye! I'll be in touch. Have a safe trip."

As I watched the train's doors close, I felt this wave of gratefulness sweep over me. Tears of joy welled up in my eyes as I thought about how blessed I was to be on my new sound healing adventure. It all started by putting those first words Sound Healing in big letters on my business card. It seems simple enough. I'm going to give you some things to think about as you consider updating your business card or even creating your first. Keep your soul-aligned business in mind. What are you passionate about? How to let the world know that's what you desire and the direction you want to go?

# THE STRATEGY

My medicine is sound healing. I was able to pivot from massage to sound healing with Tibetan Singing Bowls by rethinking my business card.

Let's look at your business card.

First of all, your business card is the first impression you make on a new client. It's your representative. It's an extension of you. Did you get your first business card online for the cheapest price? Now's the perfect time to make a change. Take a deep dive into what's on your card. As soon as you look at your card, do you love it? Does it reflect who you are? What you do? What you are looking to do in the future? Is it going to excite your ideal client? Will they give you a call as soon as they see your card? Does it capture the energy and vibe you give out? Most of all, you want your card to stand out.

What you need:

- Paper and pen to make some notes and do some drawings
- A comfortable chair with good support
- Desk or table nearby
- All your business cards, past, present, and others that inspire you
- Colored markers or pens
- Various colored papers you like. Better yet, colors you love
- Your favorite photos
- A few minutes of quiet time in your day

1. Find five to ten minutes when you feel that you can just sit and take a break from your busy day. Have your business card nearby and a piece of paper and a pen. Sit for a minute or two with your eyes closed. Take a few deep breaths. Once you feel relaxed, open your eyes. Look at your card. What's your first impression? Do you like it? Is it still current with everything you're doing? Does it need an update? Write down any thoughts you have. Draw a sample image.

2. Today there are so many different shapes and sizes of business cards. Don't be afraid to experiment. Be brave.

3. Consider a card with either a colored background or colored type. Does a particular color reflect your personality and what you do? What about the texture and feel of the card stock? What kind of typeface do you love? What had a tremendous impact for me was to put what I wanted to do most, Sound Healing: Tibetan Singing Bowls, in large type to draw the viewer's eyes. What words do you want to stand out? Emphasize them in size and type!

4. In what direction do you want to take your business? Perhaps you aren't quite sure how to put it out into the world. Are you ready to risk transitioning to a bolder personalized card? Does putting a photo on it appeal to you? A photo of yourself or something that reflects your business. I chose to put a photo of myself with four of my Tibetan Singing Bowls on my business card. I paid a professional photographer to take a series of photos, and I chose a few to put on my website and one for my business cards and stationery.

5. Once you love your new business card design, find a local printer. (It's always nice to give the business to another soul-centered entrepreneur-I used Grey Printing in Cold Spring, New York.) They will translate your wishes into your dream card, making a mock-up of their interpretation of your card and showing it to you for your approval. Does it make you smile when you look at your new card design? Does it reflect the feeling you want your ideal client to have? Would you pick up that card if you saw it? If yes, go with your new design and have it printed. If you still can't find a printer, you can ask friends and business associates who they recommend. If you love a particular card, call and ask who printed it for them. You can also go online, read reviews and choose that route. You could also add a virtual e-card.

6. Once you have your new card, hand it out freely. Where do you want to place it for folks to see? Do you have a favorite cafe or restaurant? Where does your ideal client spend time? In a gym? (There are bulletin boards in many places.) A Yoga Studio? Use your intuition to help guide your choice of where you leave your cards. What kind of energy does each location give off? Choose the

places that resonate with you. I will always remember the story my chiropractor told me about when he opened his office. He'd put pins in a map over the New York tri-state area where chiropractors' offices were. He chose to open in a town with no chiropractors. He was paying office rent and had no clients. Everyday he'd close his office from 1:00–3:00 p.m., and he'd go to local banks or grocery stores and stand in line. He'd turn to the person behind him, introduce himself and give them a business card. He continued to do this every day, and soon his phone started ringing, which was the beginning of his very successful 30-year Chiropractic practice.

7. Good luck. Have fun and know that you will attract clients that are aligned with your energy and love being around you.

Master Sound Healer **Michelle Clifton, LMT,** is an expert energy healer with over 30 years of study who uses a powerful mix of modalities to help her clients experience healing and transformation. Michelle transitioned from a massage and bodywork practice to sound therapy.

Michelle's passion is placing bowls on participants and playing the bowls, creating an environment in the body for deep healing and profound relaxation. She provides private and group sound meditation services. Michelle has worked with families, cancer patients, autistic adults, and the aging, among others. Her Sound Bath birthday parties are lots of fun.

Michelle is a teacher/trainer for the Academy of Sound Healing (IASH). Do you want to learn all about sound healing and how to play Tibetan Singing Bowls? Michelle is your teacher. She teaches privately or in group workshops and certifies you in IASH's sound healing course. One of her students said, "Michelle is an amazing teacher with great passion and love."

Michelle's artwork has been exhibited in the Smithsonian and is in the permanent collection of the Museum of the City of New York. She designed the Sneaker Bed featured in Bloomingdale's Designer Rooms. As a filmmaker, Michelle co-founded the Emmy Award-Winning Hudson River Film and Video Company. She produced numerous films and was a sound recordist for her company and major television networks.

Michelle lives in the middle of the woods in the Hudson River Valley. She provides sound healing in-person in NY, NJ, CT, and online.

Connect with Michelle:

On her website: sonicbowls.com
On her Resources page: https://www.sonicbowls.com/resources
On Facebook: https://www.facebook.com/michelle.clifton.397/
Via email: clifton.michelle1@gmail.com

# CHAPTER 22

# THE ROOM OF INDECISION

## FIVE UGLY TRUTHS TO ORGANIZING

Gayle Gunn, Organizing Strategist

# MY STORY

I once had an entire room completely taken over by piles of random stuff. Every time I would open the door, there it all was, just like an unwelcome surprise party. It was staring me in the face, saying *surprise! We're here. Surprise again! We're still here! Surprise! We're not going away!*

Ugh!

All my life, I'd had a space like this—a closet, the floor, and now a whole room overrun by stuff. What was particularly ironic to me about struggling with stuff in my personal life is that things were always perfectly in place in my professional space. My work area was always neat and tidy.

I knew where everything belonged, and I loved that. Yet, when it came to my personal space, even if I knew what was hiding in every pile, box, or bag, it was never organized. It just gradually accumulated. I'd tell myself, "I'll get to it later" or "I'm too busy to take care of that." Anyone who has ever said I'll get to it later knows that later rarely or never comes, and finds themself facing an overwhelming pile of clutter. The door gets closed, and the unwelcome surprise party is in full swing!

What's more, all these prized possessions (aka stuff) I couldn't part with, or couldn't face, moved with me from place to place.

It wasn't until my life was turned upside down, like *turn the box over dump out the content's* kind of upside-down that I realized it was time for something to change. Between 2004 and 2006, I lost my career, my candle-making hobby, my husband, my house, and my dog. Well, I didn't actually *lose* any of them. I knew exactly where they were; they just weren't part of my life anymore.

I'd reached rock bottom before, but this was a whole new level of rock bottom. As I was knocking on the door of turning 30, the only thing I was able to hold on to was what little courage I had left to face another day and all the years of baggage—figuratively and literally!

After getting my feet back under me and semi-settled into a new space, I thought it best to put everything I didn't need in a separate room to deal with later. My list of priorities was far bigger and more urgent than making decisions on all that stuff. Besides, with it tucked out of sight, it would be out of mind, right?

Wrong!

Over the next two years, while getting my life back on track, establishing a new career, avoiding relationships, and hibernating in my new little quiet space as much as possible, the items in this room weighed on me. Even though I couldn't see them on a daily basis, I always knew in the back of my mind it was all there. I would often wonder, what was all that stuff in that room? Why did I have it? How come it was there?

Ever play a game of 20 questions with yourself? So many more questions! When the surprise party analogy hit me, I realized I was done. It turns out I don't like surprises—especially not this kind.

I'd finally reached the point in my life where I knew I needed to do something about the mess. It was time for more major changes. I had been through enough! Now it was time to purge. I remember thinking, *if I'm so organized at work, how come I can't be organized at home?* Knowing my new location was temporary and wanting to be ready for the next move, the only thing I could think of was to box it up, label it all neatly and have it ready to go. I bought at least three or four dozen white bankers' boxes, some yellow sticky notes, and dove right into my organizing project.

I enjoyed the process and the end result. When I was done with the whole room, I stepped back and looked at my beautiful wall of boxes. They were all labeled, neat, tidy, and finally organized! It looked amazing, and I was so proud of myself. For a moment, I thought I'd conquered the world.

Then the strangest thing happened!

About six months later, as I was moving on with my life, something was wrong. Even though I loved the way it looked, and even after spending all those hours sorting, organizing, boxing, labeling, stacking, and investing my time, it hit me: *I didn't truly feel any better.*

How was that even possible? How could I go through all this effort and hard work only to find I *wasn't happy?* Just because I made it look pretty and more organized didn't take away the fact that it was all still there. The slew of questions returned. The biggest question of them all erupted out of me. What is all this crap? Wondering, *had I just gone from being a messy hoarder to an organized hoarder!*

Looking back, I can recall it was an assortment of things. Things that I loved, wanted, or thought I wanted. Things I'm pretty sure I'd be okay without, *if* I could let them go. Yet, I couldn't bring myself to get rid of any of it. Even beautifully organized, *this was now my Room of Indecision.*

# THE STRATEGY

This experience led me to the first ugly truth about organizing:

**#1. Organizing isn't the answer!** *Dang-it!* I thought to myself. *Now I have to go back through everything.* I started the real work of the painstaking process of deciding what to keep, what could be donated, and what needed to be tossed. The true beauty and freedom of organizing was purging and paring down. I saw that I could live with much less without depriving myself of what made my space functional or what made me feel good about myself. There was comfort and confidence in keeping only what was most important.

I would work on one box at a time, looking at each item and sitting with it. Did it have a place in my space? Was it something I wanted to hold on to? Was it something I needed to hold on to? When I thought about it, was it something that I didn't like, didn't need, or would *never* use again? As I allowed it to be a process, I discovered that letting go was also a process, and having it *be* a process made it easier *to* process, which brought me to the second ugly truth to organizing.

**#2. Organizing is a process.** Anyone who has ever organized their space and maintained it knows organizing isn't a one-and-done.

Well, isn't that the truth! Organizing takes time and attention and deciding what goes where.

I started asking myself, *Where does this stuff or this item live? Where is its home going to be?* I began living by two important ideas: a) If something doesn't have a home, it doesn't come home with me; and b) if I already brought it home and it doesn't have a real home, then maybe it needs to not stay. I noticed that once stuff moved in, keeping order in my house was difficult if they didn't have a planned place. Apparently things not having a home, mixed with I'll get to it later, leads to a room of indecision. No more of that for me! I would decide right away on where things will live.

Then, the third ugly truth to organizing emerged.

**#3. It isn't just stuff!** Why can't I get rid of my stuff? This old t-shirt? Those pants that don't fit? All the books I've read or have yet to read? That random thing? You know, the one I might need someday? Or the other one, which has *as soon as I get rid of it, I know for sure I'll need it* written all over it!

Well, guess what, people, it's possible that what some consider to be stuff is actually more than just stuff. It's a t-shirt from a concert I attended with my best friend. Even if it was a gazillion years ago, when I see the shirt, it brings me back to those glory days and makes me smile. Who cares if it's several sizes too small! How about those sweatpants? The ones with the worn-out waste band, the holes in places that make them questionable to wear in public. Yes, the ones that saw me through every feeling fat day, need a hug from my clothes day, can't get out of bed day, or just loving life and wanna be comfy day.

This stuff is memories of times gone by. It marks a time of change in my life. Some changes I didn't ask for and some changes I'd been looking forward to. That stuff is a way for me to hold on to what was and a vision of what someday might be. That stuff is a gift or thoughtful gesture. That stuff is a possibility for what the future has in store. It's a sentiment from a loved one that is no longer with me.

My dear friends, *that* isn't just stuff. Those are experiences that I want to hold on to. My room of indecision was the story of my life, where I'd been, and the people I cared about.

So now what? What was I supposed to do with the stuff I didn't think I could part with or now saw was more than just stuff?

I took one last good hard look at the roads I'd traveled in my life and decided at that moment, does *all* this stuff go with me into my new life? I only had three choices. 1) I could ignore it and let Mother Nature or acts of God like fires, floods, natural disasters, or mold and mildew take care of it; 2) Haul my wall of boxes around with me for the rest of my life, leaving it for loved ones to deal with after I died; 3) I could take ownership and action for myself.

As lovely as the first two options were, I chose the third and went back through *every* single box. As I worked my way through each of the boxes, I asked myself if I needed it or wanted to keep it, let it go, give it away, sell it, trash it, or leave it. I paired 40 bankers' boxes down to what I absolutely loved and wanted to have in my space, transferring the rest to six small plastic bins. There were two beige bins for my seasonal holiday stuff, two maroons for some housewares and the costumes I'd made, and two lavenders for my memorabilia. Everything else was gone, and I *felt amazing!*

I'd cleared out my room of indecision *forever,* and I was never, ever going back—*so I thought!*

This entire process became one of the foundational principles in my philosophy on the organizing journey. Being organized isn't about having things perfectly in place. It's about being at peace with what we choose to keep in our life and how we choose to live.

I discovered the next two ugly truths to organizing when I was a few years into being a professional organizer. I would look through magazines and catalogs. I would wander around retail stores with aisles of containers and storage options. I looked at one particular magazine and thought, *Wow, that set-up must cost a fortune!* I added up a rough estimate of what each container would cost. As simple and as beautiful as it was, it would cost someone over $500, just in food containers! And there it was, the fourth ugly truth to organizing.

**#4. Organizing isn't cheap!** I'm not a fan of the word cheap. I associate this word with poor quality, low value, discount, and other less than ideas. I prefer to think of organizing as high value, and a quality investment.

I like to uplevel the perception of organizing into three categories: 1) inexpensive DIY, 2) high-quality and going all out, and 3) getting guidance on the journey by working with a professional organizer, designer, or coach.

Some people love to do organizing on their own and can find a quality, low-cost storage option. A few small purchases here or there may be all it takes. Then there are those of us who would go all out with bins, containers, decorative labels, binders, plastic sleeves, and more. All of that can get quite costly. However, it adds to our sense of order and joy, making it a worthwhile investment. Others decide to invest more in themselves by working with a professional to guide them through the journey.

So, how do you decide if you need to hire a professional? Isn't organizing something anyone can do on their own?

The answer is yes!

Anyone can be organized. The challenge for many is more about the when. When will you carve out time? When will you work on it, and how will you tackle the overwhelming amount of stuff that isn't really stuff? How will you stay focused on your organizing project to get it done?

The best professional organizers will support you through the decision-making process. They won't tell you what to keep or get rid of. They will gently encourage you to make the decision that works best for you. At least, that is what I do with my clients. I am there, by their side every step of the way. I have been in their shoes! I know how it feels, and I know it's a process. So, there is no pushing or forcing, like some family members or friends may do. *You know the ones…* The ones who harshly say, "Why can't you just get rid of that?" Or the "I can't believe you won't just toss that out." As loving as they are trying to be, sometimes it's not the right kind of support. They just don't get it!

Whether you do it yourself in simple ways, light up at uniform and orderly containers, or decide to let a professional help you, you may encounter the fifth ugly truth to organizing.

**#5. Organizing systems change.** This, for me, gets a raised palm of the hand to the forehead. A slap every time it happens. This ugly truth came to me as I was working on one of my own organizing projects, trying to print, save, and store all the material I purchased for a course. I thought it would be brilliant to print it out because I am a paper-in-hand kind of gal.

What started as a few pages and maybe a three-ring binder or two turned into 12 mini leather binders, over 600 mini plastics sleeves, and probably four reams of paper. It was originally a decision I was making as I went because the first plan of printing and tossing everything in a folder wasn't going to work. The second plan was to digitally save everything instead, but as I was going through my modules, I found it difficult to follow along or find anything easily. So, I shifted my system *again!*

This started the process I share with my clients—let's see what you have or are planning to hang on to before we purchase the containers or storage bins. If we pare down first, then we know what the best system is. Of course, as we grow and expand, so might our system, but we are always gaining traction by having a simplified starting point.

Accepting this concept that things change also inspired my routine to follow up with clients two weeks after a final session to see how the system is working. This way, if a change is needed, we can catch the need early and make tweaks, helping my clients stay encouraged and feel great.

What I have learned and love about being organized personally and professionally is that when we pare down to what is most important, give things a proper home, and set up systems or processes, everything else in our lives begins to fall into place. I now call this the Outside-In Approach to clearing clutter from our space and life. It's the core principle of the work that I do with my clients and the soul-aligned business I have created. I help heart-centered professionals overcome the ugly truths of organizing so they can clear the clutter from their space and simplify their lives to gain confidence, clarity, happiness, and success.

The other thing that I have learned and experienced over the years for myself and working with clients is that rooms or areas of indecision still appear—bringing me full circle to these ugly truths. Organizing is not a one-and-done. However, now that we know the ugly truths exist, what they are, and what they mean, we can work together to overcome them with options to move you forward. Knowing them is only half the battle. The other half is the practical application and taking inspired action.

If your space is overrun with piles of indecision, please reach out to me at soulaligned@gaylegunn.com to learn more about how we can help you say goodbye to those unwelcome surprise party guests!

**Gayle Gunn** is an Organizing Strategist who specializes in space utilization. She offers a unique outside-in approach to decluttering that awakens the mind, body, spirit, *and space* connection.

Gayle's gift of spatial acuity, along with her personal journey and her design experience working for Crate and Barrel, and Bassett Furniture, inspired her to launch her own business. She blended her passion for organizing, coaching, and design to create Ener-CHI Organizing. She now works with women and new home-based businesses, guiding them on a journey to organizing their space, helping them set it up in a way that inspires, motivates, and empowers their success.

Today when she is not at home with her family or visiting loved ones, you will find her helping her clients discover and let go of what no longer serves them.

To learn more about transforming your space to change your life, please visit her website: www.gaylegunn.com.

# CHAPTER 23

# DISMANTLING THE SUPERWOMAN MYTH

## MAKING AN AUTHENTIC TRANSITION FROM CORPORATE TO HEART-BASED ENTERPRISE

Lily Gibarac, Ph.D. ABD, M.Ed., LPC, CEC

*In a haze of lies, we can't know the truth. In a quagmire of shame, we cannot know authenticity. Much of what we have been conditioned to believe in is false. The quest for our essence begins in this discovery.*

~Dr. Shefali Tsabary

## MY STORY

A picture of a successful businesswoman is glamorous and graced with a crown of super competence, high achievements, and elegance in balancing competing needs, roles, and demands, right? You are a responsible woman who feels the pressure to do it all—juggling family, career, and social activities while attending to the needs of everyone around you.

Did you know that being a Superwoman and people pleaser can actually kill you?

As a sensitive, enthusiastic, and ambitious female with a big heart and dreams, I found myself thrust into a cold world of deadlines, structure, expectations, and delivery that slowly but consistently took me further away from the longing of my heart. When I closed my eyes, I'd drift away to dream of helping people come alive with passion and joy—watch them have a breakthrough as they realize that they are magicians who can bend time and space and harness the energy of their desire in the most powerful way. Tethered by increased demands and pressure to perform, I assumed I had to sacrifice, put my dreams on the back burner and compete to make it in the corporate world. After all, that is the way to climb the corporate ladder.

Chronic exhaustion, stress, overwhelm, and burnout forced me to make futile attempts to numb them away in Epsom salts, baths, and lavender oil. Looming over my head like a guillotine, the primary breadwinner's responsibility time and time again lured me back into trying harder. This rigid, uncompromising approach usually solicited a surge of fresh energy supply and secured a smooth sail for a bit longer.

Meanwhile, the relentless onslaught of demands continued to pile up, exerting chronic fatigue due to the inability to prioritize self-care, set limits, delegate tasks, or ask for help. As the insidious cycle of things staying the same under the guise of good enough, a question crept into my mind like an invisible net holding me hostage: *I am taking care of my family? I should feel happy and proud.* While deep inside of me, I was dying a slow death by a thousand cuts.

Can you relate? Did you find yourself shaking your head in agreement? I'm sorry. I had no idea about the dangers of people pleasing either, not until I found myself having to fight for my right to live.

It was an early afternoon in May of 2012. The soft glow from the window accentuated shadows on the walls. My mind played with these images as my doctor's voice echoed in my ears, "Your antibodies are as high as the lab would measure. There is no cure."

I faded away, disappearing together with the remainder of his monologue. I already knew, with every fiber of my being, that I was in trouble. I didn't need him to tell me. Fever and rage rippled through my body while I shook uncontrollably. My old friend's fear, guilt, and shame feasted on my conscience, lashing out with a vengeance as my body crumbled into disobedience. Abandoned, hurt, and betrayed by myself and my own body that no longer wanted to bend into compliance, I sobbed softly.

This disease of people-pleasing began early in my childhood. The cultural experience of being raised in a rigid patriarchal society, made oppression, abuse, beating and shaming a socially accepted model for enforcing respect and obedience for my parents, as it did for many generations before them. "Children are to be seen, but not heard," my mother repeated often.

Unpredictability of emotionally scared and parents, and conflicting messages induced emotional anguish, a constant state of fear and anxiety that made it easier for my parents to maintain power and control even into my adulthood. Oppressive behavior routinely inflicted in my childhood became a deeply embedded part of my psyche. Like a haunted animal, I developed an acute ability to read the body language, facial expressions, and on the spot contrive a strategy to please my unforgiving mother. *Mama, dearest Mom, I'll be whatever you want me to be, just don't beat me,* I begged with eyes filled with hope that somehow, I might avoid yet another violent eruption.

I learned how to be independent, self-sufficient, and take care of others all through surrendering my personal power and obfuscating my needs, voice, and authenticity. From there on, this people pleasing behavior, like malignancy, bled into every aspect of my life. It became an integral part of my acquired personality, an unconscious survival mechanism, and a long-stemming way of interacting in the world that preserved an illusory sense of control, safety, and connection.

Deformed sense of self image, and identity molded by mindless crimes, messages that were lavishly gushed my way cut deep into my innocent mind. I can still hear my exasperated mother's voice ringing in my ears, "Oh, you are so useless! What a nuisance! It would have been much better if I had a rock instead of you, at least there would be some use for it—pigs would have something to scratch their butts on."

What we don't learn we repeat. One line of oppressed, traumatized generation produces another line of innocent victims. Adversity, entrenched patriarchal standards, and age-old misogynism held a tight grip on me, molding me, like so many other women, into an expendable, compliant wife and Superwoman. One who would unquestionably shoulder a towering set of expectations and competing needs, while stifling her truth and diligently applying herself to earn a place at the table. Chronic business and doing meant safety, temporary reprieve. With the lack of proper modeling, that's what it appeared to be.

Back in the doctor's office, I heard him shuffle papers as he continued to mumble, but my mind was preoccupied with something else. I was heading down memory lane. There I was, barely five, still lying in bed. As I sleepily rubbed my eyes, a tantalizing smell of freshly baked bread filled my nostrils. I eagerly jumped up and ran to the kitchen. My mother was hovering over the stove, her face flushed from the hot oven. I rushed toward her, extending my arms wide into a hug as I imagined sinking my teeth into this crunchy piece of delicacy. My mouth was watering as I imagined it dissolving and rolling down my tongue when my mother's somber voice stopped me in my tracks, "What did you do today to earn something to eat?"

I stood there with my arms still open, feeling a pang in my belly. I wanted to cry, scream, and throw a tantrum, but instead, I just stood, frozen with a blank stare.

As children, we cannot control most of what happens to us, nor can we self-advocate. At moments like these, primal fear of abandonment and rejection is intolerable for a child. Hence, we make some crucial decisions and conclusions about who we are, our values and worth, and what these events mean about us and the world. The incident in the kitchen marked a defining point for me, one where I concluded that it was not safe to be myself and have needs. To win my mother's approval, I abandoned my inner core and ability to trust myself. This hideous beast of focusing externally usurped my innocent mind and became an unconscious block, a self-limiting pattern that held me back from the life I desired.

To compensate for an underlying fear of worthlessness, I armored myself with overachieving tendencies, people-pleasing, and a heavy emphasis on embodying strong, masculine traits. At eleven, I was told that I'm old enough to become a fully contributing member of the family and dragged to work in the cornfield at the crack of dawn. And it didn't end there. At fifteen, I was working hand in hand with the grown man carrying bags of cement, hardly distinguishable among them with my short hair. Working hard, suppressing emotions for fear that "I'll get something to cry about," was addictive. This emphasis on doing opened the doors for me and secured recognition and approval from the inner circle of family, friends, and coworkers – a luxury I was seldom afforded. My hard work and determination served as a testimony of a worthwhile person. I carried laurels such as my son, trophy wife, Superwoman, and more academic degrees than I care to list, with pride like a badge of honor.

The façade of over-competence and high achievement masked my unmet needs and hid internalized disarray, disconnect, and misalignment. I became so good at playing this make-believe game that no one, not even me, suspected dissonance nor the depth of discontent for abandoning my truth. Deeply seated suppressed shame and crippling lack of self-worth became my long-lasting companions, fueling my insatiable desire to reach the highest of the high and earn that place at the table.

That early afternoon in May of 2012, while still at the doctor's office, I became aware of how this childhood adaptation to an adverse experience, while ingenious at the time, inflicted a mirage of erroneous perceptions of my self-identity. As this awareness navigated through my body and consciousness, it dawned on me: *I've never allowed myself to release the fear of that terrified five-year-old girl.*

This raw, pent-up feeling and trauma unconsciously dictated my choices and prompted me to make decisions that ultimately held me back, playing safe and small.

I remained frozen in time, with my arms still outstretched.

Suspended, I was waiting to receive permission to be worthy of happiness and enjoy life with an invigorated sense of aliveness. Suddenly, even a moment longer was too long, and I resolved to free myself, and dismantle the shackles of conditioning that had created a fertile ground for this illness.

A strong negative mental pattern lingers and embeds itself into the body's tissues and causes disease of all kinds. Healing comes from awareness and releasing harbored feelings. I had to make things right. What choice did I have? I could either accept that my autoimmune condition was as incurable as the doctor was telling me or allow my old self to die—to shatter a dysfunctional pattern of self-abandonment and release things and people from my life that reinforced this behavior.

Right there and then, for the first time, I chose to make a vow to myself. *No, not like this; I will no longer abandon myself and keep myself small for fear of making someone else incompetent.*

While shadows continued to bounce off the walls in a wild, ecstatic dance, I let out a long sigh as an act of surrender. With knowledge comes great power and responsibility to act upon it. I watched in my mind's eye as the generational inheritance of guilt, shame, and trauma began to crumble.

As Maya Angelou said, "You can't really know where you are going until you know where you have been." Leaning into the possibility of tomorrow, I felt my body shift - my breathing became deeper, and my shoulders let go. The raging war was over. Although unaware at that time, I had instructed every cell of my body to renew itself with love and acceptance and to stop producing the antibodies destroying my organs. This was the first step toward healing.

Over the next few years, I realized that qualities of compassion, empathy, altruism, and a desire to make a great impact in the world are not universal qualities. These are traits of people who are on a certain level of consciousness. The fact that you found your way to this book and are reading these words tells me you're one of them. I want you to know that it takes an incredible amount of courage to follow your heart and choose this path. Honor yourself for that.

As an aspiring, conscious business owner, you know that you have the potential to make a great impact and achieve true financial abundance so you can harness the life and career you desire and deserve. Yet, you find yourself feeling trapped and invisible in a maze of corporate ruts, sucking you dry, inducing stress, anxiety, depression, and perhaps some health challenges. Your heart calls you to excel at the highest level possible, but you find yourself drained, losing power, passion, and purpose. An endless emotional rollercoaster of indecision and self-doubt keeps you up at night. Can you make the transition? Do you have what it takes to run a successful business? Is that going to be financially viable?

Despite the chatter of your mind's critic, deep down in your heart, you know you're ready to up-level, optimize your emotional state, and shift the paradigm of success. Author Patrick Overton reminds us that when we reach that critical point and come to the edge of all that we know, we must believe that we will have something solid to stand on or learn how to fly. When you step into faith, the outer world reflects and supports the authenticity of your inner alignment. Here is a little secret. You already have the wings! Let's dive in and see how you can use them to manifest your soul-aligned business.

Can you, for a second, take a mental inventory of those dreadful thoughts that sneak out when you're at your lowest and want to hide from the world? I'm sure you know what I'm talking about. These fear formations take different manifestations like people-pleasing, perfectionism, procrastination, and self-criticism. They grow like cancer, feeding off your life force. Naturally, we respond by repressing them for fear of being discovered and unmasked. This internalized feeling of dread keeps us contracted, separated from what we value, and trapped in a scarcity mentality. Hence, keeping out of reach what you crave the most—meaningful connection, unconditional love, and a fulfilling and uplifting life.

Your willingness to transcend these core wounds, whether from this lifetime or generations-old beliefs passed down, can unlock the door to alignment and authenticity. There is no way around them. They are the way. This wounding is the place where light enters.

When you lean into these core emotions of guilt, shame, grief, or fear and welcome them in with compassion, acceptance, and forgiveness, you reclaim disowned parts of self. To extinguish darkness, you must turn on the light. To remove obstacles and reach clarity, you must move beyond your thoughts. To see the truth of your essence and your potential, you must tap into your heart's energy. This energy unlocks the door of infinite potential and up levels your consciousness. When you boldly and unapologetically step into your heart's truth, your soul-aligned business becomes an extension of who you are, an authentic way of honoring yourself and the divine.

Kahlil Gibran wrote we are "the sons and daughters of Life's longing for itself." We come through our parents, but we are not from them. Have you ever wondered why you had the sense that you did not belong in your family? What if that is because you're the divine spark of the Creator itself, longing to blossom into your fullest expression. Your birthright is the perpetual state of abundance. To allow your cup of life to overflow, you need to first safely arrive in your body, support your neurological system into healing overwhelm, and practice the ability to receive.

As an aspiring and successful business owner, how much light can you receive without shrinking? Marianne Williamson says it so beautifully, "Our deepest fear is not that we are inadequate. Our deepest fear is that we are powerful beyond measure. It is our light, not our darkness that most frightens us."

At this evolutionary time, the world needs as many awakened, conscious leaders and business owners as possible. In a world where you're free to become anything you want, who would you like to be? What you cultivate is what you offer to the world. Your life is a gift to be shared. Maya Angelou said, "People will forget what you said, people will forget what you did, but people will never forget how you made them feel."

What are you sharing? Who are you touching? In her unforgettable keynote speech at the recent Presidential Inauguration, poet Laureate Amanda Gorman proclaimed that "If you merge mercy with might, and might with rights, then love becomes our legacy." What will be your legacy?

Before we transition to the tool for clearing stuck emotional patterns, accessing your heart-based intelligence, and optimizing your container for love and light, I want to thank you for allowing me to guide you on this sacred journey.

# THE STRATEGY

## HOW TO EXPAND YOUR CONTAINER FOR LIGHT AND CAPACITY TO RECEIVE

Learning how to generate an expansive state by accessing heart intelligence can help you crack open the door of infinite potential. It invites the energy of gratefulness, kindness, and resonance with love. When this energy consciously amplifies and radiates through the prism of your authenticity, you build a business from the essence of who you are and energetically attract clients, opportunities, and sales aligned with what you stand for.

1. Take a seat in a nice comfortable space where you will not be disturbed for the next 20-30 minutes. You can do this practice sitting in a chair with your feet flat on the floor or in any other position comfortable for you. Having your feet flat on the ground is the most preferred way.

2. Mentally surround yourself with silence, like you're in a soundproof bubble.

3. Follow the sensation of your breath and feel the air traveling through the nostrils, lungs, and all the way down to your belly. With each in-breath, feel your belly expanding like a balloon, and with each out-breath, feel the contraction. Gently stroke and rub your skin all over.

4. When you feel fully present in your body, tense all of your muscles, legs, arms, shoulders, torso, jaw, and back as hard as you can. Make fists and hold this position for the count of five. Relax. Exhale and repeat this three times.

5. Feel your body completely relaxed. As your breathing becomes deeper, imagine roots growing out of the soles of your feet, reaching to the core of Mother Earth—she's waiting for you, with a big smile, ready to embrace you. All worries melt away in her loving presence as you surrender to her arms.

6. Emotions of sweetness, acceptance and loving forgiveness emanate from her as you feel the wave of bliss sweeping over your entire body, and from the top of your head, like a fountain shooting that energy into the sky.

7. As you continue to feel this loving attention, a globe of golden-white light starts filling in your belly and growing bigger and brighter. Consciously continue expanding it until it surrounds your entire body—big enough to fill in the entire bubble.

8. Feel the flow of love pouring into you and getting bigger. Intentionally expand it until it fills the entire room, your house, city, state, country, and the world.

9. Soak in this beautiful flow of luminescent light, taste its sweetness like honey rolling down your tongue, and focus your attention on your heart space. Pose a question and let the answer come to you. Don't think. Feel it.

10. Take in your heart's intelligence, express your gratefulness for yourself, Mother Earth, and this life-sustaining love. Slowly begin to return your awareness to your body, feeling renewed.

11. Practice taking in this expansive love and consciously radiating it wherever you are, especially when you find yourself contracting and shrinking.

When you learn to receive, you consciously co-create and get into the flow of all life has to offer to you. Acknowledge, remember, appreciate and be grateful for what you have and how far you have come. Gratefulness will shortcut your path to success and condense the timeline.

**Lily Gibarac,** Ph.D. ABD, is an expert Leadership Consultant, Heart-based Mentor, Creative Business Strategist, certified executive coach, and licensed professional counselor.

She works specifically with conscious woman entrepreneurs and professionals who need help challenging their Superwoman script so they can operate from the place of authentic alignment and create greater impact, influence, revenue, and life they deserve and desire. She's passionate about transforming lives in her presence and helping them step from the brink of burnout so that they can harness the power and possibility within.

For more information about Lily and her full bio, please visit https://bit.ly/3qqwbM9

For a free information kit on Dismantling the Super Woman Myth, visit https://lilygibarac.isonline.page/Superwoman

Connect with Lily:
On her website: www.LilyGibarac.com
On LinkedIn: https://www.linkedin.com/in/lily-b-g-913a9ba9/
On Facebook: https://www.facebook.com/lily.gibarac

## CHAPTER 24

# FUEL FROM WITHIN

## HOW TO BUILD YOUR BEST SELF
## WHILE BUILDING YOUR BEST BUSINESS

Kiki Magnuson, MS, PN1

## MY STORY

"When are you going to get a real job?"

"Honey, I'm concerned about your future. Why don't you get a stable job that has benefits?"

These were the questions my parents asked me after they found out that I'd decided to open my own business and embark on an entrepreneurial path. At this time of my life, I'd moved in with my boyfriend, who they did not approve of, and they'd cut me off financially. I had moved to a new city with no connections, and, on top of all that, I decided to start my own online nutrition business.

*Was I making the biggest mistake of my life?*

Starting a business is hard. You don't have all the answers right away, and it's a lot of trial and error. But there were times when I felt alone, trapped, with no real direction or help to know if what I was doing was right or not.

"Get a business coach," they say. "Have a mentor," they say. "Surround yourself with those more successful than you," they say. But how?

I knew this journey wasn't going to be easy, but man, I had no idea how impactful it was on me mentally. I often cried in my car or the shower, just so no one knew how bad I felt. I was constantly stressed out about getting clients and making enough money, and there were times when I felt lonely and hopeless. I felt like I couldn't talk to my family or friends about my struggles because they wouldn't understand me, or they'd blame me for choosing this path. I compared myself to friends and what I saw on social media. I knew if I kept this way of thinking, I would go down a path that was going to be very damaging.

My boyfriend struggled, too. He found a strength coaching job that required long work hours and did not pay well.

*Brrring!* The alarm clock sounded at 4 a.m. The door slammed, and there he went off to work. Around 8–8:30 p.m., the door creaked and opened, then a thump as he plopped onto the couch.

"Time for dinner," I called out. "Okay, yea. Be right there," he said. But I was frustrated and asked. "Why are you always glued to that TV?" "It's my way of decompressing, that's all." His answer didn't satisfy me. "I guess I am having a hard time seeing any motivation come out of you right now because that isn't how I was raised." "I see. I am trying here." He said defensively. "I just cope differently than you do."

Deep down inside, I felt like I was the one that was supporting both of us, and he wasn't as driven. It got so bad that I had a calculator out and added everything up while grocery shopping to make sure I didn't overspend and stayed within budget. Who does that?

*Okay, Kiki, this isn't the life you want to live. You have to change the things you can control. Start applying the things you teach your clients. You can do this!*

I didn't realize that owning a business was a lot like losing weight and maintaining it. As an online nutritionist, I teach clients every day how to apply small habits that compound over time. There is no instant gratification here, but we want it now like everything we do in life! We want to see results immediately. We want to see change and progress instantly. We think we are failing without these things, and we give up because we believe it's no longer working. However, even the smallest change we don't realize can eventually build to something greater. But since many of us don't like playing the long game, the ones who quit early don't get the opportunity to see the change manifest. It's like the quote I often tell my clients, "If losing weight and keeping it off was easy, everyone would do it." Just like that, my mind was blown!

*If owning a business was easy, everyone would do it, too.*

Wow, how did I not see this earlier? I am part of the long game. I had to change the way I saw my challenges and obstacles. In the book *Mindset* by Carol S. Dweck, Ph.D., she states, "People with the growth mindset know it takes time for potential to flower." I needed to change my mindset and habits and apply the law of attraction if I wanted to have a successful, fulfilling business and life.

So, I started with myself. Working out was a habit that had always been ingrained in me. That has often been a saving grace. But my nutrition had taken a turn for the worse. My boyfriend and I would binge drink on the weekend, have unhealthy foods in the house, and obviously, my mental health was declining. So, I started small. I started cooking more nutritious meals with all sorts of colors. I started reading more personal development books and even got myself into a room with successful people to find mentorship. I knew that fueling my body from within was my secret weapon to keep me healthy and show that anyone can change their trajectory just by applying simple tools that don't take a ton of time and work.

Talk about the law of attraction! As I lost weight got stronger and leaner, and I received more comments from people. Even my clients were amazed by the story of my journey. I woke in the morning with more energy and purpose. I carried my body differently and had a great relationship with food. My performance went up, and I was applying new techniques to not overwhelm myself as my business continued to grow.

I am at a place now where I don't have that stress about *how will I get that next client?* I've been able to create different programs, online cooking classes, and my boyfriend and I worked things out. We're happily married and can't wait to grow our family.

So how do you not gain weight and stay sane and healthy while building a business? Here are some simple strategies you can start applying immediately to start building your best self while building your amazing business!

# THE STRATEGY

Most people believe that staying healthy is hard while building a business. Popular excuses I hear are, "I don't have time to cook" or "Meal prepping sounds daunting." However, it doesn't have to be that way. It all starts with how you value food and your health. If you see food as nourishment and a blessing to your body, you'll see it as a priority.

My goal isn't to change your entire life but to move the needle a little bit so you can have the energy to perform at your optimum level or fit into that business suit you love wearing. As I mentioned before, small choices you make every day can direct your path to thrive and be your best self verse dragging your feet, feeling heavy and lethargic.

So, let's start small:

## 1. PLAN, SCHEDULE, AND TAKE ACTION

We all have to take the time to eat food every day, so why don't we take the time to choose healthy quality foods that actually benefit us? Feeling busy and always on the go is the norm in the 21st century, so making time is imperative. But like I said, start small. Adopt a daily or weekly ritual with your routine. Pack your lunch the night before. Buy chopped vegetables that you can grab immediately (My favorite is the veggie trays you buy at parties. Who said you couldn't buy them for yourself?), or even make Sunday family quality time while batch cooking for a few days of the week. Again, nothing so vast that you crash and fail because it was completely unattainable.

## 2. CHOOSE NUTRITIOUS FOODS MORE OFTEN

This is an area where I find people are more challenged. People come to me thinking they need to change their diet completely, be entirely perfect, and never eat junk food again. If you didn't realize, we don't live in a perfect world, and we are all human. I'm not saying never eat that donut or birthday cake again. I am saying choose healthier foods more often and save the not-so-healthy foods for those rare occasions. There are simple ways to make healthy substitutions. For instance, switch white rice for brown rice in your burrito bowl. Or switch sugary breakfast cereal for steel-cut or old-fashioned oats with fresh fruit and chia seeds since you don't have time for a sit-down breakfast. If you can eat less processed foods and replace them with healthier alternatives, it helps you shrink your waistline, gives you more energy, and allows your body to get rid of and prevent diseases.

## 3. MOVE WELL AND OFTEN

Have you ever heard the term, "If you don't use it, you'll lose it?" Movement is so important. I would say, just as important as brushing your teeth. Seriously. The power movement has on the body is so impactful that it blows my mind when I have clients tell me they don't exercise or it's been ten years since they stepped into a gym. Why do you think movement is such a big deal? Well, let me tell you. Just by moving your body daily you can lower your chance of chronic diseases, boost your immune system, improve memory and brain function, reduce anxiety and depression, improve your bone density, not to mention improve your quality of sleep.

Try things like walking the dog, walking around the block with a neighbor or friend, jogging, hiking, swimming with your kids, or playing community games. Did I mention, there are a lot of these things you can do for free. So why not do them?

## 4. REST AND RECOVER

I'm sure you're wondering what this has to do with nutrition? Believe it or not, how you sleep and recover can be greatly impacted by what you eat and drink. Allowing yourself good quality sleep gives your body and mind an opportunity to recharge, feel refreshed, alert, and stray off diseases. If you didn't know, a high sugar, high processed-food diet is linked to disrupted sleep, making it harder for the body to heal and repair. Poor quality sleep can also lead to weight gain, sickness, brain fog, and more.

## 5. BUILD SUPPORTIVE ENVIRONMENTS

Many facets make up our environments, including physical spaces like our home, kitchen, and workspace, and who is in those spaces like family, friends, roommates, and co-workers. How about our relationships and who we hang out with often? Even our culture and background influence these environments. Make it easy on yourself by being transparent with your environment. Getting everyone on board will make things easier than trying to do things alone or having to hide them from others. That will only build shame and disappointment. Other ways to fill these spaces positively are reading personal development books or listening to motivating podcasts. Even hiring a coach to keep you accountable is very powerful. However, you decide to create these healthy spaces, make them so they keep you supported and motivated to stay on track.

If you'd like to have more laser coaching on your nutrition and guidance around how to customize it to your life, head over to www.livingwellwithkiki.com and sign up for free discovery. Call me. Let's get you to that place where you're creating the best version of yourself while changing the world!

**Kiki Magnuson,** MS, PN1, is a Certified Nutritionist who has a huge passion for helping people find a way to eat well and keep those techniques for the rest of their lives. She works one-on-one with people who want to learn what real nutrition looks like and to be free from the diet mentality stigma. She doesn't believe in restrictions or crash dieting. She believes in balance and having the ability to enjoy all things in life. Kiki has been in the fitness industry since 2012 and has focused on her nutrition specialty since 2016. She has seen people struggle with restricted diets and does not want to be another try-then-fail program.

Kiki is a foodie, loves to cook, and likes to try new things. Her background is Panamanian and Greek. She loves everything that comes with discussing culture. One thing she loves to do for fun is to offer her online cooking classes, which encourage cooking all sorts of different, exotic recipes that are easy-to-follow, delicious, and nutritious. She is also into fitness, and her exercise of choice is Olympic weightlifting. Her favorite lift is the snatch, and she loves the idea of getting strong and challenging her body in this healthy way.

In her spare time, Kiki loves reading personal development books, traveling the world with her husband, and going on hikes with her dog, Suzy.

Connect further with Kiki here:

On her website: https://www.livingwellwithkiki.com/
On Facebook: https://www.facebook.com/livingwellwithkiki
On Instagram: https://www.instagram.com/livingwellwithkiki/
On YouTube:
https://www.youtube.com/channel/UCJqmEIBWKSLDrFvhD1UC4HQ
Join her Free Community - Secrets to Becoming a Fit Foodie:
https://www.facebook.com/groups/1179015675765062

# CHAPTER 25

# LEADING WITH SOUL

## HOW TO BRING YOUR UNIQUE GENIUS TO LIFE

Robin Mooney, Purpose Coaching

## MY STORY

What's your purpose? Why are you here? What do you want to bring to the world?

My purpose, since I was a very small girl, has been to make the world a better place—to be the change.

Can you relate to this? For my entire life, I have intentionally put myself in the position of risking my vulnerability to step into a typically male role. I've always had the deep *knowing* I could help transform teams, culture, performance, engagement, and growth. That is if I was invited to share my knowledge, question the status quo, and invite blue-sky thinking. Together we could design a new way forward. Somewhere in my soul, I knew my uniqueness was needed and could help change the world. Not despite my uniqueness, but because of it.

It takes willing, not reluctant, participants. The latter destroys the energy, attention, and alignment needed to create a safe space. I refer to this as permission space, the foundation for inviting others to dig deep into their courage and begin exploring what is my *why*, my purpose. Some ask: "How come I am feeling so empty and unseen? Why can't I bring my brilliance?" I believe it's because they've never asked themselves, "What is my *why?*" "What is my brilliance, and how do I want to share it?" Have you ever asked yourselves these questions?

Let me set the stage. It's important to share that my spirit was tapped at a dangerously low level. I could feel it happening but couldn't control it. The finely tuned intuition that began as a young child helped me trust my *knowing*. This happened when I loved myself enough to stop everything, get grounded, breathe into my body, and just listen. This connection to the Divine that was ignited when I was two or three years old when my childhood consisted of constant fear, violence, scarcity, and uncertainty. That connection saved my life. Here's what happened.

## UNDER THE BED

I was just a toddler the day I heard from God. It was confusing, but the experience directed my life's trajectory. I was hiding under the bed alone with my hands clasped to my ears as tightly as I could to muffle the screams, but it didn't lessen the terror. Why did God let us live in this unending fear? Why? Daily trauma leaves its mark until it's healed.

God, his angel, or something Divine must have heard my cries and spoke to me while I cowered under that bed. It was a loving energy that enveloped me. It said, "Robin, do not be afraid. I am with you. You're more powerful than you know. You're here to help save the world. You're stronger than you know." And then, it was gone. I felt an overwhelming sense of peace despite the chaos around me. I felt comfort and curiosity.

That message became my mantra. I finally began seeking answers to my *why* in my early twenties. *Why did God or his angel speak to me?* I'm just a girl from the other side of the tracks who still hasn't made a difference in this world. I'm not Gandhi, the Dalai Lama, or Oprah! Here's the miraculous thing—the energy and the voice stayed with me, calling and guiding me and reassuring me to this day. I call upon it when I am exhausted, feeling vulnerable, or not aligned with my soul's calling.

The question I kept asking was: *How exactly am I supposed to save the world? I'm not equipped. I have no tools.*

I now know I dragged that voice, message, calling with me throughout my entire life. Everything I did, I held up to that "Robin, you're here to save the world" message. That voice became a millstone around my neck, almost like a curse. I was hunched over from carrying that weight my entire life but never told anyone about the voice for fear of ridicule.

I have frequently heard, "Robin, your head is in the clouds. Come back to the real world. You're not Gandhi." After years of being dismissed and unseen, I was resigned to setting my aliveness aside and did what my grandmother and mother told me to do. "Put your head down and work hard. Never ask for help. Get it done whatever it takes." That's just what I did. I put my head down and got things done. That is, until the day of my accident.

If you were to ask, "How did that accident even happen?" I would tell you the Universe pushed me into a glass door in a last-ditch effort to *save my life.* I honestly believe I would have eventually died from a disengaged and broken spirit.

The Universe had succeeded. Whispers, nudges, taps, and shoulder-grabbing had not woken me from the stupor I walked through in my boring, uninspiring, and disconnected work. But then, I believe the Universe saved my life. I was in a spiritual desert, and I had been living in my head for most of my life as a learned survival response. Divine discontent was winning. Spirit could no longer armor up.

## THE GLASS WALL

The two years that followed were unimaginable. Upon impact, I lost my identity, and my life changed forever. I'd suffered a TBI (traumatic brain injury), and was no longer the Robin Mooney I had been. I couldn't share just how injured I was with my own family because my brain didn't connect the dots. I couldn't articulate my experiences and have conversations that made any sense. God bless them for their patience and love.

I was no longer that small but mighty, high-performing sales executive, mother, daughter, sister that would pursue the most challenging opportunities others feared. I had to abandon my life studio drawing class which provided a beautiful, healing, creative outlet and much-needed stress relief. The rigorous daily workouts in the pool disappeared. Power walks and talks changed from invigorating and creative connections to dangerous excursions. Walking, a sacred ritual, became unsafe.

Excruciating headaches, neckaches, dizziness, and nausea were all ongoing in my life. My body had become a vessel emptied of its previous life, spirit, and brain functions. *Nothing* worked the way it had before the accident. My cognitive, memory, visual processing, reading, balance, emotional health, and physical abilities were all broken, as were my confidence, resilience, curiosity, and problem-solving skills. The joy of connecting with others was all gone.

I had become The Gone Girl. At least, that's the belief I once held.

Can you relate to any of this? Have you felt unfilled, aching for something more, but paralyzed with the lack of tools or a path forward? For years, I'd been seeking a way out of that false version of self. The TBI wouldn't have been my first choice to awaken to my life's true direction. But in the end, it *was* my choice.

## REBIRTH AND REDEMPTION - THE PIVOT

I am *not* a quitter. I was determined to push myself to do the therapies despite the consistent and recurring symptoms and would not settle for a lesser version of myself. On some level, I knew I was called to use this journey to help others learn how to be seen. My TBI made me feel invisible, but eventually, I would learn how to navigate my healing, insights, and tools to bridge the much-needed conversations that impact our personal and professional lives. To help others uncover their genius and purpose and step into being seen.

I would not concede to the doctor's statement. "We expect you to get better, but we just don't know what that looks like."

"How long will it take?" I asked. "When can I get back to work? I have a vacation coming up."

The doctor said, "Robin, I know you. You want to flip a switch so you can go back to a job *I suspect* (don't you just love a good marmoset insight?) isn't fulfilling or healthy for you. There is no switch to flip. It's one day at a time. You must do the work. If you do, you will heal, and regain your confidence again over time. But it could take 18 months or longer. It may take the rest of your life. With the brain, we just don't know. There may be abilities that you might not regain. It's just too soon to tell."

My mouth dropped to my chest, and my breathing became shallow and rapid. The ringing in my ears was screaming. The room was spinning. Everything around me seemed to fade away like the end of an old silent movie.

The tears and shaking stopped because I fired rapid questions at my doctor and his assistant. He turned to face me squarely and said, "Robin, I don't find myself saying this to very many patients, but you, Robin, are an exceptional person. You need to hear this. You *have* a TBI. You're *not* your TBI." A pregnant pause hung in the room.

I could have been knocked over by a feather. But I regained my composure, looked at his kind, wise eyes, and thanked him for reading me so well and for his gift of tough love. I needed it. Again, Divine intervention saved my life. I was listening with my heart because my head was out of order. This was new for me. It was a strange and wonderful gift.

Here's the most miraculous thing—remember that voice and energy of God, my higher power or the Divine? I call upon it when I am exhausted, feeling vulnerable, or not aligned with my soul's calling. Up until the TBI (which I now refer to as my Tremendously Brilliant Invitation), I lived in that spiritual desert, unwilling to admit that I was going through the motions, sleepwalking and miserable. When I was working, I kept taking on more to distract myself from my discontent. My light was waning. I didn't want to admit that I was sick of myself for not standing in my bold, beautiful, creative, intuitive self.

Have you ever loathed yourself for allowing dismissive family members or colleagues to treat you as if you were unimportant or unseen? Do you detest retreating to that smallness of self that feels safe yet powerless? I was sick of not being seen, allowing myself to be invisible, and resorting to crawling under that *Harry Potter* cloak for safety.

Why didn't I do anything to change my story or how I showed up in the world? Why haven't you?

Why? Because, in my case, I didn't have a roadmap. The road, my hero's journey, had been arduous as I felt my way through the risky terrain. I had been beaten up and beaten down on that journey. What hero's journey are you on? Do you need a guide, a Wayfinder, or a lighthouse?

I was aching to *know what lit my internal flame;* that gift *I knew* could light the way for many others just like myself. In seeking my brilliance, inner genius, and the things that make me uniquely amazing, I've learned that these help me make a difference in the world. And the world is aching to learn how to come alive. And I knew I would eventually help guide the way.

I was paralyzed because I didn't know I had a unique genius. Nor was I aware that everyone has a unique genius. To uncover it, you must call on your courage and become your hero, willing to crack open your story, old beliefs, and programmed behaviors to uncover your brilliance.

That's just what I did. I came home to myself and my heart. And you can too.

The coaching tools I've developed are now familiar friends to me. I use them with myself frequently. They have helped me heal, uncover my genius and claim my purpose. Not only did my brain heal, but my heart was also cracked open to healing, forgiveness, and love. My internal homing device has been switched on. It's become effervescent. I want that for you!

My calling is to help you, women, and men uncover your brilliance and to help you create a path to live that into your lives and work.

I have the tools to help you get there.

# THE STRATEGY

## UNLOCKING HEROES – IGNITING YOUR SPARKS OF GENIUS

Here are five questions that will help you *begin* to unlock your unique genius. Your purpose-work is woven throughout these questions. When I work with clients, I take them through a series of exercises that will begin to peel away the stories they hold onto that prevent them from allowing their genius to come to life.

Please grab your journal and create a minimum of 15 minutes for this invitation. Set an intention to create a sacred space for this exploration. Light a candle. Shut your door and ground. As you read each question, give yourself permission to feel the question. More importantly, identify how you feel about the question and what it means to you. Capture your feelings and insights in your journal.

Your unique genius is that feeling you have when you come alive. Your light is on. You lose yourself in what you're doing. You step into your personal power and use your voice. Leading with vulnerability and unabashed courage is your foundation. You have identified the qualities, energy, activities, people, and passions that buoy you through challenges. You find yourself aching for not doing these things. You may or may not be doing these in your job, but your life would feel so much richer and more joyful if you could. Being seen, valued, included, contributing are some of the gifts that emerge with my clients as a result of doing this deep work.

Unlocking your unique genius starts with a series of soul-searching questions:

1. What is the theme or consistent thread that has been present throughout my life that speaks to my gifts?

How have you consistently shown up throughout your life's experiences? I call this your Let your Life Share exercise. You will be writing your major life events in a series of seven years. Identify what the theme or word is for each seven-year period. Write those themes or words down. Do you see a pattern or recurring descriptor? What insights have you uncovered?

2. What lights me up to where I lose a sense of time, space, fear?

Recall memories from the above exercise and journal on everything that brought your joy. Did you love gathering family, friends, or colleagues to create, commune or heal? What did you get pulled into that you loved?

3. Which of these gifts have I hidden for fear of ridicule, shame, vulnerability?

Why did you hide these gifts? What happened to cause you to set them aside? How did that make you feel? Do you still hide these gifts?

4. What lessons keep showing up for me to learn?

Think back to the Let Your Life Share exercise above—what continues to show up that you keep asking yourself, "Not this again—why does this keep happening?"

5. What can I not, *not* do?

What is that thing that is a deep ache inside of you that you have hidden and long to do or play within your life? This is one of the most powerful questions to ask yourself. Try to sit with it. Play with it. Dream it. What is that big, hairy, audacious goal that is aching to come to life?

What thoughts, feelings, and sensations do you have in your body after taking the first bold, courageous steps in excavating your purpose and soul's calling in sitting with the questions above?

Please capture what you notice about the insights you've observed in your notebook. *Notice what you're noticing.* Are there any surprises? How does that make you feel?

What ache do you have that's just beginning to reveal itself to you? It's not what your head and ego are telling you. This is your *soul* speaking, and it's probably been trying to get your attention for your entire life.

*You* are the answer to the questions you have been asking.

The world needs your brilliance.

*You* are the magic the world is waiting for.

What are you waiting for? Bravo! You have taken the courageous step to opening your heart and listening to your soul, and I'd love to help guide you on your path!

*Live the questions now. Perhaps then, someday far in the future,*
*you will gradually, without even noticing it,*
*live your way into the answer.*

~Ranier Maria Rilke

**Robin Mooney** is a modern-day Joan of Arc who has armored up throughout her life to slay the dragons of human struggle and workplace survival. After her traumatic brain injury, Robin catapulted herself into her calling of unlocking the heroes within us.

The accident led to the invitation and gift of self-love through excavating her purpose, unique genius, and brilliance. Her On Purpose program brings coaching and wisdom to individuals and teams, helping them find, embrace, and grow their unique genius through 1:1, group, and team coaching and facilitating, workshops and retreats.

To explore unlocking your genius and human magic, please reach out to Robin at:

Robinmooney57@gmail.com
www.robinmooneycoaching.com
Instagram – @robbimastr
Facebook – robbimastr
Linkedin – www.linkedin.com/in/robinmooney1

CLOSING CHAPTER:

# SURROUND YOURSELF WITH SUCCESS

## THE IMPORTANCE OF A LIKE-MINDED COMMUNITY

Camille L. Miller, MBA, Ph.D. ABD

If you want to create your soul-aligned business, built on your passion, and in complete alignment with your vision and truth, you must surround yourself with others who think the same way and hold space for you to achieve.

Business is about relationships and the energetic exchange between us. The company we keep affects our ability to be successful and reach our potential.

Our need for connection is human. We all long for support, understanding, love, respect, encouragement, and validation. We build alliances in life and business to expand ourselves personally and professionally. You can't be successful if you're hanging around unsuccessful people. You need the constant encouragement and support of like-minded souls to help you hold your vision so you can reach your highest potential, and only in the energy of your highest potential can you achieve ultimate success.

It takes courage to create a business around your dreams, to dovetail all the things you want in life, and to be seen as who you authentically are. It takes bravery and involves risk and uncertainty to do it unconventionally too. I can't stress enough the importance of surrounding yourself with nonjudgmental peers who think like you do and give you strength and encouragement when you have doubts or need a confidential sounding board for a new idea. Find a professional community of soul-aligned professionals that are there to lift you up and advocate for your success. They should help you navigate your questions and offer accountability. Look for a community with high-achieving role models you can emulate, and that provides mentors and accountability partners who understand where you've been and offer the space and critical support for working through important business decisions.

*The better you are at surrounding yourself with people of high potential, the greater your chance of success.*

-John C. Maxwell

I heard Tony Robbins say in 1999, "Success leaves clues." I was embarking on a new real estate career at the time, so I started studying successful salespeople. Guess what? I became a highly successful salesperson, which morphed into a national sales trainer position and a branch manager position for a local real estate company. I opened my own brokerage firm a few years later. So, when I decided to create NLBP, the first thing I did was study successful membership models. Today I study the greatest CEOs and constantly read books on leadership and building businesses. You might say I have a hyper-learning problem, but I love it, and I get to share it with others in my professional community.

When I started NLBP, it was to find people like me. I knew I needed a community of like-minded professionals to surround myself with—professionals who believed in the same core values I did and who wanted more for themselves. I was searching for a very rare, evolved professional who could co-design the future organization with me. It wasn't to make money or go global. I never even imagined the global organization we have today. I did want to surround myself with success and genuinely help others bring their gifts to the world.

At the time, I didn't believe I had any gifts in the spiritual sense (that would prove to be very wrong years later), but I knew I was good at building successful businesses. My thought was to help those with the gifts to build businesses from an aligned place to help others. In my mind, it was my way of giving back to the world.

*You are the average of the five people you surround yourself with.*

-Jim Rohn

I struggled for a long time growing NLBP and even considered closing some mornings, but something inside me said, *keep going; this will pay off; the world needs this.* We stayed a small boutique community for many years because I felt small. I struggled internally with *who am I to run a global professional organization,* and *what if people realize I'm not that smart?* Yup, classic imposter syndrome. It wasn't until I started doing deep inner work on my own self-worth issues that I was able to grow the community and start to demand a price that reflected the value each member was getting. Every time I would raise the membership price, I held my breath until the first person bought in. *Was I worth it?* Now I look back and see what an amazing bargain our charter members received, but I'm also sincerely grateful for their belief in me and the mission of NLBP.

To finally step into my power, I surrounded myself with people who had a bigger vision. I needed to shift my mindset, but I also needed to find mentors who were already running successful companies and coming from that same place of alignment I wanted in myself and in the community. Once I made that shift, I easily aligned with other leaders, attracting a more high-achieving entrepreneur to the NLBP community. As you can imagine, I took another leap of faith when we launched our Six-Figure Souls Inner Circle for Soul Professionals making over $150,000 per year. Again, I held my breath, but it quickly gained momentum and once again showed me I'm worth it. Now we're in the planning stage of a new membership level for those who have built soul-aligned brands nearing or breaking the million-dollar mark and wish to lead in a conscious way.

*In The Compound Effect, Darren Hardy points to research by social psychologist Dr. David McClelland of Harvard that states, "[the people you habitually associate with] determine as much as 95 percent of your success or failure in life."*

The vibration of the NLBP community is hard to define unless you experience it. I often tell people "It's like a giant hug." In the beginning, I wasn't quite sure what was happening, but I knew when we all gathered, I felt a shift in who I was. I was not in tune like I am today, and I now know that it's the vibration of the collective that I feel. The energy and joy I receive from the NLBP community is my true north, constantly directing my path and pulling me forward.

NLBP was created for like-minded professionals that embrace both science and soul. However, because the community attracts high-vibrational beings, we collectively began to resonate at a higher level and attract more of the same. Now we only co-create with love, respect, and admiration for each other. Since our opening, I have not witnessed a jealous indignation or feeling of competition within the community or its members. It's not a you-or-me approach; it's a you-and-me understanding. We are not transactional; we are relational. It's spiritual energy lifting all of us to grow successful businesses.

Your professional circle should want to see you succeed and actively co-create with you. Successful people never stop learning and growing. Successful soul-aligned people never stop trying to reach a higher vibration and stay in alignment. There is a wonderful parable in Napoleon Hill's *Think and Grow Rich* called *Three Feet from Gold*. In the case of this parable, it was a gold miner who gave up looking for gold after years of disappointment and then sold the rights to the land. The next miner sought an expert out for advice and found the gold three feet from where the previous landowner had stopped looking. The moral of the story is to not give up in the face of temporary defeat. Many entrepreneurs give up right before they hit gold! Look for advice and mentorship from others who've been where you are and have the experience and know-how to help you move forward.

*Surround yourself with the dreamers and the doers, the believers and thinkers, but most of all, surround yourself with those who see the greatness within you. Even when you don't see it yourself.*

~Edmund Lee

Entrepreneurship is lonely. I found it even more lonely when I couldn't connect with someone from a spiritual perspective. We're not in competition with each other. No other person can ever be you. Even if they do the same thing, they don't attract the same clients. When you work from an abundance mindset and help others reach their potential, you'll quickly supersede yours.

If you are an introvert like me, your energy and mental time are finite. Spend it with people that get you. Spend it with people that mirror you, that are high quality, high-vibration, and authentic.

I invite you to join me at an NLBP Meet and Greet to learn more about our unique Soul Professional community and to see if you are aligned with our goals and values. You can find the next meeting by going to www.SoulProfessional.com.

You can also join our *free* Global Collaborative of soul-aligned professionals on Facebook and connect with the other authors of this book and me at www.facebook.com/groups/nlbpglobalcollabortive/

# CONCLUSION

Phew!

What an amazing book! I want to thank all the incredible authors who contributed. I'm sure your head is spinning from all the stories, tips, and strategies you received too. I hope you feel this was a great investment of your time. It took a lot of our time to create it for you.

Use this book as a reference guide as you build and grow your soul-aligned business. Reflect on each chapter and go over and over the strategies until you feel you have it. If at any time it doesn't feel in alignment with your soul, recreate it. You have the right to change what you want any time you want. In the words of NLBP member Paul Taubman of Digital Maestro, "[your work should] make your heart sing."

I invite you to listen to individual author interviews on my Six-Figure Souls: Doing Good and Making Money® podcast at SixFigureSouls.com.

I also invite you to connect with other amazing soul-aligned individuals and me in our free Global Collaborative on Facebook www.facebook.com/groups/nlbpglobalcollabortive/.

If you loved this book, please do a shout-out in our Global Collaborative with the hashtag #UltimateGuideBook1 and tell us what you loved. Feel free to tag an author too.

This is the first book of a series, so I invite you to share the book with friends and colleagues and then look for the next edition to be coming out in 2023.

## Natural Life Business Partnership®
*Purpose Beyond Profit*

A non-traditional professional organization and business incubator for the soul-aligned business owner, entrepreneur, and conscious leader who wants to build wealth and impact the world by awakening their financial and spiritual potential.

# JOIN THE MOVEMENT
## SOULPROFESSIONAL.COM

GET CONNECTIED TO THE

# NLBP GLOBAL COLLABORATIVE

JOIN FOR FREE!

Get connected to the FREE NLBP Global Collaborative Facebook Community and expand your network with other soul-aligned professionals. Gain instant access to Camille, other authors in this book, and mentors from around the globe. Connect, collaborate, and ask questions with like-minded professionals who believe in the same core values and are committed to building soul-aligned businesses—just like you!

As a Global Collaborative Member, you will enjoy

- Weekly business building tips from Camille
- Inspiring discussions forums
- Listening to live Community Shares with NLBP members
- Exchange of ideas and information with other readers
- Exclusive access to networking events and free programs

Camille and the NLBP community are committed to helping you build a soulfully aligned business. We want you to find joy and inspiration every single day you are working and beyond. As a member you belong to an ecosystem of soul professionals with an abundance mindset, who want to build innovative, robust businesses that impact the world.

**Find us on Facebook**

VISIT FACEBOOK.COM/GROUPS/NLBPGLOBALCOLLABORATIVE

# NLBP GLOBAL COLLABORATIVE

# TIKTOK

FOR DAILY BUSINESS
TIPS AND
INSPIRATION FROM
CAMILLE L. MILLER

FOLLOW

# YOUTUBE

SUBSCRIBE 🔔

SUBSCRIBE TO NLBP.TV
ON YOUTUBE TO GET
AUTHOR INTERVIEWS,
DISCUSSIONS, BUSINESS
TIPS, AND FREE
MASTERCLASSES FROM
INSPIRING NLBP
MEMBERS

TIKTOK: @CAMILLE.L.MILLER
YOUTUBE: NLBP.TV

# Six-Figure Souls®

### Doing Good & Making Money

## LISTEN TO AUTHOR INTERVIEWS FROM THIS BOOK

AND OTHER SOUL-ALIGNED ENTREPRENEURS WHO CRUSHED THE SIX-FIGURE CEILING AND FEEL IN ALIGNMENT WITH THE UNIVERSE AND THEIR PURPOSE.

**SIX-FIGURE SOULS** WEEKLY PODCAST HIGHLIGHTS SOUL-ALIGNED PROFESSIONALS WHO ARE PUTTING PURPOSE BEYOND PROFITS. THE INTERVIEW SERIES BEGAN IN 2020 AS A RESULT OF THE WORLDWIDE PANDEMIC AND QUICKLY BECAME ESSENTIAL FOR THOSE LOOKING TO DOVETAIL WHO THEY ARE WITH WHAT THEY DO. LISTEN TO CAMILLE FEATURE **100S OF ENTREPRENEURS** FROM AROUND THE GLOBE SHARING THEIR **INSPIRING JOURNEYS**.

SUBSCRIBE TO THE PODCAST TO GET WEEKLY DOWNLOADS ON YOUR FAVORITE PROVIDER.

## HOSTED BY CAMILLE L. MILLER

CAMILLE L. MILLER'S

# SIX-FIGURE SOUL BOOTCAMP:

## Break Through Your Money Fears & Earn What You Deserve

**8-WEEK FINANCIAL BOOTCAMP
LEARN THE INNER WORK, OUTER WORK,
& HIGHER WORK IT TAKES FOR SUCCESS**

IF YOU ARE AN UNDER-EARNER, LIVE IN
FINANCIAL CHAOS, DON'T CHARGE
ENOUGH, SELF-SABOTAGE, IN DEBT,
PROCRASTINATE, CAN'T SEEM TO
PROSPER, DISORGANIZED, OR
RESISTANT TO ANYTHING
FINANCIAL...

**THIS COURSE
IS FOR YOU!**

JUST 8 WEEKS TO RESET YOUR
MINDSET AND EARN WHAT YOU
DESERVE!
- INTENSE HOME STUDY TRAINING
- PRIVATE STUDENT DISCUSSION
  GROUP
- SHORT DIGESTIBLE LESSONS
- COMMUNITY SHARING OF
  EXPERIENCES AND BEST PRACTICES
- ABILITY TO UPGRADE TO 1:1
  COACHING TO ENSURE YOU STAY ON
  TRACK AND COMPLETE THE WORK IN
  8 WEEKS
- DOWNLOADABLE WORKSHEETS AND
  EXERCISES
- THE BEST OF BOTH TRAINING: DO AT
  YOUR OWN PACE AND COMMUNITY
  SUPPORT AT WHATEVER STEP YOU
  ARE ON.

**GET 50% OFF THE BOOTCAMP
WHEN YOU APPLY THIS CODE:
UGCSAB50OFF**

LEARNINGACADEMY.SOULPROFESSIONAL.COM
/COURSES/SIX-FIGURE-SOUL-BOOTCAMP